100 Great Jobs and How to Get Them

Other Books by Richard Fein...

101 Quick Tips for a Dynamite Resume

101 Dynamite Questions to Ask At Your Job Interview

111 Dynamite Ways to Ace Your Job Interview

Cover Letters! Cover Letters! Cover Letters!

First Job

100 GREAT JOBS
and How to Get Them

Richard Fein

IMPACT PUBLICATIONS
Manassas Park, Virginia

100 Great Jobs and How to Get Them

Library of Congress Cataloging-in-Publication Data

Fein, Richard, 1946-
    100 great jobs and how to get them / Richard Fein
      p. cm.
    Includes bibliographical references
    ISBN 1-57023-116-8 (alk. paper)
    1. Job hunting—United States. 2. Vocational guidance—United States. 3. Career Development—United States. I. Title. II. Title: One hundred great jobs and how to get them.
    HF5382.75.U6F445 1999
    331.7'02'0973—dc21   99-24356
                                                    CIP

Publisher: For information on Impact Publications, including current and forthcoming publications, authors, press kits, bookstore, and submission requirements, visit Impact's Web site: www.impactpublications.com

Publicity/Rights: For information on publicity, author interviews, and subsidiary rights, contact the Public Relations and Marketing Department: Tel. 703/361-7300 or Fax 703/335-9486.

Sales/Distribution: Bookstore sales are handled through Impact's trade distributor: National Book Network, 15200 NBN Way, Blue Ridge Summit, PA 17214, Tel. 1-800-462-6420. All other sales and distribution inquiries should be directed to the publisher: Sales Department, IMPACT PUBLICATIONS, 9104-N Manassas Dr., Manassas Park, VA 20111-5211, Tel. 703/361-7300, Fax 703/335-9486, or E-mail:100greatjobs@impactpublications.com

Book design by Kristina Ackley

Contents

In Memory of Leon Frankel
and
In Memory of Isidore Fein

Acknowledgments

I want to thank each of the 100 people whose story appears in this book. Their time, reflections and ideas are all deeply appreciated. Thanks also to my publishers and editors, Ron and Caryl Krannich and Kristina Ackley.

There is a life outside of writing. My deepest gratitude to my wife, Rhonda, and my daughters, Lauren and Gabrielle for being supportive while I was engrossed in this project. To my assistant, Janice Dagilus, my deep appreciation for making my life at work so joyful.

Richard Fein
March 19, 1999

100 Great Jobs and How to Get Them

Meet 100 People

100 Great Jobs...

Have you ever noticed that some people truly love their job, while others barely make it through the days, months and years until retirement? This book is about 100 people from across the nation and a wide spectrum of professions who think that their job is great. You will feel good when reading their stories, but that is not at all my purpose.

By reading these stories, you will have a clear sense of what people do and enjoy in various jobs. That insight should help you decide what your next career step will be and the skill sets you will need to land the great job you want.

When I started research for this book, I wanted to find out what it is that makes jobs great. I discovered that very few people mentioned money — although that does not mean they would volunteer for a pay cut. Instead, certain themes were expressed with great frequency:

▶ **Making a difference:** People wanted to know that their work has a positive impact. This was as true for highly technical people making commercial products as it was for people in the helping professions.

▶ **Gaining respect:** The positive feelings of colleagues and clients seem to have been a major source of satisfaction. Being appreciated by superiors and others was also important.

▶ **Using skills:** Whether it was engineering, computers, writing or other types of training, many people said they gained major job satisfaction by using skills they had acquired. Learning new skills was cited as a source of satisfaction, in addition to being a professional necessity.

▶ **Meeting Interesting People:** A writer enjoyed meeting the people he interviewed. Service providers enjoyed interesting clients and scientists enjoyed highly intelligent colleagues.

▶ **Responsibility:** People found satisfaction, rather than a burden, in the responsibilities they were given or sought. Promotional opportunity was sometimes a related virtue.

▶ **Autonomy:** Two types of autonomy were frequently mentioned. First was the ability to make decisions based on their own judgement. Second was the flexibility to schedule their own work day.

▶ **Variety:** "No two days are the same," "there is a mix of projects," and "every assignment is an eye opener" were typical topics. People found variety through multitasking, a change of responsibilities over a time and a mix of clients.

▶ **Newness:** A desire for the new was expressed in terms like "innovate," "create" or "cutting edge issues".

Most of these characteristics that make a job great *could be present* in most jobs most of the time. To make your job great, or at least better, pursue qualities that matter to you personally, rather than those that simply advance your career. Your manager may listen carefully to your suggestions to make your job a great one. After all, an employee who thinks his/her job is great produces more and stays with the organization longer.

...and How to Get Them

Each person in this book has worked hard to get where they are and none have stopped working hard yet. They have developed the skills they need through a combination of education and experience. Some caught a lucky break along the way, but none have their job through sheer luck, favoritism or privileged background. Most stay current with their field by continuous reading and interchange with other professionals. None is a single dimension person, for example, having technical knowledge but lacking interpersonal skills. *The bottom line is to have a great job, you need to do a great job.*

While writing a good resume and knowing how to interview are important skills for all of us, there is nothing in these stories about slick resumes or practicing interview jujitsu. Instead, these are people who acquired the skills they needed, developed a solid professional reputation and pursued opportunities through the means available to them. Usually, a great job was both earned and sought. In some cases, the people in these stories generously provided contact and background information for their companies.

Whose Stories are Told in 100 Great Jobs and How to Get Them?

Over a nine month period during 1998, I interviewed people recommended because they thought their jobs were great. Most of these people were called to my attention as a result of a questionnaire sent to approximately 1,300 human resource professionals. These were my criteria for conducting each interview: First, a variety of professional fields, career paths, educational levels and length of time in that career were represented. Second, the interview would capture what the person does, the skills s/he needs, what they like about their job and how they got there. Third, to the extent possible, these stories would represent 100 people in their own words. I asked each interviewee for comments, corrections, changes and additions to my drafts. Being a layman in every field but my own, I wanted to assure accuracy of terminology, concepts and nuances while also telling about each person's career development as they themselves experience it.

The division of these 100 stories into chapters was a difficult task. Many stories could fit well in more than one chapter. Perhaps this reflects the fact that real jobs often don't fit neatly into tight categories.

As this text was being readied for publication, several people moved on to other positions. The good news is that people advance or simply change jobs. The bad news is that employing organizations can go under. Even then, those who have done a great job stand a good chance of landing another great job.

This Book is Important to You If:

These stories cover people with experiences ranging from one year to 30 years. They will be important to you if:

▶ You are planning your next career move. This book will help you think broadly about your options and realistically about the steps you need to take. You will also have a better sense of what to expect when you land the job you want.

▶ You are thinking about starting or restarting your career. You will be able to identify the skills you need to acquire and what avenues are open to get the job you want.

▶ You simply want to know why people think their jobs are great and how they got there.

▶ You always wanted to know what other people do for a living.

For me, writing *100 Great Jobs and How to Get Them* has been a great experience. I have been introduced to some wonderful people whose enthusiasm for their jobs was an inspiration to me. In addition, learning about the worlds of 100 people opened windows which would otherwise have remained closed to me. It is my fervent hope that you will benefit as much from reading this book as I did from writing it.

A Note on the Resource Pages

At the end of each chapter, I have included resources in a "What to Do Now" section that you may wish to use in pursuit of your own great job. Professional organizations are included because they are a great source of information about their field and a fertile source of contacts. Publications are important to stay current with the field the way a dedicated professional does. Both organizations and publications may have links to Web sites containing information about job opportunities. I encourage you to utilize these resources.

1

Computers

Making a Living in a Wired World

We hear a great deal about the importance of computers in today's work world and their significant presence at home. In this chapter, we will hear from computer specialists who have made working with computers their profession. These stories are about the kinds of people you would enjoy meeting at a party. Terms like "geek" and "nerd" simply don't apply.

Some of these stories tell about people, such as Robin Krantz and David Rippy, who studied computer science and fell in love with their first exposure. On the other hand, Marla Derosa was a math teacher and her first job in computers was in computer support. Louis Matrone was an accounting major.

As important as technical skills are, they are never sufficient. Interpersonal and communication skills are a big part of the job. So are time management and dealing with stress. But the rewards are challenge and change in an expanding field.

Our computer professionals tell us about working in air traffic control systems, computer security, building program architecture, geo-spatial applications and researching how customers actually use computer technology.

5

Robin Krantz
Software Engineer
Raytheon

We all take aircraft for granted. They are almost always on schedule and are one of the safest means of transportation. In large measure this is because air traffic controllers have sophisticated computer systems developed by specially trained software engineers that provide them with extensive and accurate information. Robin Krantz is one of these engineers.

Robin came to the Raytheon after graduating from the University of Michigan in 1995. Robin's initial coursework focused on business until she took her first programming course and loved it. Following in her parent's foot steps, she majored in Computer Science. During the summer breaks, she gained computer experience working on a nation-wide reservation system for a large auto rental company. Looking for a career position, Robin knew she wanted to work for a large company that offered a variety of challenging opportunities. She submitted a resume to Raytheon at the suggestion of a relative who was a long time employee of the company. "The interview sold me," Robin related. "Raytheon offered me the opportunity to work on advanced software systems which deliver critical information, like Air Traffic Control. In addition, I loved the Boston area."

Robin has worked mainly on Raytheon's AutoTrac 2100 program, which is a Unix-based air traffic control automation system sold to countries around the world. Specifically, she works on network and communication involving interfaces with many different external systems. Programming is only a small part of Robin's job. She is involved in every phase of the system from the start of the program through operation and beyond. Her other responsibilities include writing the requirements and design for the software. The life of a program including testing and system integration can extend over a period of one to three years.

Robin enjoys the teamwork and the opportunity to learn new technology. She also enjoys teaching others what she has learned herself. As a team leader, part of her responsibility is to assign work and to help other engineers on her team to meet their deadlines. In addition to technical skills, Robin feels that taking the initiative and asking questions is essential. Good interpersonal skills are also vital to working successfully with other team members.

In the future, Robin sees herself managing programs and people but she's likely to keep her hand on the technical side.

Robin enjoys many aspects of her job. "There is something new happening everyday, lots of teamwork and constant challenge" she told me. Her work site is highly professional yet very young, with casual dress days twice a week. Robin enjoys solving problems if they occur, because they provide a puzzle that needs to be solved. When a deadline approaches, Robin may work late nights and weekends—but that's just part of her job. "The day may be long, but it's always exciting" she remarked.

When Robin does get home, she can leave her work behind her. "I am thrilled by my job while I'm doing it and enjoy the rest of my life when I'm not," she noted.

David Rippy
Director of Consulting Services
US Web/Ensemble

The Internet is growing as a vehicle for conducting business. David Rippy is the director of Consulting Services at US Web/Ensemble, "a professional service organization that focuses on developing Internet solutions for Fortune 1000 companies." US Web/Ensemble is based in Santa Clara, California.

David came to what was then known as Ensemble Corporation after working for one of the five largest corporations in the world. "It was a fine employer," David recalled, "but I wanted to work for a smaller employer where I could truly effect the bottom line and make a difference. I felt that at a small company there would be more room for innovation, a faster pace and the opportunity to expand my skills in many areas." David's first job was being a programmer writing data base systems. In addition to honing his technical skills, David also began writing articles and even books about the computer industry and speaking at professional conferences. "The company grew from 10 to 80 employees and I grew into a more managerial position," David explained. "When Ensemble merged with US Web, I became the Director of Consulting with primary responsibility for closing the deals on new business for this 50 office, international company."

A key part of David's job is working with new clients to understand their technology needs. His goal is to build credibility and trust so that they award work to his company. "We usually gain new business by word of mouth," David told me, "often the client initiates the contact. I will take a senior technical person with me to visit the client to better understand their issues. One possible tool for me to use is walking through their data model and discussing their existing systems. Then I demonstrate our capabilities to the client. If we mutually agree that it's a good fit, I'll assemble a team of programmers to actually implement the system." As David explained it, "A large percentage of our business is developing Intranet and Extranet systems. Intranets are internal systems based on web-technologies, meaning the application typically runs in a browser such as Netscape or Internet Explorer. Most of our clients are moving towards internets for systems like Human Resources, accounting, etc. Intranets are very easy to deploy and are quickly becoming preferable to traditional client/server systems. Extranets are built using the same web-based technologies, but are intended for external users such as suppliers, dealers and distributors. These users are given special permissions to us the system while keeping the rest of the world out."

David earned his bachelor's degree in Management Information Systems at Texas A & M and worked in the information systems department of a huge natural resource company before coming to US Web.

David enjoys his job for many reasons. One is that he has a fast paced day which is guaranteed to bring with it new challenges. In addition, David works with highly talented people who are as committed to doing a good job as David is. David has clients from a variety of industries on the outside, while enjoying a relaxed, politics-free environment within the company. "We work hard at understanding the goals of each person in the company and try to match their goals with the projects they are assigned to. This company has a family feel to it."

Early in his career, David belonged to a number of local computer special interest groups in addition to an organization now known as the Association of Information Technology Professionals. "These days," David added, "I spend more time recruiting at events than attending for the content of the presentation." David also reads a number of trade publications on a regular basis. "I read *PC Week*, among other hard copy magazines, but most of what I learn is from news wires and on line publications on the Internet," David told me.

David has some good tips for getting ahead. "I've always loved to add a lot more value than my job description indicates," he said. "That way, any time an opportunity for advancement came up, I was the natural fit. After all, I had already been performing those duties in my current job." David is also a strong advocate of networking. "I am on the phone constantly with old acquaintances. Often this leads to a new hire or new business," David remarked. In the same vein, David suggests helping yourself by being helpful to others, whether colleagues, clients or friends. "Spend time understanding the needs and goals of those around you," David advises. "Teach a new skill, pass along advice, point someone in the right direction. People remember those that took time out to help them, and they will want to help you down the road."

Barbara McGann
Senior Systems Engineer
SAIC

Would you like a long title? Try Senior Systems Engineer in the Secure Solutions Division of Science Applications International Corporation (SAIC). Barbara McGann, a delightful "thirty-something" and mother of a two-year-old has the title and loves the job.

Let's take a step back for a moment. SAIC is "the largest employee-owned research and engineering company in the United States," with 30,000 employees. It offers expertise in "information technology systems integration national and international security, transportation, telecommunications, health systems and services, energy and environmental systems and engineering." SAIC was founded in 1969 by Dr. J. Robert Beyster.

Barbara has been with SAIC since 1993. Her division assures the security of computer systems for both government agencies and commercial enterprises. In brief, security means that there is no way for outsiders to break in, whether they are joy-riding hackers, commercial thieves or disgruntled employees. There are four primary components to security: controlling access, maintaining confidentiality, protecting the integrity of information and authenticating that both senders and recipients are legitimate. Security can be achieved through computer architecture (e.g. appropriate hardware, software), encrypting data and, on the less technical side, adopting secure personnel procedures.

Barbara's primary role is to be a project manager. She provides technical leadership and assigns tasks, often based on an assessment of who has the right mix of technical and interpersonal skills. Barbara is also responsible to see that the project is completed on time and under budget.

Projects can last from 3 weeks to five years and Barbara manages several projects concurrently. How is it possible to manage so much? Barbara identified having time management skills and being organized as factors. She also credited the people to whom she delegates work. "They are very bright, very dedicated and don't need a lot of supervision," Barbara told me.

Technical skills are not enough to really succeed at SAIC. Barbara does a good deal of writing, whether for status reports, technical issues or input into proposals. Fortunately, she did a good deal of writing in her first job and her technical editor was a "super asset." Interpersonal skills are also critical, and Barbara thanked her high quality mentors for her growth in this area. Mentoring at SAIC is both formal (Leadering 2,000 Program) and informal.

One thing Barbara likes about working for SAIC is the constant challenge. For example, she was the project manager for a contract to provide security for a Web-based supply chain for missile components. Barbara enjoyed ascending a steep learning curve in a hurry, which was necessary because she had little web-security experience. She also enjoyed doing background research through the Internet, soliciting expert advice within SAIC and discussing user needs with missile procurement specialists. Interestingly enough, the expertise used for this military project was completely civilian. The technology is mutually applicable both ways.

Responsibility, challenge, constant learning, and bright colleagues are all important to Barbara. But topping the list is that SAIC allows her to maintain a balance between work and family. Barbara works three days a week based on an arrangement she negotiated when her daughter was born. "I am treated as an individual, even though this is a huge corporation," she told me with clear conviction. "I feel fulfilled both professionally and personally. Being a mother has not hurt my career at SAIC."

Barbara did mention one downside to her job, " There is a good deal of stress, especially with writing proposals," she explained "You're under tight deadlines and you need to spend a lot of 'free time' to get it done."

Barbara started her career at Signal Science Corporation in 1988 after graduation from Drexel University with a Bachelor of Science in Electrical Engineering degree. This company depended on government contracts and, when business slackened, Barbara decided to move to a company which was a contractor for NASA. When SAIC bought Signal Science in 1993, she joined SAIC in part because her experiences at Signal Science had been so positive, but primarily because of the unique opportunity to work closely with a female senior manager, Ronni Wyrwas, who continues to be instrumental in Barbara's personal and professional growth.

Barbara earned a master's degree in electrical engineering, studying part time. The value added from her graduate degree stems from three factors. First, academic challenges helped Barbara keep her mind sharp. Second, her instructors tended to be full-time practitioners, so the program had a serious, from the real world character. The third reason is more prosaic. Many employers want master's degree holders because they are called for in contract specifications and foster a higher bid rate. That is, Barbara is eligible for more jobs at higher pay.

Not all of the technical people at SAIC have an electrical engineering degree, but most have some measure of technical training through computer science, information systems, business degrees or military experience. Beginning workers do not have a training program as such at SAIC, but there are plenty of training opportunities as one's career develops.

John Svedman
Technical Leader
Syncsort

Let's say your company has several hundred million bytes of information to sort and rearrange every hour. (A telephone company preparing bills would be one example). Your company would need a computer software package that maximizes the high speed, high reliability capabilities of your operating system. Syncsort of Clifton, New Jersey provides this service to 95 out of the Fortune 100 firms and it is people like John Svedman who make this possible.

John has been a Technical Leader at Syncsort for 14 years. Part of his job is to be a group consultant, that is, to be available to others who seek advice, information, or help with problems. However, most of John's job involves the research and design of primary products. "The first step is fooling around with algorithms" John explained. "There really aren't many new ways to sort data, but you need to revisit old ways as new machines come along," John told me. "Execution is hardware dependent. So if a computer maker comes out with a new model, or a client buys new hardware, I need to find the approach that makes our product work best on the new hardware." When John thinks he has hit the right algorithms, he develops prototypes to test his ideas. The volume of material in most databases is huge, so John needs to build a useful prototypes while cutting some corners as compared with a full-blown system. "Otherwise it would take six months to test a new idea and that is too inefficient," John told me. If the prototype works, John brings it to the next step, which is formal design.

John describes himself as 90% independent. His ideas are triggered by publicly available stimuli like trade magazines, reports on machine specifications and information off the Internet. These ideas are then discussed with his boss, and if approved, John can proceed with a prototype. An old algorithm might still work, but with new hardware it may take too long or no longer be the most efficient.

In John's case, his work is primarily done in the office, but his arrival. No one formally reports to John, although he may work with a few people at times.

John likes his independence. In addition, his world is constantly changing, in part because new equipment is always coming on-line. "There are a lot of manufacturers," John explained "IBM, Sun, etc. When you finish adjusting to each one's new hardware, the cycle will start itself again." "We are a high-end provider so we are constantly looking for little edges to beat the competition," John said. "That's a thrill and a challenge. I get a kick out of looking at an operating system and identifying the opportunity for us of a new input/output approach or a new way of handling memory." John is also the proud holder of a patented algorithm. "My main piece was figuring out how to implement it," John recalled.

John graduated from the University of West Virginia with a degree in computer science in 1976. His graduate school was interrupted by four years in the Air Force, but he returned to complete a master's degree in Computer Science with a focus on operating systems. "Today, Computer Science has grown to include so many subfields, you probably couldn't have such a narrow focus. But then you could and it has worked out well for me," John remarked. His first job was in general business programming for manufacturing software. John switched managers, and became more involved with testing operating systems, both equipment and software. After a few years, John took a job with a processing company and worked closely with Hewlett Packard and Prime operating systems. When the company was bought out, John started to think about finding a new home for his skills. A friend knew of his interest (even though John wasn't actively looking) and set up John with an interview at Syncsort. That led to fourteen years of independence and excitement. "As a kid I tore apart toy trucks and rebuilt them, built my own radio and go carts. I get that same joy at Syncsort," John told me. "I am like a big happy kid with a well paying job."

Tony Richardson
Supplier Quality Engineer
Xyplex

Tony Richardson is a Supplier Quality Engineer for Xyplex, "a leading provider of network access solutions…The company provides customers with fast flexible and scalable wide area network access." What Tony does and how he got there make an interesting story.

In a nutshell, Tony's job is to assure that vendors provide Xyplex with the quality products his company has ordered for Xyplex computer boards. One way to do this is to examine his huge database (485,000 records from a single year). Tony looks at his data from many different perspectives to identify the source of problems. "Something which doesn't show up when you look at raw data on a monthly basis, may become clearer when you view it quarterly. Similarly, if you organize the data by part number or sub assembly unit, you may be able to identify a pattern." Problems could have many sources and may not become evident for months. A defect could be in workmanship (vendor caused) or in initial specifications (Xyplex caused). For Tony two rules prevail. At the functional level he needs a huge database because "a problem which seems to be intermittent or random may have a visible pattern if you have enough data." At the relationship level, Tony develops a non-adversarial relationship with vendors. "We don't name call or point fingers," Tony explained. "We just solve any problems together."

Quality is also a question of "manufacturability." When the assembly workers start putting the pieces together what is the quickest, most error free process? Determining the most error free process starts with listening to the ideas of people on the bench to understand the sheer pragmatics of their job. "If a certain process is awkward or requires a lot of tool work, maybe we should redesign it," Tony said. "We also take into account possible repairs. A seemingly simple question like inside versus outside mounts can make a significant difference from that perspective."

Tony is also involved in moving from prototype to production. "The first few runs may produce 50% - 70% usable boards while the manufacturing process is being developed," Tony explained. "We want to move that to 99.6% as soon as possible." That requires identifying problems in process, materials flow or instructions and getting them fixed. "The sooner we are doing it right, the more price competitive we can be," Tony observed.

One of Tony's responsibilities is to sign-off on specifications before they get to the vendor. This can be a difficult judgment to make. "A component with one flaw per million is much more expensive than a similar component with 50 flaws per million. The decision on the quality needed for each component involves a lot of money," Tony explained. "Your product should be top quality but there's no point in adding to cost for capacity that won't be used."

Variety is one of the things Tony loves about his job "One day I am knee deep in data and the next day I am speaking with assembly workers about bolts" Tony commented. Impact is another attraction. "One little problem can cause a huge ripple effect that could hurt my company, our vendors, everybody. I am protecting a lot of businesses, which live on their computer transmitted data, and protecting a lot of jobs." Xyplex itself is an attraction for Tony. "It's a small company with a family type atmosphere. We all help each other. One of my friends just had a baby, so Xyplex arranged for her to 'tele-commute' so she could stay home with her new daughter."

Tony studied computer science at Louisiana State University for one year. "I loved computers, but it was like studying five foreign languages at once." he recalled. Tony left LSU and spent four years in the Marines as a Tactical Microvan Operator. He left the Marines and joined the Army for two years as a cryptography technician. However, "Once you've been in the Marines the Army is hard to take," so Tony left the military and got a job in hospital maintenance through an ex-military friend. He looked for something more technical, and found a position as a late shift floor inspector for a company which manufactured military equipment. "I had military experience, a security clearance and I was familiar with military procurement standards," Tony remembered. He stayed with that company five years "and saw the whole process of military manufacturing in detail." Unfortunately for Tony, the reduction in military procurements led to a downsizing and he was caught in it.

As a man who loves computers, Tony started faxing his resumes from his modem at home. In less than three minutes (Caution: Tony's story is not necessarily typical) Tony received an invitation to interview with a Technical Staff temporary employment agency.

Their client was Xyplex, and Tony quickly passed through the interview process. After eight months as a temp, Xyplex offered Tony a permanent job, which he accepted in 1994.

"I didn't earn a college diploma," Tony said in parting. "But everything I ever learned helped me get and do well in my job at Xyplex. I thank my computer courses, military experience and previous jobs for helping get where I am today."

Marla DeRosa
Chief Technologist
Lotus Development Corporation

How does a company which produces computer software direct its efforts to the needs of users and not simply the most sophisticated technical capability? Part of the answer can come from Marla DeRosa, Chief Technologist at the Lotus Institute of the Lotus Development Corporation.

Marla is a member of a research group which includes a psychologist and a business school professor among its 25 members. Together their job is to research how organizations actually use computer technology to meet critical needs. Their focus is an "knowledge management," namely the capability of organizations to pull together their intellectual assets. Marla's specific roles are to know the technological trends in the technology use and to guide software developers in working towards meeting client goals.

One fruitful approach is for Marla's group to work with a client on a shared-cost basis. The group looks into both the technology involved and the human and organizational changes in employee work lives the technology brings for employees. Then the group builds a solution for the client and takes the knowledge gained from this experience back with them to Lotus. "This exposure helps Lotus understand how technology interacts with people and their organization. We want to know if the technology can support what it is supposed to when people are not in the same room," Marla explained. "It's a win for everyone. The client gets a lower cost solution and we acquire hands on knowledge of how the technology is used," Marla continued.

Back at Lotus, Marla and her staff can spend weeks getting into the nuts and bolts of the client needs they will address. Then they build a prototype and test it. Only then will the new software technology be considered ready if a decision is made to develop it full scale. "That's far from an automatic," Marla told me. "Linking technology to a business issues is not the way software has been developed historically. Developers want to invent and create, flowing from their intellectual interests. I often need to combine my technical expertise with my interpersonal skills to persuade folks to pursue ideas coming from my group."

Marla's path to chief technologist was a bit indirect. At Colorado State University, she changed her major from civil engineering to math. Her first two years after college were spent as a teacher. When Marla moved from North Carolina to Massachusetts, she wanted a career change, but wasn't sure what kind. She found an entry-level job at Lotus in customer support for desktop applications. "It was a good break in job because I learned so much about computers," Marla recalled. Marla liked to write and after two years she moved to a group which documented problems with software uncovered through customer support. "In a way, it was my first exposure to knowledge management. Our documentation became a resource for customer support to use when problems were called in," Marla observed. In another two years, Marla became the group's manager, assuring that the documentation was written well enough to be used. Borrowing ideas gained in collaboration with the University of Massachusetts, Marla developed a retrieval system to enhance capability for accessing the content of databases.

Marla became an "internal consultant" to a new group formed to connect Lotus support centers from around the world. "We used Lotus Notes to create and edit the knowledge needed by support analysts," Marla recalled. "I especially enjoyed establishing a system that translated our content into other languages, like French and Spanish."

The experience in customer support had a significant impact on Marla. "I came to realize that you can't just give someone a computer system and say 'hope you like it'," she said. Marla's next assignment prior to her current position was in project implementation.

Marla enjoys the variety of issues she deals with in her job. "The customers are from different industries, their goals are different and so are their expectations from Lotus," Marla observed. She also enjoys the relatively unstructured nature of her work. "I need to prioritize every day," she said. On the other hand, there can be stress and disappointment. Convincing others to adopt her group's ideas is a slow process at best. "You are often talking to a skeptical audience and the results are not always what you want," Marla explained.

Marla identified presentation skills as critical to her success. "You need to boil down complex ideas so they are easily digestible, particularly with customers," she explained. Written communication is especially important within Lotus. Those skills will also be useful if Marla steps into either product development or consulting at Lotus.

Midge McGinnis
Human Resource Information Systems Manager
Philips Semiconductors

One of the interesting parts of the Midge McGinnis story is that her office is 500 miles from her company's headquarters in Sunnyvale, California. After working at Philips for fifteen years, she and her husband decided to move to Oregon. Midge asked her boss about the possibility of tele-commuting, certain that she would say "no." Instead, she said "sure." "They didn't want to lose 15 years of experience," Midge recalled, "and a lot of my work was on the phone anyway. It's worked out well for Philips, because I can do more work this way since I don't lose time at meetings or socializing. The boss knows where to find me and now I can do data crunching projects without interruption. Approximately once a month I fly into Sunnyvale for a few days of face-to-face reunion."

Midge described her first six months of tele-commuting as rough. Some people were jealous of what they considered the privilege of avoiding traffic jams. Midge also missed the camaraderie a bit and found that some folks called her night or day. "They figured that if I worked at home I was always available," Midge recounted. Further, since Midge is "out of sight, out of mind" to those outside her immediate department and since most promotions would require substantial interaction with people, Midge's opportunity for promotion within the company is limited.

The advantages for Midge predominate, however. "I'm not really a people person so much as a computer person; I like to work in perfect quiet, so isolation is a good work environment for me," Midge explained. "I also get paid Sunnyvale wages while living in a lower cost part of Oregon." Philips supplies Midge with all of the necessary equipment (computer, a printer, a fax, software, phone lines, etc.) and monthly travel expenses. She in turn works standard 8 AM to 5 PM hours. "When you have this arrangement, you must make sure not to abuse it," Midge noted.

So what does Midge do from her home office? She does a good deal of report writing in response to inquiries from all levels of human resource/payroll workers. Midge also helps her long-distance colleagues resolve software or data retrieval problems. "I know the systems so well that I can see all the screens in my head when someone calls in for software advice. I also love the challenge of merging data bases so we can 'mix apples and oranges' from different sources. My clients at Philips understand that it takes time to produce reports, so I feel a commitment but not undue pressure," Midge explained.

Midge earned an associate's degree in Secretarial Science from Pierce Junior College in Pennsylvania. Her original job at Philips was purely clerical, "answering phones, filing, travel arrangements and things like that," Midge recalled. But in four years she became a supervisor. "I saw an internal posting and felt I could do the job. It involved data entry and report writing for a new HR system. It looked interesting and I wanted a more independent contributor type position job because I hated taking orders." The philosophy at Philips was to promote based on merit, not degrees.

"In fact, it was not uncommon for clerks to be promoted to an exempt or supervisory position," Midge noted. Because Midge was known as a hard worker who learned quickly, the new position was hers.

Midge suggests that to do her job, you need a love of computers, "especially when they are not behaving." She was not formally trained in computers, but became engrossed in them on the job.

Shourya Ray
Product Development Manager
Universal Systems, Inc.

For Shourya Ray, the decision was easy. Ray, as he prefers to be called, had been programming computers since he was seven years old. He picked computer science for his college major, feeling that "high pay and job satisfaction would be a tough combination to beat." Ray described his major at the University of Massachusetts as "primarily learning the foundation of writing programs, a tool set deep in math and theory. Many students were hoping for something more pragmatic, but I can use my theoretical base forever. Specific computer programs, on the other hand, eventually become obsolete."

As Ray had anticipated, his degree was indeed a "ticket to a job." When he graduated in 1995, Ray chose Universal Systems, Inc. because "working there would give me a chance to be in product research and development. Some of my classmates went to service based 'body shops' where they rent you out to a customer. That wasn't for me," Ray told me. Product Research and Development in Ray's case means developing business applications for finance departments in Fortune 500 companies. Ray observed that large companies benefit best from changing labor intensive processes to a more efficient electronic system.

As it turned out, Ray spent six months as a "junior developer" doing customer based work like maintenance of existing programs. "It's analogous to laying bricks where the customer wants them," Ray reflected. But then he moved up to a "developer position" where he wrote his own programs. "That's like building a whole wall," Ray said, continuing his analogy. After a year he was promoted again, this time to "senior programmer." Now he was working with program architecture. "It's something like designing a building's blueprints," Ray observed. He now had full authority over the entire life cycle of a software product. "My rise was not guaranteed, but it is typical of what you can do in a relatively small (i.e. $100 million) company." Ray added a bit of advice "Don't rely on computer talent only. Even in a small company it's important to do your face-to-face networking."

Ray's "baby" was "Invoice Manager," a program to reduce sharply the labor hours needed to process an invoice. "In the beginning there were lots of trips to the customer to see their processes and understand their languages. My basic question to the customers is 'Tell me how you do your job'. From their answer I can create a more efficient means of getting the job done."

The very fact of making a process more efficient probably means a reduction in the customer's processing staff. "It can be difficult," Ray noted. "Sometimes people with 30 years of service in that department are let go. They and their friends are resistant. I often need to work through the customer's management to deal with that. The good news is that the staff which remains adapt because they have a better work day and they are improving their job skills."

Ray manages a small staff whose job is mainly to code. His own day starts at about 7:30 AM when he puts on his manager's hat, "monitoring where we are on our long term schedule and assuring that the developers are on the correct tracks. His second hat keeps Ray heavily involved in writing code.

Ray likes his job because he likes computers, problem solving and having complete autonomy. The next step is to move into either sales or upper management. "As time goes on, I will lose my competitive edge in coding to people freshly minted from colleges. So I want greater control and less coding," Ray explained.

Ray interviews job applicants at USI. "The number one skill I look for is problem solving. You could have studied electrical engineering, physics or art. The key issue is 'Can you reduce big problems to a series of *smaller* problems?' With that skill and a driving enthusiasm, you can succeed in this field."

To stay on top of his field, Ray is an avid reader of periodicals. "I read four or five technical magazines to stay current on that side and lots of business and financial periodicals to give me the more global view I need to make better marketing models for our future products."

Ray has come along way since he programmed computers as a seven-year-old. "Why not," he noted with a grin, "I am already 25."

Louis Matrone
Group Vice President
EDS

Imagine working for the same company for 20 years and still being highly energized and deeply committed. Louis Matrone of EDS fits that description perfectly. EDS is a global provider of information technology services to more than 9,000 customers.

Louis is a Group Vice President, responsible for the government sector (federal, state, and local) within the United States. He has four key responsibilities. The first is developing an overall marketing strategy, including a vision for the future and identifying markets to pursue. Second, Louis identifies horizontal synergies. "Let's take an example," Louis suggested. "Let's say we develop an information assurance package for the Bureau of Fish and Wildlife. They need it to protect the data the bureau gets from license applicants (e.g. social security number, driver's license). My job is to identify other government markets which could benefit from a similar package." Third, Louis builds a variety of relationships with vendors. Usually this involves supplying a specific service, which EDS doesn't want to create itself. "These relationships could be the deal specific or longer term," Louis told me. A fourth area is relationships with competitors. "This may seem a bit strange on first hearing it," Louis admitted "but we are competitors and not enemies. There are times when two companies have complementary capabilities and the client would benefit from a joint proposal."

Louis is the first person to hold his current position at EDS, but this is hardly his first job there. In fact, he has had nine major assignments, each lasting an average of two years. Let's go back to 1978 and see how Louis's career developed.

Louis attended Troy State College in Alabama on an athletic scholarship (for golf). He studied accounting with a thought to building his career in that field. Interviewing on campus for EDS' Accounting Development Program (ADP), Louis was impressed by the entrepreneurial spirit the company exuded and the high quality of the people who interviewed him. He was also impressed by a slogan that was at the company headquarters 'Eagles don't flock, you find them one at a time.' They made me feel that I was special already, just by receiving an offer from this company" Louis recalled. He accepted an offer to be in the ADP, based in Dallas.

Going through the accounting program, Louis began to sense that the company's business was really in the field, with the clients. " In order to process the payable, I had to confirm the charges with the EDS account managers. Speaking with them I began to realize that you had to add value to the client to generate revenue." Seeing Louis's interests, a mentor gave Louis the opportunity to be a staff accountant for an account in Alabama. "I loved dealing with customers, and I started to run the back end business," Louis recounted. "After a couple of years in Alabama I was offered an opportunity to manage finance for EDS' government units, and back to Texas I went. This position gave me financial oversight responsibility for lots of customer accounts." In 1982 EDS moved its headquarters for state and local governments contracts to Washington, DC and Louis made that move along with it. After two years, he assumed responsibility for Federal contracts as well.

Texas was calling again, however. Louis was offered the opportunity to be CFO (Chief Financial Officer) and subsequently deputy account manager for EDS' insurance subsidiary. In addition to managing operations, Louis was also responsible for 600 people. Success there led to an offer to handle the Medicaid contract in Connecticut. "It was my first account solely by myself," Louis explained, "so this was an important step." The experience in Connecticut was followed by a return to Texas in order to secure business with the Texas state government and grow other business in the Southwest. Louis was now responsible for six states. "All my past experience came in handy," Louis explained. "The accounting, finance operations, and marketing all help to understand the needs of your customers and that understanding is key to success." Louis was later promoted to Vice President for Business Development from the US, state and local government unit.

Louis's next move was to run the law enforcement and public safety sector as general manager responsible for all operations, sales and marketing. He was also called to work on a "mega deal" with the State of Texas. "Although the federal government eventually nixed the deal, my work there resulted in an offer to be CFO of EDS' Government Group. That experience led to my current job," Louis told me. Louis had to move around to move up (Alabama, Texas, Washington, DC, Connecticut). "Personally I enjoyed it all," Louis said, "I don't like to let grass grow under my feet. Every assignment brought new challenges and exposed me to new areas I needed to experience in order to grow. My mentors took me out of my comfort zone repeatedly and pushed me to the maximum. I always had a strong work ethic and never asked for a raise or for a new job." Louis continued, "Instead my success produced new opportunities and personal growth."

Reviewing his success and happiness on the job, Louis gave a great deal of credit to his mentors. "Mentoring wasn't someone's job description. I am referring to people who wanted to help me. Sometimes it was good advice, sometimes a morale boast and sometimes a kick in the pants, but it was always sincere and based on a desire to help. I believe that every relationship should be win/

win. Balance is a basis for loyalty. The company gives me compensation for the results it gets from me. The client gets what it needs in return for what it pays; I won't ask a staff member to do what I wouldn't do myself. This balance is an important value to me and it helps to explain why I am still with EDS," Louis concluded.

WHAT TO DO NOW

To help you prepare for a career with computers, the people interviewed for this chapter recommended organizations you can contact, as well as publications and Web sites that may prove useful in your search:

Organizations:

Association Information of
Technology Professionals .... www.aitp.org

Customer Support Consortium .... www.customersupport.org

Center for Intelligent Information
in Retrieval .... ciir.sc.us.edu

American Association for
Artificial Intelligence .... www.aaai.org

Association for
Computing Machinery (ACM) .... www.acm.org

Association for Information
Technology Professionals (AITP) .... www.aitp.org

Association of Online Professionals .... www.aop.org

Association for Interactive Media .... www.interactivehq.org

Association for Women in Computing .... www.awc-hq.org

Institute of Electrical &
Electric Engineering .... www.ieee.org

Publications:

EE Times .... www.eet.com

Info World .... www.infoworld.com

Internet World .... www.internetworld.com

CIO .... www.cio.com

Fast Company .... www.fastcompany.com

PC Week .... www.zdnet.com/pcweek

Information Week .... www.informationweek.com

Web Sites:

www.computerjobs.com

www.engineeringjobs.com

www.ispbusiness.com

2

Consulting

Expertise for Hire

Consulting sounds glamorous and maybe it is. Of course, there may be downsides as well. What kinds of business needs are met through consultants, what is their workweek like and what range of skills do they need to succeed? The consultants in this chapter will address those questions as they discuss their jobs in logistics, pension plans, shared service, transportation, Internet solutions and making business strategies work.

Consultants develop expertise through a combination of education and experience. However, we can see from each story that expertise is always necessary and never sufficient. Interpersonal skills are important for motivating consulting teams and eliciting vital information from clients. Persuading clients and their employees to embrace change requires the ability to overcome a self-protective aspect of human nature. Consultants work long hours, are frequently away from home and handle multiple tasks simultaneously. They enjoy variety, a fast paced work life and the professional company of talented, high-energy people.

Establishing and expanding a viable client base is the only way to stay in business. A consultant must have a marketable skill that is marketed well.

Jane Griesinger
Manager
Kurt Salmon Associates

When you order a widget from a catalogue, you expect it to arrive on time, in mint condition. If you need to contact your car insurance company at 2:00 AM, you expect a sympathetic ear and a pleasant person to take your accident report. The company that owns the widget distribution center or the insurance call center also wants you to get those things because they depend on providing fast, quality service to stay in business.

Jane Griesinger is a manager in the Princeton, New Jersey office of Kurt Salmon Associates, a consulting firm established in 1935. Working in the logistics practice at KSA, Jane helps clients make decisions which will make quality service possible and profitable.

There are several aspects to Jane's guidance. On the technical side, there is finding an optimum location, designing a new center, increasing efficiency in an existing center, and designing a transportation/distribution strategy. Jane needs to take into account space, the cost of labor, cost-effective equipment and the best operational approach. To do this job well, Jane uses her problem solving skills. She defines these as "thinking logically, creatively and flexibly to get to the end result."

As challenging as the technical considerations are, the most difficult part is the implementation. "People may not jump at the opportunity to change," Jane advised. "What I need to do is bring about a major change in thought patterns. In general, I focus on one of two themes: Why the client can't stay where they are or why the change will benefit those affected. To do this I meet throughout the project with the client's employees and keep them involved in all stages of the implementation."

With all her technical skills, Jane still needs her interpersonal skills to get the job done. "The most rewarding projects are those where you affect not only the operations in a facility, but the way that individuals approach their work." At one client distribution center managers who were initially very resistant to change evolved into sponsors of the change initiative and proactively sought out improvements. After they saw how the changes would benefit them personally, they embraced the initiative and looked for more. For Jane, that is the exciting part. "I love teaching people something that will change their lives, even if they are reluctant at first."

Jane typically manages 2 or 3 projects at a time, usually a mix of productivity improvement, distribution center design and logistics strategy. She manages several consultants on each client site who are there full time for the duration of the engagement. Jane herself spends about half her time at the client sites, traveling as required, and the other half in the Princeton office analyzing data and detailing designs. A standard week is 50 hours, but as deadlines loom, a 60-70 hour week is common.

There are many things Jane likes about her job. First, she truly enjoys her clients and working with them to obtain a defined goal. "Every client has different issues and approaches things differently. There are no cookie-cutter solutions at KSA." Second, Jane likes using the combination of intellectual and interpersonal skills her position requires. Third, "At KSA, everyone is treated with respect. You can walk into anybody's office without an appointment, sit down and exchange ideas. If you have a good idea, KSA will stand behind you to implement it. KSA gives you plenty of professional development and every opportunity to become a Principal in the firm if you perform well." Jane also spoke highly of her co-workers. "I am amazed and awed at how talented they are. Yet they are down to earth folks on a personal level."

Jane came to KSA after graduating from the University of Wisconsin in 1991 with a degree in Industrial Engineering. She had a large number of job offers in technical sales and line management, but accepted KSA's "because the values of the firm matched my own. Specifically those of putting the clients' interests first and having fun." Jane worked in four other locations prior to becoming a manager in Princeton. "I wanted to see the country, so relocating was a plus for me," Jane said. "If you don't want to relocate early in your career and travel about half the time later on, another firm or career may make more sense for you."

People interested in a consulting career like Jane's should carefully consider the firm's culture and the experience, (educational; professional) of those who have succeeded there. "At some firms your technical skills are paramount, at some a mixture of communication and interpersonal skills is central." In addition, there is a life-style question. "You need to enjoy travel, love working with people to solve problems and relocate when necessary," Jane advised.

Outside of work, Jane is a member of the National Catalog & Operations Forum and the Council of Logistics Management. Jane puts her volunteer time into service organizations and is an active alumna of her University. "I can't just be a member. I need to put my heart and soul into it."

Jody Larson
Actuarial Consultant
Hewitt Associates LLC

Let's say a pension plan guarantees vested employees a defined payment, often based on years of service and earnings history. Making sufficient payments annually to cover anticipated liabilities is a significant financial issue for corporations sponsoring such plans. Actuarial consultants like Jody Larson of Hewitt Associates LLC calculate appropriate contributions, determine accounting charges and assure compliance with government regulations.

"There are a number of factors to consider," Jody explained. "Mortality, disability and turnover rates are based on overall demographics as well as the company's past experience. In some calculations interest rate assumptions are government mandated." Jody's calculations must assure at least a minimum company contribution ("The government is very protective of people's pensions") without exceeding the government established maximum ("There are tax deductibility issues involved"). Every year, the differences between forecasts and the actual experience of a given company's plan are analyzed.

"Our regular office hours are 8:30 AM to 5:00 PM, but often times those hours vary based on client needs. Summers are especially busy because valuations for most plans need to be completed and government filings need to be prepared," Jody noted. She works on seven client accounts of varying sizes simultaneously, so the notion of a typical day doesn't really apply. "Variety is one of the fun parts of this job," Jody told me. However, time is generally divided among three kinds of activities: Working with other associates on client teams, consulting with clients over the phone and running applications on the computer.

Jody had considered an actuarial career as far back as high school, and chose Drake University in Des Moines, Iowa for its actuarial program. The large number of insurance companies and consulting firms in the vicinity make it relatively easy to acquire practical experience through internships. One of Jody's experiences was with a pension consulting firm in Chicago. Other internships were with insurance companies. When it came time to interview on campus, Jody preferred pension consulting to the insurance actuarial work with which she was also familiar. "I had several offers, but I preferred Hewitt," Jody recalled. "It was a good match for me because I liked consulting, wanted to live in a suburb of a big city and knew there would be many other young people starting at Hewitt with me."

"I was nervous at the beginning, because I had some fear that I would be number crunching all day," Jody remembered. "In reality, I have a chance to use my interpersonal and communications skills working with my team and with my clients. Learning how to present complex information in the best possible way is very important in helping our clients make decisions relating to their benefit programs." A good deal of judgement is involved, especially when new pension regulations are proposed. In addition Jody may need to work under intense deadlines. For example, when there are union negotiations or merger talks, she may need to help her client determine the answer to a pension question within thirty minutes.

Like many actuaries, Jody studies for professional exams required by the Society of Actuaries. "At my stage, there is an exam every six months. It's a bit like being in a graduate program," she mused. "The exams provide professional designations," Jody continued. "When actuaries sign-off on a report, we are saying that it was done to the best of our professional judgement. There is a lot at stake for me professionally, for the company financially and for the covered employees in terms of pension security."

Hewitt Associates, a global human resource consulting firm, is headquartered in Lincolnshire, IL, where it has 5,200 employees. Of these, 160 are pension actuaries like Jody. There are Hewitt offices throughout the country, and around the world.

George Heath
Director
The Amherst Group Limited

Should a company's internal support staff operate as an independent business? George Heath is a director of the Amherst Group, a management consulting firm which teaches people in support functions, or "shared services" to do exactly that. A function is considered support if it doesn't produce the actual product or service sold in the market place. Examples are finance, marketing, MIS, public relations and human resources unless they are the company's actual line of business.

"We believe that the overall company can benefit if the support services run like a business of their own," George explained. "That means treating the other units of the company like a customer. Instead of telling them what you can provide, ask them what they need." George helps his client develop metrics to measure the cost of an operation relative to the satisfaction delivered. This is done by developing formal surveys and engaging the internal customer in dialogue. "Eventually, we want the client to move to charging for shared services based on services provided and a defined cost. In terms of pricing, we help the client determine whether an hourly fee or a retainer makes the most sense," George told me. "Traditionally, efficiency principles have been applied only to 'outward facing' functions (those which more directly produce the product or service) only."

George divides shared services into four categories: "Governance" services, which satisfy organizational continuity and regulatory requirements; "Business Direct" services, which are unique to discrete business unit imperatives; "Expertise" services, which are knowledge or expertise-based; and "Volume-driven" services, which are volume intensive or transactual in nature. In George's view, expertise and volume-driven services should be competitive with outside vendors. "We want to put management practices in place which will make, let's say payroll, competitive on cost and quality with an outside vendor. If it isn't, the company could be better served by the outside vendor," George observed. "We are not trying to get rid of the payroll department. Instead, we want them to know their business impact and be able to produce a competitive value."

George acknowledges that the employees in a shared service function may have a great deal of anxiety about a consultant being present. "Many times they are concerned about a shift of power away from them to others in the company. Often they feel that we might be just another consultant coming in with the *panacea du jour*. Of course, people may also fear for their jobs," he said. "One way to deal with those anxieties is to focus on the goal, namely productivity gains. People tend to understand how important it is to stay profitable in a competitive marketplace," George suggested. "We are a work solution, not a people solution. Still, jobs may be at risk. We try to show employees the whole process and where it is going. Being brought into the picture and understanding the changes tends to lessen anxiety."

There is another factor in overcoming any resentment toward his firm. "As part of our engagement, management must communicate with employees and say 'This is management's decision. Amherst Group is here to help implement it.' "

As a director, George has several responsibilities. One is to solicit business. Of course reputation does generate its own referrals, but Amherst Group also sponsors seminars which attract potential clients. "If a company pays to attend our seminar, we know they have a business need or interest. We follow up with attendees to see if contracting with us makes the best sense for them," George said. When an opportunity is identified, George develops a proposal to the client which includes goals, methods and pricing. He also manages the overall process of the client engagement. "I spend about 65% of my time on billable activities. The rest is devoted to business development and internal business processes of the firm," George said.

George earned his bachelor's degree at Michigan State University in 1975 with majors in marketing and psychology. He began his career with an industrial market research firm in Chicago. Three years later, he started an MBA at the University of Michigan, focusing on finance and policy. "I wanted a broad business education and strategic planning issues were of the greatest interest to me at the time," George recalled. Upon graduation, he accepted a position with A.T. Kearney, a general management consulting firm in Chicago, in their Business Strategy Group. "Our primary focus was in business or market development such as entering a new market or perhaps an additional line of business. We looked at various possibilities, considering both external and internal growth options. For example, if the client made tiles for the OEM market, it might be worth considering expanding into the 'after market' with products and/or services such as installing floors," George explained.

After six years, George moved to Connecticut to become a principal in a small business services group. "They were in management consulting, but wanted to add capital and real estate development. Those were hot areas at the time," he recounted. "Unfortunately, our growth came at a faster pace than we could adequately fund. Networking through his connections with two previous consulting firms, George moved to a chemical processing focused consultancy in New York. "I was in the management, rather than technical side," he explained. That firm ran into internal troubles, and George saw the wisdom of networking his way to something else. He is now with The Amherst Group Limited, founded by Dr. Leland Forst, with whom George worked at A.T. Kearney.

George told me that he likes being with a small firm. "The firm has a clear sense of mission and I have a hands-on impact," he explained. "I know my work with our clients will be implemented, at least in part. At previous strategy firms, your best efforts could end-up locked in a file drawer 'for future reference'." George also likes taking marketing and business planning principles and applying them to the client's support functions. As a matter of life style, George told me that he has a lot of freedom to build a flexible schedule, within the content of a 10-12 hour work day. On the other hand, job security and income flow can always be a source of concern in a small firm.

John Takvorian
Associate
Reebie Associates

When I spoke with John Takvorian, he was one week shy of his first anniversary as an associate at Reebie Associates. Reebie is a 15 person consulting firm based in Connecticut which sells data and consulting service dealing with transportation. Clients could be freight carriers, shippers, departments of transportation (DOT's), and state and local governments.

John's primary responsibility at this stage of his career is to analyze data dealing with the flow and volume of commodities from origin to destination. Reebie has a huge data base called Transearch™ which is one of the tools John uses. He generally handles several projects concurrently and each can be of a different duration. "My long term projects are three months to a year; a short term project could be a day or two," John told me.

Let's take a simplified look at John's work. One of his clients, let's say a container shipping company, is a major player in a certain area of the country. They are examining the potential of developing an air cargo business. The question for John is, "Is the market such (based on volume; competition; synergies) that air cargo could be profitable?" To answer that question John will do a market segment and a ground level analysis. At the same time, a state government is considering a major investment in road building. John will examine the volume, content, origin and destination of current cargoes to evaluate the proposed road building project as a cost/effective public policy.

John is also getting a bit into marketing, a necessary skill to advance in consulting. This includes selling data to other consulting firms, and generating ideas for the firm's principals. "They are very open to questions and answers addressed to 'what next' issues. These include marketing current products better and developing products for new areas," John explained "Having solutions is necessary but not sufficient," John observed "If you have the right answers but nobody knows about it, who cares?"

John enjoys the variety offered by his company. "We are a small company, so everyone needs to take on more than one function," John told me. "This is also a creative business, since you need to find innovative ways to attack the client's problems." John manages his own schedule and projects which fits his personality. "I am a self starter who doesn't like rules and red tape," John said. "At Reebie the idea of cooperative effort is very real. There is always someone to answer questions or provide assistance," John stated.

Reebie is John's third employer. After graduation from Penn State in 1986 with a degree in Quantitative Business Analysis, John served four years with the US Navy. When he had fulfilled his military commitment, John started to work for an air borne freight carrier. There he was a loadmaster, a supervisor and hazardous material expert. "I developed my managerial skills there and had a chance to apply my analytical training to determining route structures," John remembered. "It was great for a while, but I plateaued. I wanted a more thinking kind of job." As good fortune would have it, the State of Connecticut instituted a program to pay full tuition for veterans who had been on active duty when Iraq invaded Kuwait. "That's my ticket to an MBA," John thought to himself and he enrolled at the University of Connecticut in 1995. That spring, John saw a posting from Reebie seeking a full time employee. John needed a summer time job only, but he didn't stand on ceremony. He applied for a three month position and was hired on that basis. A year later, Reebie hired John full time.

To enter a position like John's, it is helpful to have computer programming and/or transportation experience. "It would be tough to enter Reebie as your first job," John remarked. Writing skills are a major asset, as are speaking and listening. "To understand your client's needs, you have to engage in a dialogue that you can turn into a productive project," John observed. Intellectual curiosity is also very helpful. For example, John often reads trade publications to generate ideas and researches the Internet to identify ever more sources of data and other useful information.

Linda Ronan
Associate Partner
Andersen Consulting

Let's say that you meet Linda Ronan at a college alumni reunion. "So Linda," you might say, "what's up with you professionally? When you graduated in 1982, you were going to Andersen Consulting if I remember." "You have a good memory," Linda might reply. "The firm has changed a bit over the years and so have I. When you last saw me, I was off to training in Chicago as a staff analyst. Now I am an Associate Partner." "Oh yes," you might respond, "Your firm installs computer programs." "Do you have a little time?" Linda asks, "It's a bit more involved than that." Linda then proceeds to describe what she does:

"When companies want to affect a major change, they often turn to a consulting firm to help them define and implement an appropriate strategy. At Andersen Consulting we focus on Business Interaction; linking people, processes and technology to make the new business strategy work. Let me give you an example."

"A client in the health care industry has a business issue; they want to improve their customer service. Given that goal, Andersen Consulting, first works with the client to understand the business problem, define requirements and options, then work with the client to develop a detailed plan to implement the strategy. 'OK, this is what you need to do.' As a project director, I work with the client and the Andersen Consulting team to make sure that the client's expectations are met and to guide the team through the implementation. This involves being a bridge between Andersen Consulting and the client and between the various members of the Andersen Consulting team."

As you're listening to Linda, you might interject: "How do you do all this?" Let me tell you what we usually do: First we try to really understand the problem, from the client's perspective. What are they trying to solve or make better? Are calls taking too long to be answered? Do the people answering the phone have the skills to answer the questions? Does the customer service process cost too much? What is the real issue to be solved?

"If we find that the client wants to reduce the amount of time a customer call takes then we begin by looking at the process. In the example of customer service, we look at what happens when someone calls in. The client wants the call to be handled in the shortest possible time with the highest level of performance value to the listener. We observe with questions like these in mind. How is the call answered? How and why is the call routed to someone else? What is the content of the service the customer gets? What we then do is ask what needs to be done? In this case, based upon our experience on other projects we might recommend different training for the staff, a caller ID system and computerized medical records to meet the client's goals. We look to give John Doe, customer service representative, the tools and training he needs for the up-graded service."

Relieved that Linda will improve your productivity, you ask some more questions. "How do you allocate your work time, Linda?" Linda's response is something like this:

"You can think of my week in thirds. One-third of the week is spent with the executives of the client reviewing progress made and identifying any needed adjustments. I also work with our managers making sure that we have the right resources in the right places and helping to solve problems that have come up. Another third is spent with the staff to keep them motivated."

"That sounds good," you might say, "But some of the client's people may not be thrilled to see you there." Linda knows that situation well and describes it:

"Not everybody in the organization wants 'help.' Maybe they are afraid of losing their job. Perhaps they are just comfortable with things the way they are. Change can be unsettling and we understand that. Our approach is to work with the client's staff, explain what we're doing, and involve them in the process. That tends to alleviate fear. As much as possible, we want the client's people to work on implementing the changes because they are the ones who will work with the new process."

"This has got to be expensive," you wonder out loud, "and time consuming as well." Linda understands that the client may have constraints in terms of budget or time frame. "In many cases we use a phased strategy where you say, 'Given what you need and the operating constraints you have this is what we recommend doing now. The client can then start with smaller units of change and build from there." We try to focus on those areas which provide the highest value, first.

You ask about the skills Linda needs to do her job as Associate Partner well, and Linda gives you a reflective answer:

"You need to have leadership skills to move a team forward in the most productive manner. Part of that is being upbeat: when we hit roadblocks, we'll find a way to knock them down. Part of leadership is being able to articulate a vision towards which the team can work. You also need to have knowledge of the client's industry, like key factors in the market and significant trends. Being a manager means you can implement the 'change journey' so you have to know how to establish and analyze project milestones. You also need to keep your staff happy and excited."

"You seem so enthusiastic, Linda. What do you like about your job?" might be a logical next question. "Glad you asked," Linda responds:

"The two top reasons are that I love the autonomy I have and I love working with the people at Andersen Consulting. The firm gives you lots of autonomy, while holding you accountable for results, of course. They also give you the resources you need. It's kind of like running your own business with someone else's capital. The people are bright, energetic and committed, so they are fun to work with. There is also a touch of glamour in this business. You are working on critical issues and often work with very senior and talented client executives. You can also look at your accomplishments. My first project was working on a regional airport expansion project. More recently, I worked on a 'greenfield project' (i.e. a start-up business within a larger firm). The information technology and processing we helped to put in place contributed to part of this company's competitive advantage in the healthcare marketplace."

"I am an early bird, so I like to start work about 7:30 AM and wrap it up by 6 PM. One of the things I like about Andersen Consulting is that when my kids came along, I was able to work with Andersen to find projects which could enable me to better balance my work and home life."

Intrigued by what Linda has said, you ask a last question. "What advice would you give to someone considering your field?" A lot of people speak with Linda about that and she responds this way:

"If you are a recent college graduate, be flexible. There is a lot of travel and some very long, intense workdays. If you have industry experience and want to get into consulting, think about how you could use your experience to benefit a client and look to shift your focus from day-to-day operation to project work."

Linda's career at Andersen Consulting began in an interesting way. She was interviewed by a perceptive recruiter at Arthur Andersen, a public accounting firm of which Andersen Consulting was then a component practice. Linda had written on her data sheet that she wanted to be in consulting in five years. "You can actually do that right now if you want," he suggested. So when Linda graduated from the University of Massachusetts with her degree in accounting, she went to Chicago for training and started work as a Staff Analyst programming and installing software. "I had taken Cobol in college so that gave me a head start," Linda recalled. After a few years, she became a "Senior" with a staff of three to supervise. She then became a "Manager" with more responsibility including the entire implementation of payroll/HR project. After nine years she became an Associate Partner. "My duties now span the spectrum," Linda noted. "I'm still pleased I started by working at the detail level. I've worked in many roles, on many projects, and I feel like I have the experience I need to make day-to-day decisions as a manager and to be a credible project leader."

WHAT TO DO NOW

To help you prepare for a career as a consultant, the people interviewed for this chapter recommended organizations you can contact, as well as publications and Web sites that may prove useful in your search:

Organizations:

Andersen Consulting .... www.ac.com
Organization Development Network .... www.odnet.org
Institute of Management Consultants .... www.imcusa.org
Society of Actuaries .... www.soa.org

Publications:

Consulting News (Kennedy Information) ..... www.kennedyinfo.com
Consultants and Consulting Directory 1999
(19th Edition, Gale) 1-800/877-GALE

Web Sites:

www.ncni.com
www.handilinks.com/cat1/Employment.htm

3

Environment

Science, Business and Government
Protecting Mother Earth

In this chapter we will take a look at a variety of jobs focused on protecting the environment. Three combine training in natural science with a business function. The fourth provides a fact-finding service in earth and natural science areas. In all of these cases, technical training is important to make a living that supports a personal environmental commitment. Those who love Mother Earth should consider some study in natural sciences if they want to have a hands-on environmental job. Public advocacy and fund raising careers are not covered in this chapter.

These four stories reflect problem solvers who are ready to ask hard questions when necessary, have the ability to multi-task and possess a knack for dealing with scientists, public officials and business professionals.

A range of environmental issues are addressed. These include contamination clean-ups, clean water, business liability scientific investigation and monitoring natural hazards. These environmental professionals enjoy their working environment, in addition to their cause.

Shiela Chrisley
Federal Client Service Manager
Montgomery Watson

Caring for the environment is a business as well as a cause for many companies. A case in point is Montgomery Watson, an international environmental engineering technology construction services and management firm. Shiela Chrisley is Montgomery Watson's Federal Client Service Manager in the Northern California office. Her job is to market Montgomery Watson's services to agencies of the federal government who need to clean up some type of environmental contamination. These contacts are typically in the range of tens to hundreds of millions of dollars.

"Much of my job is internally based but externally focused," Shiela told me. Most of Shiela's time is devoted to writing proposals and developing strategies to win government contracts. Shiela needs to find the right message in order to strike a responsive chord with government decision makers. Her proposals, prepared in response to a notice that the government is accepting bids, range in length from 45 pages to seven volumes. (The super long proposals are less frequent now because the government is streamlining its procurement process to rely more on past performance than on volumes of text.)

Shiela is part of a core team of 8-10 marketing professionals and proposal writers, each with years of experience. If the company decides to submit a proposal, Shiela typically has 30-45 days from the time the proposal was requested by the government to produce a final product. These deadlines can require fourteen hour days and seven day weeks, so the process can be stressful. Once a bid has been opened for proposals, the government can respond to requests for clarification but will not address issues beyond that. Therefore, Shiela needs to rely on her own experience and the ideas of others at MW for developing the proposal.

Shiela enjoys the opportunity to be creative and told me that "it's fun to strategize." She likes the deadline-driven nature of her work because she is eager to produce her product and see its result.

About 30% of Shiela's job is outside marketing and related activities. In addition to finding new clients she attempts to find ways to maximize work under Montgomery Watson's existing government contracts. Most contract vehicles in this field are pre-approved so that an agency could utilize Montgomery Watson for its environmental clean up on as as-needed basis. Shiela loves the work with clients, existing and potential. Especially rewarding is "cutting to the chase" to identify and solve problems.

Four years ago, Shiela came to Montgomery Watson in a technical capacity as a hydrogeologist. She had earned a bachelor's degree in Geography and another in Geology at San Jose State University. While in college, Shiela worked for another environmental consulting firm. Shiela wanted a change and a large international company was very appealing. Through friends in the industry, Shiela found out about an opening at Montgomery Watson, applied for the job, and was hired.

Shiela was actively involved in site clean-ups ("heavy metal, solvents, fuels, pesticides, you name it," Shiela recalled) and became a field and project manager. Along the way, she worked on some proposals and enjoyed the work. Shiela announced her interest in moving into a more formal marketing role and the company agreed. "Montgomery Watson has been good to me," Shiela stated. "They gave me a new opportunity when I asked for it, and that's just one example."

Shiela has completed a master's degree in Geology while at Montgomery Watson. Her technical education has been a major asset, although not an absolute requirement to her marketing position. Some of Shiela's colleagues moved into proposal writing from marketing or writing positions but it can be harder for them to deal with technical issues as quickly and succinctly as they would like.

Staying current with the field is an on-going process. Shiela is a member of two professional associations: The National Water

Well Association and the Association of Engineering Geologists.

People interested in a job like Shiela's should obviously have good communicating and writing skills. In addition, they must not be afraid to ask necessary questions and take lots of initiative. "You need lots of energy and a desire to put in what it takes during crunch time," Shiela related.

Tommy Sisson
Regional Business Manager
OMI, Inc.

On a beautiful Georgia day in 1990, Tommy Sisson went to his job as a chemist at the City of Warner Robins waterworks. But this was not a day like all days. The city announced that it had contracted with an outside management firm, OMI (Operations Management International, Inc.) to run its water supply and water purification plants. "As workers, we had two choices: go with the new firm or try to find another job. In a small Georgia town, that amounted to one choice," Tommy recalled.

Tommy became the "lab director" for OMI in the Warner Robins plant. "I didn't complete my college degree, but I had taken every chemistry course available," he told me. Within three years, Tommy moved up through two levels of Assistant Plant Manager to become the Project Manager in his plant. "I had 15 years of experience in the waterworks system, so I could trouble shoot problems," Tommy said. "For example, let's say our tests show pathogenic bacteria in the water. We need to find the sources and a solution. We also contact our clients and the regulatory agencies. We have high ethics, so we report problems even if it's not mandated." Tommy also got involved with new issues like budgets. For example energy costs might be exceeding the budget. "Maybe we can find ways to reduce energy usage. But if the problem is caused by increased demand for irrigation water due to a drought, we need to work on some kind of cost sharing with the client," Tommy explained.

In 1995, Tommy was promoted to his current position, where he supports eleven different project managers throughout four southern states. Support can mean helping with written communication or advice on staffing issues. "Our project managers generally went to high school but not college. I may need to review draft memos to make sure they are professional in content and grammar, then help iron out any staffing conflicts," Tommy indicated. At the same time, Tommy may be dealing with service issues. "Let's say we have opened a new facility and the town it serves grows more rapidly than anticipated. Treating a greater amount of waste water may really push our system to the limit. I'll request information about facility size, load amounts and equipment types and see if I can suggest a solution," he explained.

Tommy tries to visit each facility at least every other month to look at quality control, quality assurance and maintenance issues. He also stays in touch with political issues. "Our typical clients are municipalities with populations ranging from 2,000 to more than 50,000 people. I look to develop personal ties with mayors, town managers and council members partially because I like them and partially because it makes resolving client issues much easier," Tommy noted.

When he is considering potential new project managers from among OMI plant workers, Tommy looks for people with good interpersonal and managerial skills, a familiarity with computers, strong math, and communication abilities plus a high level of integrity. In addition, anyone wanting to enter the field would need certification from their state in water and wastewater management.

Tommy told me that he enjoys the working atmosphere at OMI. "There is no sense of boss or subordinate here. Every effort is a team effort and anybody can talk to anybody about anything," Tommy said. "Plus I'm empowered to make my own schedule and there is nobody telling me what, when and how to do things." He could potentially rise an additional level, but is hesitant because of the increased business travel that would involve.

Looking back at that frightening day in 1990 when Tommy learned that he would move from the municipality to OMI as an employer, he feels that things have worked out well. "I had a low self perception, in part because no one told me I could better my-self professionally. OMI gave me a chance to move up that I wouldn't have otherwise. In addition my salary increased approximately two fold in 4 years. That's a significant increase for almost anyone. As a regional business manager, I make even more. Personally, professionally and financially, it was a great move for me," Tommy concluded.

OMI, Inc. is a subsidiary of CH2M Hill, based in Denver, CO.

Jane DeRafelo
Environmental Insurance Underwriter
ECS Companies

When you think about environmental careers, you may consider jobs that contribute to envrionmental protection; environmental insurance underwriting probably wouldn't come to mind.

Helping companies manage their environmental risk is how Jane DeRafelo contributes to protecting the environment. Jane is an environmental insurance underwriter for the ECS Companies headquartered in Exton, PA.

Jane joined ECS Underwriting in 1994 as an underwriter, applying her background as an environmental consultant to the business world of insurance. She rose through the ranks to become a senior underwriter and was recently promoted to Managing Underwriter. Jane works in ECS' Industrial and Commercial facilities underwriting unit, assessing and evaluating the risks faced by a variety of clients, including banks, colleges, hospitals, manufacturers, property owners/developers, warehouses and even pig farms, among others. Insurance brokers send Jane submissions, which she evaluates and assesses. If the insurance submission is for a manufacturing facility, for instance, she might evaluate the chemicals and materials stored on-site and how they're used in the facility's production processes. She'll also want to find out if the facility is near a body of water or the proximity of neighboring businesses or operations. Based on this kind of information, Jane will assess the facility's potential for causing a pollution condition that might require cleanup, contaminate surrounding properties or water bodies, or affect the health of workers and the public. Considering all of the facility's potential environmental exposures, Jane decides if ECS should insure the facility and, if so, the terms and conditions of the policy.

Clearly, Jane's background is critically important to effectively assessing and evaluating environmental risks. She holds a BA degree in Chemistry and is currently pursuing a master's degree in Environmental Engineering. Her previous career experience includes environmental consulting and waste management for a landfill. Once she joined ECS Underwriting, Jane was trained in underwriting, rounding out her technical background with insurance experience. Learning about insurance is a continuous process in which underwriters can test their knowledge by earning certifications in various underwriting disciplines. For instance, Jane is currently pursuing the Chartered Property and Casualty Underwriter (CPCU) designation.

While a technical background is important, excellent communication skills for negotiating and presenting are essential. In addition, an underwriter must be able to handle multiple tasks simultaneously. Jane is always responsible for a number of projects in different stages of development. "I see each project from start to finish," said Jane, "but you can't finish one project before starting several others." For a job like insurance underwriting, flexibility is important since a planned agenda is likely to be interrupted at any time.

Because an underwriter's job can be hectic, it demands the ability to juggle multiple tasks and responsibilities—from negotiating with insurance brokers and attorneys to servicing clients and performing technical underwriting. In addition, Jane also makes public speaking appearances to explain ECS' products to insurance brokers and to educate potential clients about coverage for their environmental concerns.

Despite the frenetic pace, Jane finds her job as an underwriter both challenging and rewarding. "When the negotiations are complete and I've underwritten an environmental insurance policy that helps our client turn an impaired property into a viable site for a school or homes or a new business," said Jane, "I get a great sense of accomplishment knowing that I've helped turn an impaired property into a productive asset."

Jane enjoys her job and values ECS as an employer. For Jane, ECS stands out from other companies in several areas: fully-paid health insurance, excellent 401K program, flexible work schedules, subsidized on-site daycare, quarterly performance reviews and education reimbursement. ECS provides Jane with the opportunity to continually enhance her knowledge and skills which, in turn, will contribute to her career growth. The ECS Companies provide *integrated environmental risk management* solutions through insurance, consulting and claims management to a wide range of businesses. These include everything from environmental consultants, engineers and laboratories to general contractors, transportation companies and real estate developers.

Barbara Ryan
Associate Director for Operations
United States Geological Survey

Barbara Ryan has been serving our country and our planet at the United States Geological Survey (USGS) for a quarter century. Since 1994, she has been the Associate Director for Operations, which includes managing a $1.1 billion budget, 10,000 employees and 400 offices located in every state. "The USGS is a Gateway to the Earth," Barbara explained, "and a gateway to information about processes in, on, and around the Earth."

The USGS does not manage Federal land, nor does it have any regulatory responsibilities. It does not serve as a policy advocate, or have its own specific policy agenda. Instead USGS provides, an objective, scientific, fact finding service in four earth and natural science areas: geology, hydrology, biology and geography (national mapping). The agency assesses natural resources, living and non-living. It also monitors natural hazards like, floods, volcanoes, and earthquakes. "If you live in California, you often think of us as the earthquake agency. In other states, you might think of us as the Nation's mappers, or if you're concerned about water quality and water quantity, the Nation's hydrologists," Barbara explained.

Barbara began working for the USGS in 1974 after receiving her undergraduate degree in geology at the State University of New York (Cortland). She came up through the Water Resources division and has lived and worked in seven different states and Washington, DC. To enhance her technical skills, Barbara earned a master's degree in geography from the University of Denver and a master's degree in civil engineering at Stanford University. The first half of her career was highly technical. She started out as a technician and later became a project assistant, project manager, and finally a ground-water specialist or senior advisor for water issues.

In the late 1980's, Barbara decided to continue her career on the administrative side. This has been and still is quite a challenge. "Scientists are an independent lot," Barbara told me. "You need to give them enough freedom to be creative while keeping them within the scope of our agency's role." One way Barbara does that is by getting the scientist involved in the proposal process which precedes any project. "If they get excited by the proposal, they'll put their knowledge and creativity into the project. This process bridges the scientist's allegiance to their discipline of interest and his/her devotion to the task at hand."

As technical as USGS work is, communication skills are critical. Since state and local communities (2,000 partners nationwide) often co-fund USGS projects, it is critical to explain to the community what they can expect to get out of the project and how it will be done. "If the community doesn't support the project, it may not happen," Barbara said. "Also, if we cannot identify an appropriate national need, we don't accept the project. Instead, we may recommend contacting a private consultant."

Barbara's role has two aspects. One is the business side of managing finances, optimizing facility utilization and paying bills. Good management is as important for the agency as good science.

"We achieved our first clean audit report in the history of the organization because I appreciated the significance of sound fiscal management and was backed by a very dedicated staff," she said.

In addition to being highly talented, Barbara is also deeply committed to USGS. She puts in her typical 12 hour day not merely to keep the agency running—she is building for the future. "USGS was founded 119 years ago and we can be proud of our accomplishments. However, if we want to be here for another 119 years, we need to learn from our past and adapt for the future," Barbara explained. There are huge opportunities for growth and creativity at the intersection of our four divisions," Barbara said. "Until now, our divisions have largely kept to themselves. In the future there will have to be more interaction. The earth is an integrated system. Big issues like climate change, ecosystem health and sustainable development can't be confined within one discipline. In order to adapt for the future we can learn from the past by using tools that are in and of themselves integrative. We do a lot of 'hind casting,' that is looking backward by studying ice cores, tree rings and sediment cores. We can see better where we are going if we understand better where we have been."

It's clear that good technical training is important at USGS. In fact, 15% of the employees hold Ph.D.'s; 20% hold master's degrees. However that wouldn't be enough, especially on the operations side. Barbara pointed to excellent communication skills, both written and oral, to relate scientific research to the concerns of the public. Barbara is also guided by the belief that everyone at USGS is a professional, from secretary to scientist, and should be respected as such. "This job requires high energy and commitment," Barbara concluded. "After all, I want USGS to be here for another 119 years…and the planet needs the USGS."

Lynn Taylor
Manager for Environmental and GIS Division
PAR Government Systems Corp.

Lynn Taylor has had three employers in thirty-three years, each of which has been in a similar field. Let's take a look at how Lynn developed his career and what he is doing now for PAR Government Systems Corporation. Lynn earned his bachelor's degree from Southern Illinois University in 1966. His major was earth science with a specialty in cartography and course work in aerial mapping. Upon graduation, Lynn took several graduate courses in regional planning, but took a position as a computer systems analyst with a defense contractor, rather than completing his graduate program. His specific function was defense mapping, which made good use of his specialized college courses. "You need to account for all kinds of things, for example the terrain, soils, vegetation and 'cultural' information aspects like transportation routes," Lynn told me. "With that information, you can make decisions on where to place troops and how they can maneuver across the terrain."

A friend left the company to start his own firm and Lynn joined him as a vice-president. "This company was also in defense R & D (research and development). I knew the president and after 11½ years with my first employer, I needed a change. Besides, becoming a Vice President was kind of appealing," Lynn recalled. He was again involved in computer mapping, which was now being called GIS, and planning and directing projects. The new firm worked on commercial applications of its technologies in addition to defense projects. After 9 years the company moved out of state, but Lynn didn't want to disrupt his family with a relocation. PAR was a "friendly" competitor of his old company, and taking a position there was a good match for everyone.

At PAR, Lynn develops project plans and markets projects and proposals. There are two broad service areas. The first is Research and Development for the Department of Defense. This includes building data bases and software to provide computer maps for a variety of military applications such as line of site and troop positioning planning, among other things. "Geo-spatial applications require a huge amount of data," Lynn explained. "As the power of computers has increased, we are less concerned about constraints imposed by computer capacity. That's a major change from when I first started my career and has enabled substantial growth in the GIS business sector."

The second service area is applying defense technology to environmental applications, especially water resources. "For example, we model watersheds for state and federal environmental protection agencies and do flood mapping for FEMA (Federal Emergency Management Agency)," Lynn told me. "Using advanced software to apply GIS and GPS (Global Positioning Systems) technologies, we can support the characterization (detailed mapping of the watershed and hydrology) for even a large river system. Remote sensing data is also very helpful in that regard." It is interesting to note that the Department of Defense encourages and supports the transfer of technology to civilian uses." The GIS technology which lays out military invasion routes can also plan school bus routes," Lynn said.

On both the defense and environmental service side, Lynn is deeply involved in front-end project planning like pricing, assigning tasks and scheduling. He also monitors technical plans, the direction in which the project is unfolding and accomplishments to date. "I can influence our technical approach to projects in part because I understand client needs and in part because of my experience in information technologies and data base development," Lynn told me.

Lynn also markets to clients. A good source is seeking out up-coming projects with current clients. Government opportunities are published in trade journals and the Internet. Lynn attends technical conferences both for networking and to see new methods being development and new requirements being sought. One improvement in marketing tools is to use demonstration projects for client presentations. "It's much more effective than using viewgraphs or the old paper proposal approach," Lynn noted.

The constant improvement in technology and methods provide a challenge that Lynn enjoys. "Invent, improve, apply, it's a constant cycle," Lynn told me. "Further every contact and every contract is unique, so variety is part of the job." In addition, Lynn enjoys solving problems and satisfying his end customers.

Both technology and project management skills are important to do a job like Lynn's well. "A sound foundation in the geosciences is essential," Lynn said "That could include remote sensing, GIS and GPS, and geo-spatial data bases in addition to geology or geography. Surveying and mapping are very helpful and knowledge of computer technology is a requirement." On the program management side, Lynn uses his computer tools to lay out plans, budgets and progress. Communication and interpersonal skills are also a part of the mix.

Even with many years of experience, Lynn says it is still important to take courses and attend conferences to stay current with his field. "The technology is changing dramatically," he noted "We always have new and improved technologies to integrate and apply."

WHAT TO DO NOW

To help you prepare for an evironmental career, the people interviewed for this chapter recommended organizations you can contact, as well as publications and Web sites that may prove useful in your search:

<u>Organizations:</u>

National Safety Council Environmental
Health Center .... www.nsc.org/ehc.htm

National Water Well Association .... www.ngwa.org
.... 800/551-7370

Association of Engineering Geologists .... www.acgwe.org
.... 978/443-4639

National Environmental
Training Association .... www.envirotraining.org

Water Environment Federation .... www.wef.org

Environmental Sensitivities Research Institute .... www.esri.com

National Association for
Environmental Management .... www.naem.org

National Association for
Environmental Professionals .... www.naep.org

Environmental Industry Associations .... www.envasns.org

Publications:

Recycling Times ...... www.wasteage.com/RCT/RecyclingTimes.htm

Sierra Magazine .... www.sierraclub.org/sierra

EPA Newsletters .... www.epa.gov/epahome/newslett.htm

Web Sites:

www.eco.org

www.awwa.org

4

Natural Science

Out of the Lab and Into Our Lives

This chapter is a bit unique in that it includes stories of three Ph.D.'s. No, they are not college professors, although they could be. Instead they apply their expertise, research capabilities and interpersonal skills to develop new products — whether pharmaceuticals or household goods. There is also an interesting story about applying bachelor degree level physics to unmanned submarines.

The scientist's work is not just theory. Dr. Kendrick Curry gets his ideas from both the laboratory and business needs. As Bill Scheper put it, seeing a positive end result is one of the profession's satisfactions.

As their career progresses, scientists begin to wear a second hat — namely manager. For example, Denice Spero manages a staff of 17, including 6 Ph.D.'s.

Derek Paley does most of his work independently, while the other people profiled work in teams. In either case, one of the great joys of a scientist is being around bright, highly motivated people.

Dr. Kendrick Curry
Project Scientist
Union Carbide

Dr. Kendrick Curry is a Project Scientist in Research and Development for Union Carbide. He works on developing new or improved chemical catalysts and providing manufacturing support. "One of the things I love about this job," Dr. Curry told me, "is that I see catalysts from their conception at the lab bench to the manufacturing plant... from conception to implementation."

Chemistry sometimes leaves our mind after our last science class in school, but it is very much an instrument for pushing society ahead. In Dr. Curry's case, he develops formulations for production processes of the future. He gets his ideas either from laboratory observation or in response to business needs (e.g. increasing capacity and developing new routes for getting into a chemical). A small staff of technicians reports to Dr. Curry. He designs and plans experiments, often using statistic methods, for the upcoming week or month. The technicians carry-out the experiments and report their data to Dr. Curry. They are very skilled observers. The technicians look for and record the normal and peculiar operation of the equipment/machinery that they operate. Technicians are often time versed in with the chemistry of the process in addition to the actual operation of the instruments. The chemistry background of a technician is definitely a plus when it comes to doing research and interpreting data. I believe that the combination of a willingness to learn, an observing eye, a good, solid chemistry background and good mechanical skill will describe the technician of the future," Dr. Curry told me.

Bringing a project from bench to plant involves a number of steps. As an example, a catalyst might be used in powder form at the bench, while industrial usage requires extrudates or pellets. Dr. Curry's operation must provide the bridge from one process to the other. This involves testing the powdered catalyst to determine its properties, finding ways to improve it and then "scaling it up" for plant use. Dr. Curry also conducts validation tests to make sure that the new catalyst is plant ready. "There is a great feeling of satisfaction," Dr. Curry told me, "in developing the yield of a chemical product which meets and exceeds targets."

Team work is an important part of the job. For example, at the start of a new project, Dr. Curry may have brain storming sessions with other members of a research cluster including the technicians. When it's time to "scale up" a project, he may meet with the plant manager, logistics staff, process engineers and business personnel, in addition to other research and development colleagues.

Dr. Curry is a man who loves the challenge his job entails. Because he is a catalystic person that happens to be a chemical engineer, he is really positioned to understand both laboratory and production plant issues.

Dr. Curry told me that there can be a great deal of stress in managing multiple projects, especially the time critical aspects. At the same time, he sees the stress as a challenge which helps him to maintain his focus. Further, if one project is stymied, he can still make progress on another. This ability to shift focus becomes a good way to relieve stress. Dr. Curry spoke enthusiastically about the broad base of projects he can grow with at Union Carbide and the satisfaction he feels at making a valuable contribution.

Dr. Curry earned his master's degree and doctorate in chemical engineering at the University of Michigan. He told me that a master's degree might be sufficient for some research and development jobs, but "your head could bump-up against a lower glass ceiling than Ph.D.'s." A Ph.D. "gives you a license to create," Dr. Curry remarked. "It gives you training in addressing open-ended research questions, by forming hypotheses, looking for meaning in the data (hypothesis verification or contradictions), drawing conclusions and writing up the results."

The Ph.D. is such a useful tool in this field that Dr. Curry recommends going straight through to earn it without stopping between degrees for a full time job. "There's too much chance that one could get side-tracked and never finish," he warned.

At one time, Dr. Curry considered a career in academia, but he enjoys the practical outcomes of what he is doing. "In the future," Dr. Curry predicts, there will be more collaboration between industry and academia in fields like chemical engineering." Dr. Curry has done some teaching in math and science at a small local college while at Union Carbide. His purpose in teaching is to return some of the knowledge that he has obtained to society.

To you who are considering a career like Dr. Curry's, he recommends exploring specific niches such as synthetic organic chemistry, corrosion science and materials engineering—perhaps through internships. "Having a clear focus you truly love is part of what makes you marketable."

Derek Paley
Analyst
Metron, Inc.

If you combine analytical training in the physical sciences, intellectual curiosity and a facility with computer programs, you could have a job like Derek Paley's. Derek investigates applications of distributive robotics for oceanography and national defense at Metron, Inc., a consulting firm in Reston, Virginia.

"This is a cool place to work," Derek, a 1997 Yale graduate with a degree in Applied Physics, told me. "It's half-way between a regular corporation and a graduate laboratory. My project manager, like most of the people here, is a Ph.D. He outlines a project for me and the appropriate algorithms (e.g. procedures for solving a mathematical problem in a finite number of steps) and I take it from there."

Derek was initially assigned to an in-progress project in periscope detection. "By using sophisticated statistical inference algorithms which Metron has developed, I tested the ability to filter-out clutter, estimate a target's position and the probability of detection." To do that, Derek wrote computer code, compiled it and configured the parameters. "The volumes of data are huge. Sometimes, I run the data all night and examine the results in the morning," Derek explained.

For a second project, Derek worked on hypothetical issues related to unmanned submarines called Autonomous Underwater Vehicles. Each vehicle runs its own software and has to plan its own route. However, each AUV must also transmit some data to others participating in a broader task. "I have done some reading about geese and other creatures in nature because they exhibit a similar behavior," Derek said. "Each bird is concerned with its own height, speed and distance from the center. Yet we don't say 'there go twenty birds.' We say 'There is a *flock* of birds.' A group behavior emerges from many individual behaviors." Of course, for this project Derek doesn't observe birds in flight. Instead he utilizes "heuristic optimization methods," like genetic algorithms simulated annealing and tabu search.

If you are a layman like me, Derek can provide a simplified explanation for his technical terminology. Genetic algorithms are a member of a class of evolutionary algorithms that emulate the biological process of natural selection to evolve near-optimal solutions to complex problems. Simulated annealing adopts principles from statistical mechanics to find global extrema. Tabu search is a randomized optimization method that keeps track of attempted solutions to guide future attempts.

Derek enjoys his job for several reasons. One is that "it's fun to be around so many bright people who are equally happy giving you a personal lecture on the finer points of mathematics as they are helping you with a specific problem." In addition, Derek is interested in distributive robotics as a field. "It could be geese or submarines as far as I'm concerned," he suggested. The analytical issues and hypothetical questions are what Derek enjoys most. A typical project extends for several years, so there is time to explore and investigate cutting-edge issues in depth.

At Yale, Derek became interested in physics because of an especially talented professor. "Before that, I was thinking of medical school," he noted. To avoid "a horrendous lab section" and be able to do research instead, Derek pursued the applied physics track. That decision helped make Derek attractive to Metron when it recruited on campus, and the fact that the recruiter was an enthusiastic Yale alumnus helped sell Metron to Derek.

The two computer languages Derek uses most, C++ and Java, were learned on the job. "It was one week of intensive classes in C++, then a lot of hands-on," Derek recalled. He already had experience in C, so the transition was not that difficult. Derek learned Java because of its value for making presentations. In general, Derek feels that computer skills are a helpful tool for him rather than any special passion.

Derek works independently most of the time, but doesn't feel alone. "There are plenty of people to just chat with if you want a break and everybody is ready to help when you need it," he observed. Compensation is by the hour, so Derek gets paid for overtime. "That feels good when you're working 60 hours during crunch time," he said. In non-crunch time Derek enjoys tennis and rock climbing.

"Working here provides the opportunity to explore intriguing issues, work with brilliant people and have a life outside of work. What more could I ask?" Derek concluded.

Dr. Bill Scheper
Section Head
Procter & Gamble

As the autumn leaves were falling at Xavier University in 1986, a senior chemistry major was sitting on a bench contemplating his future. He saw three potential career paths ahead of him, and soon he would have to choose which fork in his professional road to follow.

One approach Bill Scheper considered was getting a job with his Bachelor of Science degree. "The problem is, there would be tight constraints on what I could do professionally," Bill reasoned, based on advice he had been given. "Some of my friends are going to medical school, but that just doesn't meet my goal to continue growing as a scientist and developing a fundamental understanding of what is going on at a basic level. For me, the best path is to work for a Ph.D. One advantage is that it may be possible to work as a graduate assistant to earn a small stipend and a tuition waiver. That way, I won't have a mountain of debt when I graduate," he reasoned.

With that decision in mind, Bill sought counsel from his professors. He was advised to seek a large, highly ranked chemistry program to maximize his exposure to current research. Purdue University was a good fit, offering one of the strongest Analytical Chemistry Departments in the country and attracting world renowned scientists, speakers, lecturers and visiting faculty. Bill started a six year program there. "You don't need a master's degree — you can go straight for the doctorate," he explained. "The first year was the more heavily involved with class work. After that, the focus was more on research. I was a teaching assistant for two years and a research fellow for four. That financed my life at a body remaining united with soul level," Bill recalled. "What came out of it was this," he continued, "I learned to do independent research and think as a scientist."

Bill felt early on that he wanted to go into industry rather than university teaching. "I wanted to see a positive end result, something people could actually use," Bill told me. "A university would tend to focus on basic research to be read by a relatively small handful of other scientists. That just didn't appeal to me." To Bill's good fortune, a number of prominent companies recruited actively at Purdue. Bill was impressed by one company in particular: "Procter & Gamble impressed me with their strong scientific research programs, large research and development budgets, and outstanding people. In addition, I wanted to return to Cincinnati," Bill recalled. He did well in the interview and was hired to begin working in the "upstream" aspect of product research.

"It was a bit of a surprise," Bill related with a smile. "I never realized what it takes to put a detergent formulation together." Bill "designed molecules," which is not quite like designing jeans. "It could mean designing a new molecule or it could mean utilizing an existing molecule in a different way. In either case, what prompts the start of a new project is either a consumer need or a new chemical technology discovered by a Procter & Gamble technology group. Some of the work is pure chemistry," Bill noted. "For example, if we had more suds, we thoroughly research what has been done in the past, build technical models and identify molecules to address the technical target. Once we identify a lead to produce something more 'sudsy,' we also must ensure that our new ingredients fit well with other ingredients in the product. At the same time, we need to consider commercial viability and meeting applicable safety standards. Finally, will consumers notice and value the improvement. The path from concept to execution has many hurdles."

"The development cycle for a new or improved product can be six months to two years or more. We start with a small group and add new people as the project develops. These include natural scientists as well as business people and manufacturing experts. After all, we need to know if we can 'scale-up' from the work bench to large production at a reasonable cost and without losing the very properties we're trying to introduce."

Bill spent his first five years at Procter & Gamble "on the bench." In the first year, he did his own analytical work. However as time progressed, he spent less time in the laboratory and more time doing planning. By the end of his second year, Bill spent 80% of his time on project planning and had a research assistant to execute his plans in the lab.

In 1997, Bill was promoted to Section Head. "My two main responsibilities now are strategic planning and developing my staff. A large amount of my time is spent in groups discussing ideas, defining goals, thinking of new approaches. Working with such bright people is exhilarating. I currently have four Ph.D.'s reporting to me and additional research assistants in my section. There are no formal ceilings here. I intend to develop everyone professionally. Even someone with a bachelor's degree could rise to the highest technical levels in this organization. At Procter & Gamble, we promote from within," Bill noted with satisfaction. "This is a part of the job I really enjoy."

Bill likes many other aspects of his job as well. One is the mix of projects, perhaps five or six, in which he is involved at any one time. "It's a special pleasure to see one of our technologies going out to a consumer test and learn that our inventions are truly valued by our consumer," Bill noted.

As much as he loves his job, Bill tries to find a balance with his other "projects" — his wife and five children. "I try not to let work intrude on our weekends," he told me. "I set priorities and live with the fact that low priority items may not get done. During the week, I can work on my laptop after supper so I don't have to stay so late at my desk. After all the work I put in on various soaps and detergents, I want to leave time to see my kids in clean clothes, eating off clean plates, in a spotless house," he chuckled.

Bill reminded me of important advice about graduate school: There are two possible experiences: love it or be miserable. Don't start a program unless you're sure you love it. It is a major advantage to earn your degree at an institution where a firm like Procter & Gamble interviews on-campus. Sending your resume to Ph.D. Recruiting Office can work, but it is much more difficult.

Bill also said that your technical skills are a must, but team work and communication skills are important if you want to maximize your impact on the organization and advance. Remember that within a team, each individual is relied upon to deliver. You can't hide or ride on someone else's coat tails. To obtain a leadership position, you need a vision of how to do things better and the capability to bring the vision to fruition.

Dr. Denice Spero
Assistant Director of Medical Chemistry
Boehringer Ingelheim

Jane Austin had to take a backseat for a while, no fault of her own. It seems that an English major at Wheaton College in Massachusetts registered for a course in organic chemistry. It was a thrilling experience. There was less time for Emily Bronte when Denice Spero decided to change to a double major in biology and chemistry.

Denice went straight to graduate school, earning a master's degree at M.I.T. and a Ph.D. at Brown University followed by post-doctoral study at Harvard. In 1989 she and her husband sought career opportunities together and received three joint offers. "I favored Boehringer Ingelheim because of its open interdisciplinary atmosphere. There were positive career tracks for women and not a lot of managerial levels. The company was large enough to support high quality research, but small enough that I could make an impact," Denice recounted.

Let's fast-forward a bit to the present. Denice's mission is to discover and develop treatments for immunological diseases like multiple sclerosis, gastrointestinal disorders and rheumatoid arthritis. In pursuit of that mission she wears two hats, manager and scientist. As manager, Denice oversees the work of 17 scientists, including 6 Ph.D.'s. "They have a great deal of leeway from me and I value everyone's input. I have a very talented group of scientists in my section and they all contribute ideas. I look at the ideas and prioritize," she explained. "Every two weeks we have a strategy meeting. It's a team approach and we decide on 'where to go from here' issues. I give guidance and provide support that might include exposing them to areas of pharmaceutical research which are new for them. Most chemists in our department are trained as synthetic organic chemists. In the pharmaceutical industry, they need to learn many new areas such as biology, pharmacology and drug metabolism. I try to help them with this learning process. For example, I set up an interdisciplinary seminar series at Boehringer Ingelheim. Every month we have a different speaker from each department. One of the great challenges of working in the pharmaceutical industry is to become proficient in many different fields."

As a scientist, Denice is a project manager in charge of an interdisciplinary team, including chemists, biochemists, toxicologists and immunologists. Her goal there is to take a scientific program from its inception to its availability as a drug.

Denice explained the essence of the research process to me in layman's terms. There are specific biochemical pathways which can cause a disease. The scientist seeks a target within that pathway with the intent of being able to modify it. If one member of the pathway can be modified, it will modulate the disease. By way of analogy, if the scientist can knockout the pathway's "railroad bridge," s/he can stop the disease in its tracks.

Of course, Denice didn't start her career in her current position. Her first job was "senior scientist," and she worked hands-on at the laboratory bench on a single program. She was part of a team of scientists and had one "associate" working under her direction. This associate was very talented and she encouraged him to pursue his education. He now holds a Ph.D. from Stanford University. As a senior scientist Denice worked on the development of an anti-asthma drug and also carried out basic research.

Denice was promoted to "principal scientist" and also moved to the chemical development area. "This was pure chemistry and I also experienced downstream events, namely moving a compound from discovery to development. That exposure has helped me know what criteria a compound should meet for it to be successful in development. Working in development also provided excellent training for setting timelines and achieving goals." After four years or so, Denice was promoted to "senior principle scientist," and was quickly promoted again, this time to her current job as "associate director" in the medicinal chemistry department.

For Denice, her work is a seven day a week calling. She is at the company from 7:30 AM to 6 PM during the week. Saturday and Sunday are given in significant part to reviewing data and a continual reading of professional literature.

Denice loves science because "it provides a constant opportunity for learning." She also loves the team work environment and the constant interaction with colleagues, staff and supervisors. "There is some stress from wearing several different hats," Denice noted, "but I am well organized and have learned to prioritize." Since starting her professional career, Denice has had some twenty refereed articles published in scientific journals and has also earned patents for her discoveries.

What is the next step for Denice? She does not want to speculate but says that she will continue to work hard and see where it takes her. She has no interest in an academic career because the interdisciplinary nature of Boehinger Ingelheim is too precious to lose.

Denice said that if you want to succeed in science, you can't stop learning simply because you have earned all your degrees.If you are not sure you want to make the commitment to earn a Ph.D., work in the field at a lower level, then decide. If you are well organized, a good scientist can still find time for Jane Austin & Emily Bronte.

WHAT TO DO NOW

To help you prepare for a career in natural science, the people interviewed for this chapter recommended organizations you can contact, as well as publications and Web sites that may prove useful in your search:

Organizations:

Sigma Xi: The Scientific Research Society .... www.amsci.org

National Academy of Sciences .... www.nas.edu

America's Pharmaceutical Companies .... www.phrma.org

American Institute of Physics .... www.aip.org

American Chemical Society .... www.acs.org

American Institute of Chemical Engineers .... www.aiche.org

Publications:

American Scientist .... www.amsci.org/amsci/amsci/html

Science .... www.sciencemag.org

Scientific American .... www.sciam.com

Biomednet: The Internet Community for
Biological and Medical Researchers .... www.biomednet.com

Web Sites:

www.biospace.com/sd/career

http://jobs.cell.com

5

Manufacturing

Making the Tangible

Sometimes it is hard to remember that we produce tangible products in the United States. The manufacturing process includes many steps, such as purchasing input, agreeing to contracts, working on the shop floor and various facets of engineering. In this chapter, eight separate people describe their role in manufacturing and why they love their jobs.

Some interesting threads appear in a number of stories, such as the importance of quality. Harry Bernard points out objective factors like ISO 9000 certification and subjective factors like employee enthusiasm. Jeff Bykowski has an accuracy tolerance of .001 of an inch. For Jim Mackey, the very product he supports is designed to test quality.

A second thread is acquiring a variety of experiences. Lorie Mahoney called each of her many assignments an eye opener. Mark Snyder felt that having different jobs with one employer was like having different jobs with different employers. Jim Christie moved from working on the production floor to managing daily operations.

Beth Hinchee gave an example of a third thread: Excitement at doing things better, faster and (maybe) less expensively.

A fourth thread is change. From the way we order inputs to the design of final products, improvement through change is part of the process.

Harry Bernard
Purchasing Manager
Teradyne

Harry Bernard had an interest in the purchasing function of a business even when he was in college. "I attended Curry College, in Milton, Massachusetts," Harry recounted "One of my electives was a course in purchasing which I thoroughly enjoyed. During my last semester, I took a full time internship in a factory which manufactured machines that tested the utensil strength and fatigue of materials. When I graduated in 1981, I accepted a position in a small manufacturing facility. At age 21, I ran the purchasing department. My internship experience was sufficient background for that. Of course, that was back when we did everything by paper and it was, after all, a small company."

Harry defined a purchasing agent, or "buyer," as an agent authorized by the organization to expend funds on its behalf. "You need to spend the money as if it were your own" Harry explained. "That means be wise, not necessarily cheap. It's important to look at the total cost of ownership." Contrary to the image outsiders sometimes have, buying is a highly ethical profession. "We cannot accept gifts of value from a supplier. If we have a lunch meeting together, I am the one to pick up the check at least 50% of the time." Ethics show themselves in attitude as well. "You can't use the company's check book to act like a tycoon on a shopping expenditure. We are on a purchasing mission, not an ego trip," Harry noted.

After three years with his first employer, Harry accepted a position with Teredyne, a manufacturer of automatic testing equipment. "I was attracted by the high tech nature of the company." Harry spent ten years in the "inventory" side of purchasing, namely tangible goods directly related to the manufacturing process. He then spent three years in "services" which includes things like painting and construction.

When Harry evaluates a possible supplier, he is looking for a potential long term relationship. "I look for some objective factors like ISO 9000 certification and a TQM (Total Quality Management) program," Harry explained. "I also look for subjective factors like how enthusiastic employees are. Speaking with employees informally as you walk around can tell you a lot." Both objective and subjective factors are weighed to answer an overriding question: can this company make a *quality* product *consistently*.

"Our approach to purchasing is quite different than it used to," Harry told me "For example, we used to be orderers and hagglers. Today we are looking at the totality of a cost effective solution. We used to diversify our sources of supply. Today we order as much as possible from one supplier." There are several reasons for this new approach. "We want to take advantage of economies of scale," Harry explained. "In addition, we want to be as important as possible to the supplier. The relationship is like a business marriage. If there is trust and cooperation, both parties benefit." The trust extends to the point where Harry sends Teradyne production forecasts so that the supplier can adjust accordingly. "Neither of us wants to build up idle inventory," Harry observed.

The purchasing function itself has also changed. "We are organized more on a supply line basis, almost like an assembly line" said Harry describing the new approach. "The commodities managers who report to me make initial contacts and scope out the possibilities for the commodities they control. At my end, I help develop overall strategies. The commodity managers bring in a potential source, I evaluate the situation, then negotiate the details and pricing. In previous years, one buyer would handle any given relationship from start to finish."

Harry reports to a supply line manager. A typical day starts at 7:30 AM and ends between 5 PM and 6 PM. Harry's compensation is based on salary and profit sharing.

Harry uses a variety of sources to identify possible suppliers "We use anything we can get our hands on," Harry said. "Trade journals, the Internet, the yellow pages, people we meet at conventions. The search for a long-term relationship requires a full picture of your options," Harry noted.

One of the things Harry likes about his job is the daily interaction with so many people including, engineers, accountants, shipping, his suppliers and his own staff. "The funny thing is," Harry noted, "I used to be shy." Harry also enjoys the wide range of issues he deals with in a rapidly changing industry. "I love solving problems, and in my industry, there are always new ones." Harry makes a point of treating everyone as a customer. "In satisfying them and their needs, I find satisfaction for myself," Harry said. Working indoors is a plus for Harry. "I work 85% within the facility. That eliminates a lot of traveling in the snow and cold of a New England winter."

Common sense is an important skill in purchasing "You don't have to be a rocket scientist," Harry suggested, "but you do need common sense to be a good problem solver. Reading non-verbal communication and listening carefully is also helpful. "If you are still not sure what the client wants, you need to ask 'What do you want?' Being that direct is difficult for some people," Harry suggested. Analytical skills are also important to determining both halves of the "cost/effective" consideration.

Although Harry works for a high tech company, "You don't have to be an engineer to succeed in purchasing here. I learned enough technical matters on the job. We have an ex-seminarian and a former teacher on my staff. There's more than one way to break into purchasing," Harry told me.

Jim O'Hare
Director of Contracts and Estimating
Bath Iron Works

The Bath Iron Works is one of six major shipyards that bid on contracts, to build vessels for the US Navy. Jim O'Hare is a key player in the contract process at BIW.

Jim has three major functions. The first is to develop estimates to bid on a new job. "Typically the Navy thinks in terms of a 'class of ships'," Jim explained "That means ten to fifty copies of a similar design to be produced within 15 - 20 years. Usually four or five ships of a general class will go to bid at any one time." Jim manages a group of 60 to 90 people (one-third are direct reports; the rest come from functions throughout the company) to work on the estimate. They take into account, the ship's size, what's on it, design costs, work-hours needed and inflation expectations.

A second function for Jim is negotiations, which come in two parts. Early-on when the Navy requests a proposal, there is discussion about payment terms, escalation clauses and provisions for sharing cost overruns or underruns. If BIW's bid wins the contract, there are often negotiations regarding the pricing of changes the Navy wishes to make. "You need to remember that from bid to purchasing materials to production can take six years," Jim noted. "In that time there are lots of changes due to technological innovations which affect combat and operating systems. Changes are then called for, but we have to agree on the right price."

The third function for Jim is administering the contract. "Every ship is a floating city with complex equipment and hundreds of crew. I make sure that we are performing in accordance with the contract and are meeting the Navy's specifications."

Jim spends a good deal of time on the phone reviewing the progress of contracts in operation, contracts under bid and any outstanding litigation. This means constant contact with the thirty five people on his staff, military and civilian personnel at the Pentagon and BIW lawyers. "We usually have several overlapping production contracts under way and a few more under negotiation with the Navy or international customers. There are a lot of balls to keep your eyes on." Jim said.

"This job is very demanding," Jim told me. "That's one reason I like it so much. I need a broad understanding of operations, finance and contracts. There is a lot to do and you have to do it right. There is pressure from everywhere, especially when something is being negotiated. I need to be tough but open minded at the same time." One of Jim's proudest moments was orchestrating BIW's winning bid on a $2.1 billion contract to build six ships. "Our shipyard will be working on that contract until 2006," Jim commented.

Jim's career began in 1973 when he earned a degree in finance. For two years he worked for a bank in New York before accepting a position with a large public accounting firm in Portland, Maine. "They weren't that sticky about my not being an accounting major as long as I passed the CPA (Certified Public Accountant) exam, which I did," Jim recalled. "I didn't really like public accounting, but it was a great stepping stone for my career." The next stone Jim stepped on was three years in internal audit for a large conglomerate. In 1981, he came to Bath Iron Works as the Manager of Internal Audit. "My five years there gave me the chance to see lots of operations and to really understand how the company functions. In 1988, Jim became the Director of Estimating, his first hands-on exposure to that critical function. Over time he consolidated a number of estimating activities into his current job.

Jim's advice to college students interested in a career like his is to get intensive training in accounting or finance. "An MBA would be helpful, but I didn't get one," Jim noted "My CPA was sufficient." If you are already in the work world, Jim suggests branching out. For example, if you are in finance now, do something in the operations area as well.

Lorie Mahoney
Team Member
Osteonics

Lorie Mahoney arrives at Osteonics, a supplier of orthopedic implants based in Allendale, NJ at 7:00 AM. She is a "team member" of a four-person group investigating technologies to identify product beginning with the manufacturing process all the way through packaging. Lorie was chosen for this yearlong project because she has been "respected and relied on for getting things done throughout her fifteen years at Osteonics." The team conducts its investigation on the Internet, by screening vendors and by attending trade shows. "Like all my assignments at Osteonics, this one has been an eye opener," Lorie told me. "I hadn't been involved in such extensive research and I am learning more about production, packaging, and costs."

Lorie started in packaging at Osteonics after graduating high school in Allendale. "My sister's fiancé recommended the company and it was local, so I applied," she recalled. "I was about the 40th employee then, but now the company has grown to almost 800." After three years in packaging, Lorie moved to "microstructure," a process of applying a beaded surface to implants which help them adhere to the patient's natural bone. When several departments consolidated, Lorie returned to packaging, as a "lead person," where she assisted in supervising the packaging area. "It was interesting to me because I saw how important labeling is and I had my first chance to use a computer on the job," Lorie recalled.

After a few years, Lorie had another growth experience. She was promoted to supervisor of packaging, responsible for assembly, cleaning and labeling of medical devices. "I was getting ahead in a growing company and I experienced the budgeting process for the first time. I was now managing other employees, which was challenging," Lorie recounted.

Lorie had another opportunity to learn something new when she became a supervisor in the returned goods area. "I saw for the first time how customer service and accounting are connected," she said. The new assignment also provided exposure to automated system transactions and inventory control.

In the early 1990's, Osteonics reorganized on a "cellular manufacturing" basis. It was a team-based approach, which designated a specific "cell" for a specific product line. For example, one cell had total responsibility for hips while another was responsible for knees. Initially, Lorie had mixed feelings about the change. "I thought I had been climbing the ladder and had achieved a certain status. Now the company abolished titles and I was just a team member. My sense of purpose was shaken," Lorie remembered. However, after she saw how the new system functioned, she felt that "it was the best thing that ever happened to me." Lorie began to see what happened with the product "outside the walls of Allendale." Within Osteonics, the *physical* walls in the manufacturing area were torn down, which increased communication and provided a better sense of a common goal. Lorie was also on the floor more, which she liked. Lorie enjoyed the new experience of group brainstorming to solve problems and had an opportunity to participate in a team to transition an operation from a PC-based platform to the mainframe.

When a new team was formed for spinal implants, Lorie joined it. For the first time, she worked with Research and Development and Marketing as members of a common team. Lorie applied for a position as product inspector, responsible for inspecting implants sent by an affiliate in France. As the unit grew, she had her "eyes opened again," taking responsibility for planning the spinal inventory, which included the timing, type and quantity of devices to be ordered. Lorie also increased her communication with field staff and learned what it takes to distribute and sell the product.

Looking over her experience at Osteonics, Lorie likes the opportunities she has had to grow and to learn new things. She has seized the opportunity for additional education as well. Utilizing her company's tuition reimbursement program, Lorie earned an associate's degree in business and is pursuing a bachelor's degree with an emphasis in Management Information Systems at Ramapo College in Mahwah, N.J.

Lorie identified several skills and attributes which have helped her advance professionally. "I learned how to tap into resources to get the job done. Also I volunteer for new tasks, which shows upper management that I am enthusiastic and eager to grow," she said. "One more thing. I am very focused. I eat, drink and sleep whatever project I am on."

Lorie noted that if she applied today for her job, she would need a college degree. "I was lucky to grow into a good job with only a high school diploma. Today it would be different. If you have the chance, go to college," she advised.

Jeff Bykowski
Senior Second Pressman
Quad/Graphics

An employee has been on the job for three weeks. His son has a medical problem and the new insurance carrier won't extend coverage due to a pre-existing condition. The employee sends an e-mail about the problem to the founder and president of this $1.2 billion in sales company. Within two hours, the new employee receives his initial response. Within two days, he receives a long memo from the president explaining how to resolve the insurance problem.

Does this sound like a fantasy? For Jeff Bykowski, a senior second pressman at Quad/Graphics, (a full service printer of magazines, catalogues, books and other commercial products), that is exactly what happened. It explains part of why he travels 78 miles each way to his job when he could work for another printer three blocks from his home. "The president's personal interest told me from the start that I am an important part of this company," Jeff remembered.

Jeff works on a team which operates a web press 200 feet long. His primary job is to maintain the web color, a daunting task when Quad/Graphics can produce any color out of four primary ones through a printing process which involves, ink, water and heat to produce a perfect picture composed of thousands of dots. A single paper roll can be 3 miles long and the accuracy tolerance is greater than .001 of an inch.

Quality is just one issue. "Timeliness in another key," Jeff explained. "Time is truly money for us. It is the difference between success and failure. For example, we print several major news weeklies, with a run of several million copies. Our turn around time, with high quality and minimum waste, can be measured in hours. A full day would be a luxury."

Sometimes, 24 hours is a luxury. Jeff recalled a major news item of international interest which occurred during the night, while Jeff and his team were in the middle of a huge run. "We had to reprint the cover and insert a different lead story," Jeff recounted. "From news break to new cover, it took six hours to have a new magazine ready." Modern technology enabled the magazine to generate the new cover and story from New York and transmit it to Jeff's plant in Hartford. Jeff and the Quad/Graphics team had to do the rest.

Jeff's pride in his work was evident. "For me, printing is a passion. It's a constant challenge to perform my job, as part of a team, better than anybody else." At Quad/Graphics, Jeff told me, everyone has that drive to perform. "What's more, a team truly works together. Nobody stands on rank or ceremony, and everybody is there to help without being asked." For example, when Jeff's own press was waiting for copy, he helped start-up four other presses. "We can count on the other pressmen to do the same for us," Jeff said. In Jeff's opinion, this esprit de corps flows from the company's President and founder, Harry V. "Larry" Quadracci. "Larry sets the tone and all the managers pick up on that same approach," Jeff explained. Jeff is also motivated by the fact that he can become a manager based on performance, not seniority.

Printing started as a career of chance, not choice, for Jeff. He was a high school graduate looking for work in a time and place and high unemployment. Jeff happened upon a small local printer and "talked his way into a job" as a material handler, the lowest rung position in that field. "I was lucky they hired me" Jeff recalled, "since I was totally green." Jeff moved from material handler to running the press after six years.

Then luck rolled Jeff's way again. "My boss took me to a Buck's basketball game. On the way home we passed the new Quad/Graphics plant, which the boss pointed out to me in passing. I hadn't thought about that company since they rejected me for a job 10 years prior. I applied again, this time with lots of experience. This time, they took me on." Jeff said with a laugh. "I didn't even have to start at the bottom, which was the company's usual practice. They were growing so fast, I moved right into my current position."

Jeff recommended these criteria for people interested in his profession. "First, you have to be ready to work hard and get dirty. Second, you need to excel in a high pressure environment. We work under tight deadlines and strive to be the best in every way. This is not a country club. Third, you need to adjust to the rhythm of our work life. Each day is a twelve hour shift. We work three days one week, four days the next. Once a year the whole team (with possible exceptions for hardship, family, etc.) switches between night and day shifts." You don't need any specific license or certi-fication, "but at Quad Graphics there is lots of exceptional and useful training which mixes the classroom with on the job situa-tions," Jeff told me.

The next time you read a trade or news magazine, remember that the skill and dedication of Jeff Bykowski, along with every other Quad/Graphics employee, may have helped get it to you.

Mark Snyder
Procurement Engineer
Graco

Mark Snyder has been working at Graco, a manufacturer of fluid handling systems for industrial users, since 1980. As he sees it, however, "since I have had different jobs it's like having four different employers to work for."

In a nutshell, Mark's current job as Procurement Engineer is to reduce the cost of manufacturing products. "Previously, we tried to lower the cost of supplies by hard bargaining with vendors," Mark explained. "The problem with that approach is that every dollar we save, they lose." Today, Mark and Graco use a different approach so that everybody wins. For example, as demand for a product grows, different manufacturing processes become pos-sible. "At a certain volume we can switch aluminum castings from sand-cast to die cast molds. It's a larger initial investment, but results in a much lower unit cost to produce. The savings from lower production costs is shared by our vendors, our customers and ourselves with no loss in quality," Mark told me. Another cost saver is juggling commodity orders to align for least cost manufacturing. "Vendors who are excellent with one product many be inefficient in producing another. We need to keep an open eye on it," Mark noted. Because of his engineering background, Mark can make a knowledgeable decision about the wisdom of changes like these.

Mark also solves problems with vendors when differences arise. For example, vendors naturally make products according to the blueprint given them, and assume it is to specification. However, there are always gray areas that are not covered in any set of specifications. Mark cited the case of a "dimple" which appeared in a part. "It was purely cosmetic, but in an ideal world we would have gotten rid of it. However, that would have required sanding the parts, which is expensive," Mark recounted. "I had the blueprints clarified for future production. In terms of existing parts, I coordinated a negotiation with the vendor and with our internal departments like marketing to agree on what to do about the dimples."

Mark majored in mechanical engineering at the University of Minnesota. He graduated in 1980 and accepted a position at Graco as a "quality engineer." "I wasn't familiar with that term, but it seemed impressive," Mark recalled. "It turned out to mean determining if parts we manufactured or purchased met the blue prints." For the first nine months, Mark didn't feel that he was contributing to the firm. "Then I started having my own opinions and sharing them. It began to feel real," Mark told me. "Unfortunately, I felt that my manager had unrealistic expectations, so I looked for a change."

Mark found a position at Graco as a Standard Product Engineer and stayed with it for over six years. "If there were problems with production, I looked for possible changes that would still retain the basic design. I enjoyed the interaction with people in identifying problems and solving them," Mark noted. He credits his sense of urgency for his success in this position. "My approach was fix it *now*. That won some very favorable notice. Part of my motivation was a desire to be the champion problem fixer," Mark said.

The next job wasn't so enjoyable. Mark became a design engineer. "There wasn't any real team. At most, I worked with one other person," said Mark, reviewing that time. "In addition, I am not comfortable with large, long-range projects. For me, it's better to work on solutions which can be implemented in a short period of time." A modified assignment brightened Mark's work day. He became a Design Engineer for European Products, meaning that he modified existing products for meeting European usage and standards. "A typical project was changing a design from 110 volts to 220 volts." Mark explained. "I also made sure we were in compliance with 'CE' (compliance to the unified standards for European products) for as many products as possible." Mark interpreted standards, made modifications in existing designs and wrote the required technical file. "I liked this job in part because it's fun to work with standards and apply them. The frequent business travel to Europe lost its glamour pretty quickly, though," he revealed.

Mark took his current position for the most pragmatic of reasons. "I wanted to avoid a long commute in the Minnesota winter. This job brought me closer to home."

Although engineering is not a requirement for the procurement function at Graco, it's an advantage. "You don't have to argue engineering points because you're the resident engineer. At the same time, I enjoy explaining engineering in layman's terms. Maybe I should have been a teacher, like my father."

For the future, Mark doesn't want to move into a supervisory role, although many engineers do. "I try to keep life simple. Anyway, what I want is satisfaction and respect. They are far more important than extra money to me," Mark concluded.

Mark had a few points of personal philosophy to share, including that it doesn't pay to look for the perfect job. With hard work and a bit of luck, it will happen. Also, jumping to different companies doesn't automatically build your experience. Look (and think) before you leap.

Mark advises people to become an expert at something which can be of assistance to others and keep yourself marketable so you can bail out if you're stuck.

Beth Hinchee
Research Engineer
Caterpillar Inc.

Beth Hinchee is a research engineer for Caterpillar Inc., the huge manufacturing company best known for its tractors. Like many Caterpillar employees, Beth works in Peoria, Illinois, the company's world headquarters. Beth does most of her work for Caterpillar's Solar Turbines subsidiary, so let's pick up her story there.

"First," Beth said with a small laugh, "Solar has nothing to do with sun power. Our turbine engines are powered by natural gas and other fuels and produce up to 20,000 horsepower," she continued. "These turbines often provide local power, let's say for an electric generating company or to run pumps at an oil refinery."

As an employee of Caterpillar's corporate R&D group, Technical Services Division, Beth helps other Caterpillar Division perform advanced product research or tackle specific problems. Usually these problems relate to increasing the efficiency of a component or other means to enhance performance. Beth is frequently involved with several teams at once, each working on a separate issue. The teams may have several overlapping members or perhaps only Beth herself in common. Most of the teams are comprised of mechanical engineers, although some cross-functional people may be involved.

"Our initial step is to look at what others have done," Beth explained. "The Internet is a great source of information and databases which are publicly accessible. We even get technical journal articles and conference proceedings on line. That way, we don't spend six months finding out something already known." Beth also looks inside Caterpillar to see what has already been done or who may have some expertise she needs. "Sometimes there are even solutions from several years ago which were not implemented for reasons which prevailed at the time. They may be ideas whose time has now come," Beth remarked.

Each member of a problem solving team will have his or her own responsibilities. For Beth, these usually fall into three areas relating to proving a concept on a prototype: procurement, building and testing. Procurement may involve everything from writing the specifications for sophisticated instrumentation to communicating with suppliers to assure that needed hardware will be delivered on time. Building involves assembling the prototype hardware in preparation for a test. Testing means running the prototype at pre-determined conditions and recording what happens. "We are excited to see if our ideas work. We have a high level of confidence because the upstream analysis is so good, but you occasionally get surprises," Beth explained.

Beth graduated from Southern Illinois University in 1995 with a BS in mechanical engineering. However, her connection with Caterpillar started two years earlier. "In my third year of college, I heard about an internship at Caterpillar through the Society of Women Engineers. I was hired for the summer to work on high performance diesel marine engines. The next summer, I returned to work on gas turbine engines," Beth recalled. "For me this was an all around win. It made my class work more real, defined my professional focus and certainly helped me land a good job at graduation." Beth spent five years at SIU. One reason was the need to work 15-20 hours a week. "I self-financed 100% of my education with the help of scholarships and government grants," Beth said proudly. She also took a number of non-required liberal arts courses. "I wanted to be a well rounded person," Beth told me. Since Beth writes about four to six long reports and many short ones each year, her liberal arts courses have had the added benefit of helping her do a very technical job.

Beth feels that she has lots of future options at Caterpillar. If she stays on the technical track, she could get more involved with computer aided analysis, or testing, design, manufacturing, standards, reliability and materials. "You could have several very different jobs at Caterpillar and never leave Peoria, or if you'd like, live in several different countries and never leave Caterpillar," Beth observed.

For now, Beth loves her current job. "I work with lots of bright, enthusiastic, friendly people," Beth told me. "There is plenty of variety in my work with several projects on my agenda all the time. I am thrilled seeing all the pieces of a project come together and I get a huge rush when 'the prototype runs'. There is always something new to learn, some new idea to test," Beth concluded.

Beth has no immediate plans for a graduate degree, even though Caterpillar would pay for related course work. However, there is a good deal of internal training and non-degree directed college courses of which Beth has availed herself. Beth also stays current by reading several professional journals on topics such as automobiles, gas turbines and sensors. She has remained active in the Society of Women Engineers and suggested two other helpful professional associations: American Society of Mechanical Engineers and the Society of Automotive Engineers.

Jim Mackey
Manager, Customer and Manufacturing Support Engineering
Nicolet Instrument Corporation

Jim Mackey is truly involved with products from potato chips to computer chips. The instruments he helps manufacture test the quality of oil in potato chips and the composition of semi-conductor wafers. They are also used in pharmaceutical analysis and forensic labs. "When Princess Diana was killed, we could report, based on a chip of paint, the model and year of the car which hit her," Jim told me.

Jim manages a team of software, hardware, electrical and mechanical engineers, in addition to technical draftsmen. "Our mission is to start with a product from its inception until it goes out of use," he explained. Jim's mission begins with participating in a design team which combines client feedback received from the marketing department with the latest Nicolet technical capabilities. At the next stage, Jim's team upgrades the design to a manufacturable product. The team also writes manufacturing documentation and teaches the production team on the shop floor what needs to be done. "Since we have been involved from the beginning, we understand the product in detail and that helps in teaching the manufacturing process," Jim noted. After the instrument is sold, Jim's team teaches the outside service engineers how to service the product and write technical service updates based on feedback from end users.

Jim has not been trained to the degree of technical expertise as the engineers he manages. "I allow them to be the experts in their fields of expertise," he told me. "My job is to help define situations rather than fix specific problems. I focus on scheduling issues and our commitments to others." Jim has found that brainstorming sessions to parse out issues are a good way to keep the team focused on common goals.

Jim came to manufacturing indirectly. After graduating from the University of Wisconsin (Stout) in 1979 with a degree in industrial education, he taught shop courses for two years. "It was exactly what I always wanted to do," Jim recalled. "Except that when I discovered that the kids weren't as interested in shop as I was, I became disillusioned." To earn extra income, Jim worked summers as a supervisor in a local manufacturing plant, filling in for regular employees on summer vacation. "That's where I got my real industrial education," he observed.

Jim returned to his alma mater for a graduate degree in industrial management, a curriculum which combined engineering with business courses. Unfortunately, Jim graduated in 1982, when the American economy was in recession. It took him six months to find any kind of job. Jim moved to Boston and to be closer to his significant other and found odd jobs to support himself. From there he moved with his wife to Minnesota and then Wisconsin. Ironically, both Jim and his wife got job offers on the same day in late 1983. Jim was now a "manufacturing engineer" at Nicolet.

"I was the first person in the company to have that title, and they weren't quite sure what to do with me," Jim said. "I worked on the floor in assembly and then moved to writing documentation for new products." Jim was able to move to a position in "facilities," doing plant lay outs. "I wasn't overwhelmingly happy there, but I caught a lucky break," Jim revealed. "We used to get all kinds of magazines, including free ones. I started reading about printed circuit boards and was intrigued. Soon, I was reading everything I could get my hands on about circuit boards," he continued. "A management position came up in that area. When I interviewed for the job, I knew all the lingo and all the issues. I wasn't really the most qualified, but I got the job."

Jim loved that opportunity, which included pulling together varying equipment from different Nicolet divisions and figuring out how to make them work together. "It was fun, like running a small business," Jim recounted.

Nicolet went through a period of downsizing, reorganizing and mergers. When the dust settled, Jim's boss left the company and Jim took his place.

Jim likes his broadened responsibilities because of the new situations, and new technologies he constantly encounters. Perhaps more importantly, "I work with lots of interesting people and that really keeps me at it," Jim said. He also likes the company's values, including "do right by the customer." "We could delay, blame others, wash our hands of it, but we never do," Jim noted with pride. Jim works a 7:30 AM to 5:30 PM day, but Nicolet is flexible as long as the job gets done. For childcare reasons, I worked from 3 AM to 12:00 noon for a while," Jim recalled.

Jim remains a voracious reader, including *Quality Digest, Industry Week, Service News* and *Internet Week*. He also participates in a book club where the members discuss quality and other production issues. His next career step at Nicolet might be vice president of operations, but Jim anticipates a need to know more about business before that can happen. "I would need to look further ahead to foresee the business environment for our products and make sure we are positioned to use new technologies as they emerge," he said.

In the meantime, Jim is actively involved with the American Society for Quality. "Being able to bounce ideas off people from other companies fights against the possibility of developing an in-grown professional perspective," he offered.

Jim's commitments include his family and community. "I put my family on the schedule, so to speak. I don't have to wedge them in around my job," he told me. Jim is also a scoutmaster and maintains his church's computer system. Somehow, he finds time to train for triathlons as well.

Jim Christie
Site Operations Manager
M.A. Hanna Color

In 1978, Jim Christie dropped out of the engineering program at Fairmont State College in West Virginia. In 1995, after eight years of part-time study, he graduated. In between, Jim built a great career.

Jim's first job was on the production floor of a resin manufacturer working on *Cycolac*. After six weeks, he moved into the quality control laboratory, testing latex. "I had enough math and engineering courses behind me to do that kind of work," Jim recalled. After five years or so, Jim transferred to the analytical lab, where the operating motto was "make it, break it, bish it, bash it." "I loved the lab work," Jim told me. "I learned a lot about Polymers, laboratories and testing." Jim's job was to test the composition of products in terms of their contents and ratios. He also did some testing for the EPA to guard against contaminating groundwater with his company's effluent.

After two years, Jim was invited to the color lab as a "color matcher." His responsibilities were to match a customer's color needs by analysis and then to make appropriate formulas for production. Subsequently, as a "color analyst," Jim worked with engineers to reduce color-delaying time in manufacturing: "If there was a glitch, I researched the problem and fixed it. Down time is very expensive in manufacturing and reducing it is a competitive necessity."

In 1993, an American multinational corporation bought out Jim's company, and things began to change. "The way they did things, the job wasn't fun anymore," Jim explained. "They also had no experience working with automobile companies. We were recognized experts, but they were telling us how to do things."

The saving grace for Jim was that he learned a lot about business structure. However, when he received his engineering degree in 1995, he was still passed over for promotions. "After twelve years of work, eight years finishing my college degree, they tell me that promoting from within is not their policy. That was it; I quit to look for another job. For six years, I had been receiving calls from head hunters, but I told them I didn't want to move," Jim recounted. "I contacted one of the head hunters and in two weeks he found a company in Ohio, called PMS (Plastic Molding Supplies). They wanted a color match manager. PMS was owned by M. A. Hanna Color, a company I knew by reputation. I accepted their offer and moved 360 miles to the west."

In his new position, Jim was tasked with getting the company ready for QS-9000 accreditation within 18 to 24 months. "QS-9000 is like ISO 9000 with a tougher standard," Jim noted. At the same time, Jim was assigned to achieve "A2LA," the highest independent laboratory accreditation needed for the automobile QS9000 standard. "Years prior, I had worked with the man who turned out to be our A2LA auditor. I asked him to tell me what I needed to do to pass. Within thirty days of the initial pre-audit, we did it," Jim said proudly. The parent company took notice of Jim's success and invited him to take his current position in Arizona.

Jim's role is to manage daily operations, taking raw materials — namely plastic and pigment — and converting them into custom color pellets which are then shipped to an end use. "The customer sends us a piece of paper, a bottle cap, a compact case. We develop a formula to match the color, then put pigments into a high intensity mixer. That machine is like a giant bread dough maker. Then we have an extruder which is like a big meat grinder and finally a pelletizer to make 1/8" color pellets," Jim explained.

There are a total of 26 production employees working the three shifts and Jim spends time with them all. "This is a hands-on job. Two or three days a week I put on my coveralls and work with the folks on the floor. The best way to know people is to work with them," he said. Jim also meets with each shift every day. I am in by 7 AM so I can meet with the third shift before they leave. Then I meet with the day and afternoon shifts as they come in. Sometimes I am out by 5 PM, sometimes by 7 PM, but I always speak with everyone." Jim anticipates being in this position for 2 ½ to 3 years and his goal is to "put a team together that will carry this business for another ten years." To achieve that, Jim brings them together and makes them talk about new ideas and any complaints. Jim converts the agreed upon ideas to action items and assigns them to specific people. "Everybody knows they had their say and were seriously considered even when their ideas are not accepted," Jim observed. The plant now has a 98.6% on time shipment record which Jim attributes to his "get them talking" approach. For his next move with M.A. Hanna Color, Jim pictures a regional position in which he would visit facilities to help them work through goals and meet new mixing and extrusion standards.

Jim's job has exposed him to new responsibilities, especially with financial concepts like Value Added Margin (VAM). Because of the plant's SAP computer program, Jim now has instant access to any data he needs, even in areas which are not his responsibility. On the more personal side, he enjoys the "folks in the plant" and the fact that his product touches people every day. "I look at cars, toys, soda bottles and can remember when I did the color match and production," Jim noted.

On the down side, the job has its frustrations. "Pleasing customers is not easy. We can work hard to achieve 'a little more red' only to be asked, on second thought, 'for a little less red'. We do a 100 color matches a month and maybe one-fifth turn into large orders. But that's what drives the business," he said.

Looking back, Jim sees leaving his previous job as a great break: "I gave up security without hope of promotion for a chance for promotion without a guarantee of security. I have never regretted it."

WHAT TO DO NOW

To help you prepare for a career in manufacturing, the people interviewed for this chapter recommended organizations you can contact, as well as publications and Web sites that may prove useful in your search:

Organizations:

American Productivity &
Quality Center (APQC) .... www.apqc.org

Society of Women Engineers .... www.swe.org

American Society of Mechanical Engineers .... www.asme.org

Society of Automotive Engineers .... www.sae.org

National Association of
Professional Engineers .... www.nspe.org

National Association of
Purchasing Management .... www.napm.org

Publications:

Quality Digest .... www.qualitydigest.com

Industry Week .... www.industryweek.com

Web Sites:

www.biospace.com/sd/career

http://jobs.cell.com

6

Marketing

Who Wants What and How to Get It To Them

Marketing professionals tend to be multi-talented people. Joe Higgins is the "alloy" for E&J Gallo who fuses together sales and marketing with finance and production. Both his people management and analytical skills are central to doing Joe's job well. Wearing two hats for Datamonitor, Tim Houghton enjoys the challenge of keeping diverse personalities and separate agendas working together. John Bushee both develops strategic plans and coaches account managers for Deluxe Corp.

As in most professions, some people have an especially strong attachment to a specific company. Carrie Frankson wanted to work at Mattel so much she designed a resume package so Barbie-esque they just had to hire her. Fred Marshall loves his company, too. But he found IRI while waiting in line at a career fair for another company.

How do products get to us as consumers? Jim Aglio is responsible for 40,000 SKU's in his division at Ames. That means determining broad categories to be carried, promotion and pricing strategies. Karen Freedman was responsible for advertising, selling price and supply levels at 145 Caldor stores. As a store director for Toys "R" Us, Steve Meredith works with data, merchandising, employees and customers, not to mention 7,000 different toys.

Joe Higgins
National Director of Sales and Marketing
E & J Gallo

Steve and Terri go to a wine store looking for some chardon-nay. They notice a new product from E & J Gallo. "I like the color," Steve says. "The bottle has a unique shape," Terri says. The wine is purchased, taken home and consumed.

A story like this brings joy to the heart of Joe Higgins, who played a key role in bringing the new wine product to market. Joe is the "alloy," that fuses together sales and marketing on one hand, and finance and production on the other. Gallo has increased its distinct products from 15 to 400 in recent years, and each additional product requires significant analysis and substantial changes. "We can only move the product to market at the speed of the slowest link," Joe told me. "Every function has its own perspective, interests and modes of operation. We need to work together to produce the new products which will keep us competitive."

Let's walk through the introduction of a new product, perhaps a super-premium wine. The idea for it has probably come from the sales force. "We need to consider this carefully," Joe explained "Gallo wants to be #1 or #2 in every category it enters. We look at growth potential and profitability. Part of that is estimating market size and part is analyzing our competition and what they offer." If the project seems plausible at that point, Gallo subjects the super-premium to a panel test. If the data give a positive reading, the product will be tested in several markets simultaneously. Benchmarks are established regarding sales at various time intervals after introduction. "The test market data has the most credence at Gallo," Joe noted.

The market test in itself touches on several functions. The marketing area analyses data including taste preferences, pricing and bottle shape, while finance assesses the costs. Production needs to account for the type of grapes needed. "A new product may need a distinct grape," Joe said. "That could mean replanting an entire vineyard. If we started from scratch, that could take three years or so. If we graft the new grape on existing vines, we can cut that time in half. Sometimes, we just have to go outside of our own supplies. All of these activities must be integrated into a cohesive plan."

Joe needs a number of skills to produce that cohesive plan. One is people management. "You need to understand the other person's needs. The marketing people may see high potential in something new based on their data, but the sales people fear their distributors won't carry it. A new product may require an increase in volume of a certain grape or bottle type from the production people. I reconcile those differences so we can work together on achieving the superior resolution," Joe explained. "Change is liable to upset somebody, but if you try to make everyone happy, you'll just stagnate." What's more, if a product fails, there may be some hard feelings internally as well as among distributors. "There's a price to be paid for not trying and a price to be paid for failing with a product," Joe observed. "But if we did nothing, we would be sure to be hurt in the market place even more."

Joe uses his analytical skills to identify data which support or refute the idea of a new product. "There is a huge amount of data. It's important to find what's important in a specific situation," Joe said. "I also prepare carefully to present my arguments. That requires mining data supporting different perspectives and being able to justify my own."

Ten years ago, Joe started his career as most Gallo people do as a sales representative calling on liquor stores, club stores and restaurants. After one year, he became a sales manager responsible for five people. A year later, Joe was promoted to Area Manager, responsible for a group of districts. Then he moved to field marketing, where he surveyed trends in his area market and developed a customized marketing approach.

In 1994, Joe took a leave of absence to earn an MBA. During the intervening summer of that program, he worked internationally. "These countries had their own wine, but we played on our California mystique," Joe recalled.

Returning full time to Gallo, Joe became a brand manager, responsible for building-up a specific Gallo brand. "There are thousands of products in a wine store and I want the consumer to find mine and purchase it," Joe said. Two year's of brand management experience were Joe's final preparation for his current situation.

Joe observes that being an "alloy," the one who aligns different functions with a common business goal, will become increasingly important because of technological changes and the globalizing economy.

Timothy Houghton
Marketing Manager
Datamonitor

Can an Oxford educated English major find happiness in a highly competitive business? My conversation with Timothy Houghton of Datamonitor's New York office gave me a definite "yes" answer, and a lot more besides.

Timothy wears two hats for Datamonitor, which is an independent strategy management consultancy providing "research analysis, information dissemination and business solutions." His first hat is marketing manager for Datamonitor's eight business practices. His second is overall manager for the energy practice.

A look at the energy practice will help us understand both aspects of Timothy's job. In this practice, Datamonitor's clients are major utilities in the electric, gas and oil industries. The fundamental goal is to give their clients the information and ideas they need to market their products. To that end, Timothy manages three functional teams: marketing, analytical and sales. The marketing team defines what the audience wants. For example what would a gas utility need to know to promote converting from oil or electric for heating. In a sense, they are developing needed products to attract new business sources. The analyst team researches the areas under contract and writes the needed report. The sales team interfaces with existing clients and handles those accounts.

Timothy enjoys the management challenge presented by keeping the diverse personalities and separate agendas working together. "Teamwork is absolutely critical," Timothy told me.

Interestingly enough, other consultancies will buy reports from Datamonitor for a specific client. The reason is cost. If Datamonitor invests $200,000 in producing a report which it sells to 100 clients, the unit cost is about $2,000. Datamonitor could sell the report for, let say, $5,000 to the other consultancy and still make a profit. The consultancy purchases a report for a lot less than they could produce themselves. (The numbers given here are for example only). Alternatively, another consultancy might purchase a Datamonitor report as a bench-marking tool.

Timothy told me that he likes the "academic" aspect of his job. That is, it's a position which "provokes a lot of thinking." Innovation and speed are absolutely essential to keep Datamonitor on the cutting edge, and Timothy enjoys the combined challenge. Innovation is possible because Datamonitor instills a culture of respect for everyone. Therefore the company encourages everyone to contribute ideas and everyone to give serious consideration to the ideas of others without regard to titles and levels of authority.

Datamonitor is able to move quickly because the head of each business unit can do whatever s/he wants within the constraints of budget and ethics. Speed is critical, since the value of information depreciates as time passes. In addition, client needs are often time critical.

This is a profession with high ethical standards. The rules are a bit complicated and strictly adhered to in terms of what goes into a report and under what conditions information may be shared. Quality control also plays a major role. Before a client sees the final product, reports are carefully reviewed and a Datamonitor team does a role playing examination to identify any areas which require clarification or greater articulation.

When Timothy graduated from Oxford University he had several offers from consultancies and advertising agencies in Great Britain. Timothy chose Datamonitor because he could use his creativity to the fullest. "This is an organization that even creates its own audiences," he told me.

Timothy started out in the London office writing brochures, something he truly enjoyed. But Datamonitor is open to new ideas, and within two months Timothy was called upon to provide strategic input. Two years later he works in both the London and New York offices.

If you were interested in a job like Timothy's, what should you do? Timothy suggests looking for a company which is innovative and growing. Even more, make sure the company respects employees from day one. It is that respect which helps you stay involved and committed. In term's of education, business degrees are helpful, but a quick mind is more important than any particular major. You should also consider whether you're up for long days and tight deadlines. It's important to have strong promotional potential. At Datamonitor, they generally will not hire a candidate unless s/he appears to have the capacity to become responsible for one of the firm's businesses.

You can apply for a job at Datamonitor by contacting Christine Anello, Human Resources Manager, at 212/686-7400 or Canello@datamonitor.com.

John Bushee
Market Performance Manager
Deluxe Corporation

John Bushee has been with Deluxe Corporation for 23 years and is now a Market Performance Manager for Deluxe Financial Services. That is the division of Deluxe which serves the needs of financial institutions, commercial banks, credit unions and thrift institutions. John reports to a market manager who is responsible for all of New England and upper New York State.

"Part of my job is to develop strategic sales plans for our market," John told me. "Then we identify opportunities, set goals and develop the strategies to reach those goals." Part of John's information comes from data bases developed through Deluxe research and other sources. However, more important is the "head knowledge" he has gained by working with accounts (i.e. customers) and the feedback he constantly gets from them. "For example, a customer's needs might change due to competitive or market pressures," John explained. "I want to be there with the products which provide solutions to meet the new needs." This requires the ability to listen carefully and exercise a great deal of professional discretion. What an account tells John needs to remain confidential.

Another piece of John's job is coaching and counseling account managers. "We look at sales from a consultative process. There is a lot of listening involved," John explained. "As I coach, I also listen a lot. Together with our account managers, we review the entire sales cycle and see where there are areas to improve our product knowledge and sales skills."

A third important responsibility is responding to requests for proposals. "My initial questions are: What's a good fit? What are we being asked to do? Is this situation part of an overall relationship?" The answers depend largely on the customer's goals," John continued. "Are they looking at cost, quality, variety, or service after the sale as primary concerns? You can't submit your proposal blindly. It's all about the customer and customer needs."

John enjoys many aspects of his job. He has a flexible schedule under his control, and enjoys the people he works with—both customers and sales force. "The combination of applying your experience in different ways for different customers keeps each day different and exciting, I enjoy that," John remarked. Above all else, he enjoys Deluxe as a company. "We have high ethical standards with each other and with our customers. Everything is above board," John told me with obvious passion. "We also show every employee the greatest respect and value diversity of background and opinions." Besides, John added with a smile, "we enjoy celebrating our victories together."

John's initial goal was to become a lawyer and he majored in political science. The prospect of three years of graduate school gave John some pause, and he became a customer service representative for Deluxe. From there he moved to upstate New York in outside sales. Responding to an internal posting, he moved to Rhode Island, where he still lives.

John has a "virtual office" in his home and spends at least three days a week on the road developing sales representatives. "It is a 12 hour day," John mentioned. "You need a lot of endurance for the travel and tenacity to deal with the 'no sale' conclusions to even your best efforts." Negotiating ability is also a must to reach mutually acceptable terms on any on-going relationship. Above all you need good questioning and listening techniques. "You learn more with you ears than with your mouth," John observed.

Although John is financially well rewarded at Deluxe, he advises people not to confuse financial success with happiness. "What feels good on the inside is a lot more important than what looks good from the outside," he advised.

Carrie Frankson
Designer for Barbie Packaging
Mattel

Have you ever wondered why a girl in a toy store gets excited about a Barbie doll and is less excited about other products? Part of the answer is Carrie Frankson, a package designer for Barbie's manufacturer, Mattel.

"It's a dream job in every sense," Carrie told me. "I always played with Barbie as a little girl, and now I am actually working for the woman who designed my dolls."

The fulfillment of this dream didn't come easily. Carrie studied Studio Art at the University of California-Santa Barbara. "I learned how to draw and paint," Carrie recalled, "but not how to use it in a commercial background. Worse, I knew I wasn't Picasso so I lost confidence in my talent." As a result, she took a job as a greeter in a mall, "It was almost humiliating," she said. "I wore a silly costume and gave people directions."

Next stop for Carrie was working as a receptionist. "I have good people skills, but my artistic training was going to waste" Carrie remarked, "Fortunately, I got a job as an assistant merchandiser for a firm making boys surf wear. I got some good insights into fashion drawing and marketing, but I like feminine things." Carrie took six months off to work with a career counselor. She investigated a variety of careers ranging from flight attendant to nursing, but felt none was a fit for her. Her career counselor felt that the Graphic Design program at Chapman University would give Carrie the extra training to make her talents and interests yield a good job.

"Between my studio art and graphic design studies, I knew I was ready to go." Carrie told me "My job search list had one firm on it — Mattel."

The love affair wasn't mutual at first. "I couldn't even get a human voice on the phone," Carrie recalled. "So I did something which was truly me and designed a resume like a booklet showcasing my artwork. I developed a tag line "My mother wants to marry me off. My father wants my bills paid off. To appease both my father and mother... do you have an available job or a single brother?" To accompany her unique resume, Carrie created some Barbie postage stamps, Barbie bubble gum, nail polish and chocolate. Carrie got as far as the Mattel receptionist and had to leave her packages, addressed to no one in particular, on the counter. By the time she arrived home, Carrie had three calls on her answering machine inviting her to an interview. "My resume package was so Barbie-esque, they just had to meet me," Carrie reflected.

Carrie's job is to create the environments and play patterns for Barbie's package. "My team developed a shopping Barbie which opens into a boutique for Barbie to go shopping," Carrie explained. "Not only do we strive to showcase the product, but we also develop games & play patterns for the child to use with the doll." Generally the package is designed around the completed product, but sometimes the doll will be changed in some details to conform more closely to the package.

Carrie's art medium can be anything from a paintbrush to a computer. "I'll use whatever medium the task requires," she said. Carrie's deadlines can be extremely tight or several months out. "There is both immediate execution and long term planning," Carrie remarked, "I started work on the year 2000 in 1998."

One downside is that there is a great deal of subjective judgment involved in both creative art and marketing. "Sometimes visions clash and that can be tense. Still, being at Mattel is more like dreaming than working," Carrie concluded.

As we were going to press, Carrie shared some interesting good news: "Recently, I was approached by a legendary Barbie doll designer to come and design with her. She was impressed by the innovative packaging that I created for her doll. I jumped at the once in a lifetime promotion. The rest truly is a fairy tale. I am currently working on Barbie dolls for 2000. Since I am in Preliminary Conceptual Design, I am involved constantly in brainstorm sessions which are amazing. I must stay enlightened on the current & future technology, fashions, and styles. Consequently, we often go 'inspiration shopping' just to see what is out there in mainstream culture. We also have many guests brought in to present the latest European & Asian trends as well. My job is just so much fun—I honestly love what I do and truly look forward to going to work. This is a dream come true and can mainly be attributed to much self-introspection, schooling, hard work and hope.

Fred Marshall
Director of Client Services
Information Resources, Inc. (IRI)

In 1990, Fred Marshall was standing in a long line at a college career fair. He was waiting for a chance to speak with the representative of a consumer packaged goods firm, hoping to land an interview in the process. With time on his hands, Fred thought about the sales job he had held for 2 ½ years after graduating from the University of New Hampshire with a degree in political science. "All the cold calling and lugging that sales bag wore me down. That's why I pursued an MBA here at Babson College—to move to a pure marketing position," he mused.

While still waiting in that line, Fred picked up some literature from a nearby table. "I am familiar with IRI from class work, but market research isn't my goal," he thought to himself. Nevertheless, Fred struck up an hour-long conversation with the IRI representative and was invited to interview in Connecticut. Fred accepted IRI's offer to become an Associate Project Manager because he liked the quality of the people he met and because he was interested in how large companies use advertising and marketing as competitive tools.

"I did a great deal of work in data analysis," Fred said, "It was a way to learn about client needs and IRI products. I also wrote monthly 'top line reports' for 3 or 4 clients, giving them updated competitive market information." When Fred started at IRI, "we used to gather information from a retail client by sampling, say 15 of 100 stores. Now, with scanners gathering data at the check-out counter, we do a complete census of all relevant data from each of the 100 stores.

After a year, Fred was promoted to project director, working on site at the world headquarters of a major client in the beverage industry. He spent six years there giving market and sales support to his client, before accepting a promotion and returning to Connecticut.

As Director of Client Services, Fred manages the relationship with clients in the consumer package goods industries. One major function is to "scope-out issues" with clients to identify client goals, expectations and plans. "You need to be inquisitive like a detective and diagnostically sound like a doctor," Fred explained. "If the patient thinks he has a stomach ache, you need to make sure it's not really an ulcer," he continued. "You also need to know about client sensitivities so as not to push a recommendation if the client isn't comfortable with it."

With the client's issues clearly identified, and with the support of specialists who do high-end data analysis, Fred can provide critical marketing information. "For example, by doing trend analysis and comparing present to past data, we can suggest if pricing strategies, merchandising campaigns or in-store support are driving changes in market share."

A major second function is assuring quality control of the data gathered from retail channels like supermarkets, drug chains and mass merchandisers. "The retailers originally put in the scanners to improve front end efficiency not to provide data to IRI. So if a customer wants a 24 pack of soda, the clerk will occasionally punch in "general merchandise" if the bar code is hard to access. But we want detailed data, so we take steps to account for the 'general merchandise' factor.

A third function is very dear to Fred. "I spend a great deal of time with my staff. They have great analytical skills and build important key findings. I guide them to drawing appropriate conclusions and making useful recommendations for the client."

Fred reads publications from the Advertising Research Foundation and attends monthly seminars to stay current with the field. "For example the seminars may bring in speakers from the client side to talk about their jobs. It's a good way to learn about functions outside of IRI," Fred noted.

Fred is glad that he was stuck in a long line at a career fair nine years ago. IRI has given him the chance to manage people at a relatively young age and to gain exposure to a number of companies, industries and product categories from the earliest days of his career. He also spoke highly of IRI's People Development System. Through PDS' formal evaluation system, Fred gains valuable feedback on his career development and entree to continuous education to develop additional skills.

Jim Aglio
General Merchandise Manager
Ames Department Stores

Walk through an Ames Department store and estimate the number of "SKU's" (separate, distinguishable products). It may be surprising to learn that in the Home Lines Division alone there are over 40,000 SKU's within the four major departments (textiles, housewares, electrical appliances, crafts). Jim Aglio is the General Merchandise Manager, a senior vice president level position.

As a GMM, Jim establishes strategy and direction while supporting the four merchandise managers who are direct reports to him. Let's take a look at what this means in practice.

Jim identifies in broad terms the lines which will be carried in a given year and the extent to which Ames will promote them. He also establishes margin rates (ticket price minus the combined cost of acquiring the product from a supplier and an appropriate share of general operating costs) which position his company in the market place between lower end and high end discounters. Pricing is complex, and draws on the previous year's data, industry figures supplied by IMRA (International Mass Retailing Association) and profit per square foot of store space data. Jim also uses "market basket studies" to determine what competitors are charging for similar products. Jim sets inventory targets to minimize tied-up capital. "Sometimes we will have a sale item coming through the back door just as we are opening the front door for shoppers," Jim said.

"When I started in this business twenty years ago, selecting items and pricing them relied a good deal on your gut," Jim observed. "With today's computer driven data readily available, you tend to base decisions on the numbers."

Working with his managers constantly assures that inventory, revenue and outstanding orders "are according to plan." If not, a sale may be arranged to reduce inventory or outstanding orders to vendors may be adjusted downward. On the other hand, if a product is a hot seller, Jim may support extending the plan's inventory level so the company's stores won't be short. "If only a few million dollars are involved, I will make the decision myself," Jim told me. "If we are talking about $20 million, I need to make sure that the finance people agree. Otherwise we may be tying up capital the company wants for other purposes."

Jim reviews his sales data every day. "We live or die by that data," he noted. If the numbers are out of line with expectations, Jim may call for an adjustment in shelf allocation, pricing or advertising. These decisions are not made in isolation. Jim's day (typically 7:30 AM start; 6:30 PM finish) is full of meeting within his division or with people in other functional areas like operations (stores) systems and finance.

When he graduated from Quinnipiac College (Connecticut) with a degree in marketing, Jim began his career at Ames. "Originally I wanted to go into human resources," he recalled. "But when the Ames recruiter talked about decision making early-on and the potential for advancement, I decided on retail instead." Jim's first job was handling the paper work for weekly replenishments. "The job as I did it then has been replaced by computers," he said. Jim moved up to a buyer's slot, which he held for six years. "Today, it might be called an assistant buyer, or buyer in training. You need to know a lot more about this business today than when I started," Jim explained. The next step for Jim was becoming a Divisional Merchandise Manager, with buyers reporting to him. "I helped the buyers with item selection, inventory control and advertising," Jim said. "Advertising is critical to our business because that's what brings the customers in. The decision on how to position products in a newspaper insert can have a major impact on your business." Jim broadened his understanding of various product lines by taking responsibility for new categories like domestics, health and beauty aids, appliances and housewares. "There is so much to know about each category, you need to work with it to understand it. It was extra work, but I knew that if I didn't broaden myself, I would stagnate." Jim's hard work and broadened preparation led him to his current position. For the future, someone in

Jim's position could move up to become head of all merchandising and marketing or become the president of a small retail chain.

Jim identified a number of skills needed to be successful in his profession. "Math skill is absolutely essential and a good sense for finance is very helpful. Hard data is critical in this field," Jim said. "You also need to use your subjective judgment in item selection. The market can be fickle and your suppliers don't always deliver as promised. You have to judge how much to rely on specific vendors." Jim also mentioned that a diplomatic personality is useful with subordinates, peers and more senior managers.

As part of the turn-around team which brought Ames out of Chapter 11 a few years ago, Jim has a special accomplishment to savor. "The trade press, the industry, the banks—all wrote us off," Jim remembered. "But we gained the support of our vendors and now we are stronger than ever." Jim also enjoys making a difference every day and the opportunity to work with the leaders of his industry.

"For a person starting their career getting involved with a retail buying track can be exciting and rewarding. If you are considering a career change, it might be possible after five years in another field but practically impossible after that," Jim concluded.

Ames Department Stores, Inc. is one of the largest discount store chains in America, with more than $2 billion in sales and 300 stores in 14 states across the Northeast and Washington, DC. Ames offers a comprehensive Corporate Office Training Program designed to place talented college graduates on the fast track to success. Career opportunities are available in Buying, Finance, Information Systems, Allocation & Planning, Communications, Marketing, and Human Resources. Letters of introduction and resumes should be sent to: Ames Department Stores Inc., 2418 Main Street MS #0210, Rocky Hill, CT 06067

Karen Freedman
Director of Planning and Replenishment
Caldor

Let's say that you anticipate selling $625 million of hardlines (housewares; electronics) this year. You need to position the product in advertising, determine its selling price, time its arrival and distribution, and keep track of supply levels in 145 stores. If you want to know how doing all that is possible, ask Karen Freedman of Caldor.

Karen is Caldor's Director of Planning & Replenishment. Part of her job is to review volumes of data to forecast how much of a specific product the stores can sell. "To take a simple case, let's say there is a new type of toaster the buyers have decided that we should carry," she explained. "We'll look for a similar item and, based largely on its history, forecast how many we could sell at a price which makes profit sense for us. A careful look at history and current product trends is 90% of the decision; 10% is pure gut." Frequent discussions with venders about how they see the market also figure in her forecasts.

Karen also checks data at least weekly to spot any problems with product distribution or inventory levels in the stores. As a director, she isn't as hands on with the data as she used to be. Instead, when Karen spots a problem, she raises it with one of the managers or other staff who report to her. "They're so on top of things, they're probably fixing things already," she noted. The question Karen is likely to discuss is "Why is there a problem?" For example if stocks of toasters are too low, is it because sales are higher than expected, that advertising was more effective than expected or that shipments from vendors were late or incomplete. The solution may be adjusted toaster prices, at least in the next round of sales, or pulling the advertisement from Caldor flyers as soon as possible. Lead times are also a big factor in many decisions. "Imported products can take 60 to 90 days to re-supply. Advertising is prepared 12-16 weeks in advance. Our sales cycle goes on a five week rotation," Karen told me.

Karen's second major function is coaching her managers and developing them for future promotion. "I take considerable pride in the accomplishments of my staff," Karen noted. They have their hands on everything and produce great results."

When she graduated from the State University of New York (Albany) in 1990, Karen hadn't even heard of Caldor. "But my sister was a buyer for a retail chain and I had worked in a local store, so I had some idea about retail as a career," Karen recalled. She interviewed with Caldor on campus and accepted their job offer over several others. "It was the people who sold me. They were interested in me as a person and not just my academics or work history. They also offered a structured training program which I found very appealing," Karen told me.

"When I entered the training program in MDR (Merchandise Replenishment & Distribution), our computerized, on line systems were extremely new. I really liked being part of the evolution of the systems and being part of their development," Karen remembered. "More to the core of things, our program was split 50/50 between classroom and on the job training. We also learned how to interact with buyers and store personnel."

After the 3½ month training program, Karen joined a "buying team" as an analyst. One task she especially enjoyed was calculating necessary "safety stock," that is a margin beyond forecast sales. "There is always some variability between forecast and actual sales, and we may need to cover it. Also, you can't sell what isn't on the shelf. Therefore, to sell 5,000 toasters, you may need to order 7,000, because variability is store-by-store," Karen explained.

After two years, Karen was promoted to "lead analyst", which gave her responsibilities for an entire division and not just a department. "Although I had no direct reports, I did coordinate the activities of the analysts and was available for guidance. That part was like being an assistant manager," she noted.

Karen was promoted after only nine months to Planning and Replenishment Manager and was the youngest person to hold this position at that time. Among her major responsibilities was strategic planning, in tandem with a Divisional Merchandise Manager. During her four years in that position, she moved through several product areas to broaden her exposure.

In 1997, Caldor added a fourth director level position to accommodate a promotion for Karen. "I like the broader authority to make decisions and to empower others to make their own decisions as well. However, since my position is less hands-on than before, I have fewer tangible achievements to feel good about when I get home. I had to develop a longer time frame and less direct definition of accomplishment," Karen said.

Being self-motivated to drive business, thinking "outside the box," motivating others and being appropriately aggressive are key factors in Karen's success. She has also been proactive in managing her career. "I have expressed my goals and expectations to my supervisors," she explained. "By soliciting feedback, I was more aware of what I needed to do to move ahead."

Karen's day runs from 8:00 AM to about 6 PM. "I knew about hours in retail. The surprise is how excited I still am and the fact that I am better compensated than I expected when I started this career," she concluded.

As we went to press, Caldor Corporation made a painful announcement. After fifty years, it was going out of business. Even a great job can be imperiled by business realities. On the other hand, doing a great job increases the probability of getting another grast job with another employer.

Steve Meredith
Toys "R" Us
Store Director

It's seven o'clock on a cold morning in Syracuse, New York and you see a car slowly moving around a Toys "R" Us store. The driver is intently looking at the building and the surrounding grounds. Is this a criminal planning a break-in? No, it's Steve Meredith, the store director. " I drive around the store every morning, looking at it from the customer's eyes," Steve explained. "I am asking 'Does this store have curb appeal?' That is, if I am just in the area, would I want to drop into that store?"

Steve has barely taken off his coat when he does a self guided tour of his 30,000 square feet store "Is it attractive, orderly, easily accessible? What merchandising message am I sending a customer?" Steve asks himself. "If I want to say 'This is the store for any toy you want,' will the customer get that message clearly when s/he walks in?"

Steve is looking forward to the day with a mixture of anticipation and excitement. He has made plans for a busier than usual store weekend because a Toys "R" Us "roto" (display advertisement) has appeared in the local press. "Is my merchandise displayed the right way, is the back-up inventory quickly at hand?" Steve thinks as he does a double check. "I have my extra cashiers and Geoffrey helpers (store associates who approach customers with an 'I'm here to help') attitude lined up. I think we're ready," Steve concludes.

On the way to his office, Steve stops to speak with a part-time associate (an employee below the managerial level). The conversation flows to the associate's child who has been out of school with a bad cold. "If there's something we can reasonably do to help her out, like a schedule change or a few days off, we do it" Steve explained "I don't get involved in the daily tasks the company pays associates to do. That's the manager's job. Instead I make sure every one understands that I am personally interested in them as a person, and not just their contribution to the bottom line." Steve is responsible for 40 associates in addition to his assistant and two managers.

Steve gets to his office and accesses some data bases to determine what's selling by category and sub-category at his store and on the national level. "We have a reasonable degree of store autonomy on stocking, displays and merchandising. The data helps me make these decisions." Steve explained. Next, Steve checks his messages from headquarters in Paramus, New Jersey to find out what promotions or ideas the company wants him to carry out. Steve needs to be on top of 7,000 different toys from dolls to a video game that has its own printer. "I play with a lot of the toys myself, but never the dolls," Steve told me.

Steve graduated from the Delaware State University with a degree in psychology in 1977. "I studied what I enjoyed with no specific career goal," Steve remembered. Steve put down the collected works of Freud, and took a position as a manager for a small catalogue store of a large retailer in Reading, Pennsylvania. "Folks could buy what we had on display or what was in our catalogue," Steve explained "The problem was there was nothing higher to strive for with that company and I didn't want to plateau at age 22."

Steve answered a help wanted advertisement and accepted a position as a management trainee with a jewelry and hard goods retailer. The program was supposed to last four months, but Steve was speeded ahead after two weeks when his manager quit. "It was an intense case of OJT (on the job training)," Steve remarked. Steve became well regarded as a highly motivated self starter who didn't need a lot of managerial oversight. He moved to other stores either for a new experience (Las Vegas), to be closer to his extended family (Hartsdale, New York), or for experience in a high volume store (Portland, Maine). By way of returning a favor to his manager, Steve agreed to fix the problems of a store in Syracuse, New York.

Serious health problems and tragedy struck Steve's family. To his dismay, his employer did not show much understanding or flexibility. "All they could understand was what they wanted from me at work. "My eleven years of sweating blood for them and my family situation didn't matter," Steve recounted with some bitterness. "At about that time, a good friend kept telling me about Toys "R" Us as a place to work. At first I didn't pay attention, but circumstances forced my hand."

Steve was hired by Toys "R" Us, but as a management trainee. "It was difficult to start again, with younger people who were still 'wet behind the ears'," Steve told me.

"But I was put on a fast track because of my experience." Within three months, Steve was a manager and was promoted to assistant director six months later. One year thereafter, he was promoted again, this time to his current position.

Steve identified several skills that have made him successful at Toys "R" Us. "First is attitude," Steve told me. "I have an excellent management team and excellent associates. One reason is that each one works *with* me, not *for* me. You need to be self confident, articulate and truly have an interest in other people, including a total stranger who happens to be a customer. Second are the things you can be trained to do, like merchandising skills—driving sales through the appeal of what is on the shelf—and report writing."

Steve enjoys the interpersonal aspects of his job and the satisfaction he derives from directing a profitable operation. But more than that, he is glad to be at Toys "R" Us because of the "support they gave me from day number one during the period of my family's crisis." They would say things like 'take care of your family, Steve. The store will still open'," Steve told me. "I feel committed and couldn't even think of leaving." In addition, Steve liked the fact that his company wants employees to have a life outside of work. "We have a basic 40 hour week. I come it at 7 AM, but I go home at 3 PM or 4 PM. That's important to me."

People who have succeeded in the store environment could move up to regional manager or move over to a staff position in the Toys "R" Us headquarters in Paramus, New Jersey.

Steve is paid a salary plus a bonus based on sales and profits. A bonus is typically about 20% of base salary. In addition, Steve gets 600 stock options annually. Everyone can participate in a 401(K) retirement plan, including associates. Up to 8% of the base pay can be added to each 401(K) program from annual profit sharing. "I will not get rich here," Steve concluded "but you can say that I am quite comfortable."

Kenneth Tendo
Manager
Enterprise Rent-A-Car

To Kenneth Tendo, who had just become manager of the Enterprise Rent-A-Car branch in Lebanon, Pennsylvania, his work isn't simply a job—it's a passion. "I view it as Ken Enterprises," he told me. "Putting in long hours doesn't bother me because I enjoy what I do, make good money and have a chance to move up some more."

Ken's formal responsibility is to manage the office, hire and train employees, supervise staff and see to it that customers are well served. Doing that well takes an array of talent. A majority of Enterprise customers are looking for a replacement car because they have been in an accident. "You have to understand that the customer could be quite agitated," Ken explained. "Part of good service is understanding the client." The administrative task in insurance cases is more involved than in vacation or business rentals. "Before the customer even comes in for the car, we have already gained payment authorization from his/her insurance carrier and asked the body shop to estimate how long they need to get the repairs done," Ken told me. "That way we can estimate the length of the rental and meet the customer at the body shop with their rental. We shift that logistic issue from them to us." Another logistic issue is having the right supply of cars on hand if possible. Most customers want a comparable substitute for their damaged car, so Enterprise tries to keep a variety of makes and models on hand. The sticky part for some customers is that their insurance will cover only the cost of, say, a subcompact and the customer wants a replacement for his sports utility vehicle. "In these cases, the customer has to pay the difference, and I need to carefully explain that unpleasant reality."

A majority of Ken's time is actually spent outside the branch meeting with insurance agents and auto body shops to make sure that they have confidence in recommending Enterprise as a source for a replacement vehicle. At the branch, everyone is trained to do whatever needs to be done. If you don't see Ken behind the counter, you may well see him (or even his boss) outside cleaning cars. "You can't tell what position we hold just by watching what we do in a given hour," Ken said proudly.

Ken first became interested in Enterprise while researching the company for a class project in college. Ken was very impressed — but the feeling wasn't mutual. He interviewed for a job and was rejected. So Ken went out and sold copy machines for two years. He applied for a second time and was hired as a trainee. When I spoke with Ken, he had been with Enterprise for 17 months, and had just been promoted to manager. "At Enterprise, you move up based on producing results, not seniority," he told me.

Ken's feels well compensated, in fact he is making 65% more than the day he started. He hopes to become a city manager for 4 or 5 offices within three years of his start date. "That's not impossible at Enterprise," he told me, "although most people take six years or so to get that far.

Ken typically puts in a 55 to 60 hour week and doesn't regret it. He likes working with people and feels that he is building a kind of relationship with each one. "Everybody is different, and I rent about 25 cars a day. That keeps things interesting," he said with a laugh. "I am also building my supervisory skills by training the five people on my staff to become managers themselves. On top of that, I'm responsible for several million dollars of inventory."

For Ken Tendo, working at Enterprise Rent-A-Car is more like running his own business than just having a job.

WHAT TO DO NOW

To help you prepare for a career in marketing, the people interviewed for this chapter recommended organizations you can contact, as well as publications and Web sites that may prove useful in your search:

Organizations:

Advertising Mail Marketing Association .... http://amma.org

Business to Business Marketing www.business2business.on.ca

American Marketing Association .... www.ama.org

International Mass Retailing Association .... www.imra.org

The Direct Marketing Association .... www.the-dma.org

Publications:

Advertising Age .... www.adage.com

Brand Packaging .... www.brandpackaging.com

Brandweek Online .... www.brandweek.com

Colloquy .... www.colloquy.org

*Creative: The Magazine of
Promotions and Marketing* .... www.creativemag.com

Marketing .... www.marketingmag.ca

Target Marketing .... www.targetonline.com

Web Sites:

www.dm.world

www.anywhereonline.com

7

Sales

Building Relationships and Moving the Product

If you can't sell your product or service, you're out of business. Selling today is about raising awareness, building relationships and being a consultative resource. These stories tell us about sales professionals in action and why they think their jobs are great.

All the sales professionals related in this chapter are educated, dedicated and hardworking. In no case are they fast-talkers, making a quick hit and then walking away. For Holly Arbogast, sales means building and managing relationships for her information management company. Nicole Dunlevy enjoys solving customer problems because she likes to see people satisfied. A sales professional does not require a glamour product. Aric Philipson sells floor mats and mops while Mike Schane works with low tech approaches to bookkeeping issues.

Building relationships requires doing your homework. It can take Mike Fortner a month of research before he can present a proposal to a prospective client. Mike also cited the ability to engage in sometimes-tense negotiations as being part of the job.

Being a self-starter is part of the career. "No one is setting a schedule for you," Brian Marsella observed.

Aric Philipson
Facility Service Branch Manager
Cintas

Could you be enthusiastic about a career in the floor mat and mop service business? Aric Philipson is, and with good reason.

Aric's role is two fold. The first is expanding his client base and the second is managing the mat and mop service his clients want. "This business has huge growth opportunities," Aric told me. "Eighty-five percent of our potential customers don't have a service like ours." Aric's operation has already gained over 700 new clients, from small convenience stores to large retail chains and manufacturers. "The small client is actually the most challenging to sell. At first he only sees the cost, and not the benefit of our service. Since the money is coming out of his pocket, and not a budget, he is very careful," Aric explained. "We tend to reach them through cold calls." For larger clients, Aric develops a strategy to identify appropriate decision-makers, find out these buyers' motives, and arrange to make a presentation. "These are very busy people," Aric noted, "but they may recognize our name from its national stature in the field or because our stock is highly ranked in *Forbes*." Initially there may be a perception hurtle because Cintas charges a premium price for their service compared with a self-use product. However, when decision-makers realize the enhancement to health, cleanliness, safety and appearance, the Cintas service provides, it is quite attractive. "We are often recommended by health inspectors because our mats trap dust and control moisture. We launder and replace them every week," Aric noted. The anti-fatigue quality of the mats is significant to clients when dealing with OSHA and the fact that they are ADA (Americans with Disabilities Act) compliant is an important feature as well. "We put our mats where the client needs them most, like common entranceways, where they trap soil and moisture; cafeterias, to absorb counter area spills; and high traffic areas, to reduce wear and tear," Aric told me with great pride.

Their mop service is also important to clients because they are relived of the burden of maintaining supplies and the constant cleaning of mops. In addition, Cintas cleans up any toxic waste in the mop before returning it to service; something the client may not be able to do itself at a reasonable cost.

The second part of Aric's job is serving his customers. "It's all good and well to sell our service, but if we can't satisfy our customers each week, we'll quickly go out of business. We have to under-promise and over-deliver." More fundamentally, Aric is involved with training and motivating his service drivers who see his customers weekly. "Motivating blue collar people was a new challenge to me when I came on-board," Aric reflected. "We let them know how critical they are to our customer and pay them well. Using a computer, we role-play various customer service issues. I help get service drivers ready in both attitude and ability," Aric noted. "But hiring the right people for the job is the real key to success."

Working in mats and mops services was not Aric's goal when he graduated from college in 1991. He started out in a retail chain and then moved to a service company, which dealt in remanufactured copy toners. Immediately prior to Cintas, Aric worked for a class ring company. "I thought my next move would be to a high tech company," Aric recalled, "but an executive recruiter recommended trying Cintas and I was intrigued."

As happy as he is, Aric is realistic about the need for an above average work ethic. "This is a come early, stay late career path," he said. "I start at 6 AM and leave at 7 PM. About 35 hours a week is spent with my sales people and a good deal of time is devoted to my service people and customers. I also have a profit and loss responsibility.

Aric also reads to stay ahead, including *Business Week* and *Industrial Launderer* magazines in addition to a business-related book each month. "Our service may seem relatively simple but running the business is a challenge," Aric concluded.

Holly Arbogast
Business Development Executive
Unisys

How's this for an old fashioned route for getting into a high-tech company: Holly Arbogast connected with her job at Unisys, a huge information management company, by answering a classi-fied ad in the newspaper. Her first interview was a Transcontinen-tal phone call from Unisys' headquarters in Blue Bell, Pennsylva-nia to her home in California. Holly convinced the interviewing recruiter that he just had to give her an in-person interview. This wasn't based on pleading. Holly sent him a "Word Document," outlining her successes in life over the past ten years. In Holly's case, that took her back to junior high school! Her point was that she had always given 110% in the past to achieve her goals and she would do the same for Unisys.

After five more interviews, Holly was hired and entered into Unisys' six-month training program based in Chicago, Illinois.

If we were looking for one word to describe Holly's job, we would probably say "sales." For Holly, this means building and managing relationships. "That's as important for me as technical expertise as such," she told me. "After all, technical knowledge changes every day and we have great specialized people to sup-port us."

Holly's core product is "remittance processing equipment." Unisys makes the machines which process payments like your checks and those little slips when you pay your credit card bill. Holly has a range of machines, from ones processing 35 transac-tions a minute to those processing 1,800. Therefore Holly's clients rank from small businesses to huge corporations.

One challenge for Holly is to know how to spend her time to produce the best results. Although she enjoys her job, working 55-65 hours a week is motivated in part by the desire to earn commis-sions. If any week could be called typical, Holly spends sixty per-cent of her time prospecting for new clients, and the balance of

her time administering current accounts, pursuing already existing prospects and doing strategic planning.

Holly takes a consultative approach working with her clients. If Holly thinks she has a good opportunity with an account
she does a "business case" to determine the client's "total cost of
ownership". That is, finding the best way for Unisys technology
to solve critical business issues in a period of time that would prove
to be the most cost effective. Each "business case" is a two-way
instrument: first, to determine if the prospect is worth pursuing
and second, as a presentation document for the client. To build
and keep a client, Holly needs to differentiate her product from
those of competitors and show how she's bringing value to the
client.

Since Holly spends more than half her time prospecting, I
asked for an example. "First, you need to identify the prospect.
For my product, that means finding companies which have a need
for remittance processing, but don't use Unisys," Holly explained.
"Next, I need to find out who is in charge of that process. Some
phone investigation will usually tell me that. Third, I send a letter
of introduction followed by a phone call. If moving fast is critical,
I skip the letter."

What Holly likes best is the constant challenge. She "enjoys
getting in front of customers, building trust and thinking about
longer term relationships." Holly also appreciates the support and
respect she gets from her managers. "They are very supportive
and they're here to ensure my success in Unisys." Although Holly
travels a lot during the day, it is rare that she is not home for the
evening. Holly plans to spend the next several years in sales at
Unisys, partly because she enjoys it and partly because she believes that "there are tremendous opportunities at Unisys."

Holly told me that a job like hers requires "multitasking—
you really need to do many things all at once." At the same time
you need to take things in stride and be flexible. Even more, it's
important to keep going after a disappointment. "Let's say you
were sure a deal would be signed but it falls through. You have to
live with it and keep going. Be persistent or perish in this business," she concluded.

Unisys is Holly's second employer. After graduating from the University of Oregon in 1996, she worked for an employment agency on a straight commission basis. "I loved what I was doing but I wanted a more secure income and better career opportunities," Holly remembered.

Mike Schane
Sales
McBee

"I shake a different hand every hour," twenty-seven year old Mike Schane of McBee told me. Mike and I spoke when he had been on this job for seven months. " I love meeting new people, building relationships and networks." Although Mike's job would typically be classified as "sales", he told me that for him, it was 85% building relationships and only 15% pure sales.

Mike's employer, McBee, is a $57 million company which offers "innovative business solutions to the small business market." These solutions are often creative but low-tech approaches to bookkeeping issues. They specialize in one-write systems for manual bookkeeping operations but also offer computer check and forms compatible with any software. Clients are typically companies with ten or fewer employees.

This is Mike's second professional job; his first was in chemical sales. So what attracted Mike to McBee? Was it glamour or money? Not at all. In fact the initial reason was Colorado. Mike loves camping and skiing and moved to Denver without even having a job. After getting by on survival jobs, Mike decided to re-enter the professional world.

Mike's first connection to McBee was through a short classified advertisement in the Sunday paper. Mike applied in part just to get himself in motion again. He had never heard of McBee.

During the interview process, Mike became excited by the opportunity for daily independence the job offered. "I make my own schedule," Mike told me, "If the weather is good and I want to take a drive in the mountains, I can schedule appointments in the mountains. I can enjoy the drive while doing my job." Since most of Mike's appointments come through referrals, he doesn't need to spend a lot of time cold calling.

In addition to independence, Mike enjoys the two-way networking his job involves. Mike gave me an example: if Mike sells a product to a paint store, he will refer business to them when he hears about people planning to paint their house. Mike also enjoys grapevine networking. For example, a local bank referred a small business owner to Mike for payroll products. Mike then signed up the business owner and subsequently her accountant as well!

I asked Mike about living with rejection, a common part of a sales position. To my surprise, Mike said, "One of the things I like is my fairly high success rate. Nine out of ten businesses I visit are using an inferior product to what I can provide through McBee." Mike is probably fortunate to be in that situation! Mike also likes the fact that McBee has a district office in Denver. Even though he is usually making sales calls, Mike feels that the district office gives him job colleagues in addition to his clients.

What is the role of money for Mike? "This job pays every bill I have," he told me. (Mike's first year income will be about $26,000, an amount which he hopes will grow through expanded and repeat business)." I love my job and I love Colorado. I have been offered a more lucrative opportunity, but I passed it up," Mike revealed.

Mike was a communications major in college and several of his classes have had a direct impact on his profession. One was a professional selling class. Even so, Mike emphasizes that a person could succeed in this business with no prior sales training at all. In fact, one of his friends at McBee is a former medical school student!

Individuals interested in learning more about sales career at McBee's could contact: Cynthia Burke, National Recruiting, Training and Development Manager, McBee, 299 Cherry Hill Road, Parsippany, NJ 07054

Nicole Dunlevy
Account Manager
Pitney Bowes

It takes a tough person to do a tough job, even in sunny Irvine, California. Nicole Dunlevy, an account manager for the Pitney Bowes Copier Division, has a story to tell in that regard.

"Office copy machines are a highly competitive and difficult sale. That leads to a lot of sales staff turnover," Nicole said. "Copiers are viewed as an interchangeable commodity and somehow copier sales people are not seen in the best light." Nicole's approach is to let the potential client "buy us, not the machine." That is, Pitney Bowes people are problem solvers and relationship builders. "The customer can view us as a consultant," Nicole remarked.

In Nicole's position, the focus is on expanding sales to existing accounts. "The first thing is to give major league service to the client. If you prove yourself, you can expand the number of your machines with a client by displacing someone else," Nicole explained. "Of course, our competitors are trying to do the same thing to us," she added with a laugh.

Nicole has about 200 accounts and she makes it a point to visit each at least every 90 days. To do that, she uses Monday and Friday to set up appointments. Then Nicole spends most of Tuesday, Wednesday and Thursday in the field. During the middle of the week, early mornings and late afternoons are spent working within Pitney Bowes to make sure that what the client gets what they wanted. "The biggest skill in this business is follow-up," Nicole advised. "If you promise—you deliver. If not, you're finished."

How does Nicole keep track of so many accounts? "My lap top is my best friend," she said. "I immediately enter everything I need to do. Then I get a reminder at the appropriate time through the computer's alarm." By working "smarter, not harder" Nicole can service her accounts in 40 to 45 hours a week.

Nicole likes working with people "Some customers even invite me to lunch as if I am one of their staff," she remarked. Nicole enjoys solving problems because "I like seeing people satisfied." Even an unfriendly customer can add to her job satisfaction if Nicole can turn them around.

Nicole graduated from Loyola Marymount College in Los Angeles in 1996 with a degree in international business. Her first job was being a retail manager for a well-known apparel manufacturer. "I enjoyed the job, but it just wasn't for me," Nicole remembered. "I tried to find a new job for about a year. Ironically, I found Pitney Bowes through the most mundane method — a newspaper advertisement." Nicole related her one year search to unrealistic expectations. "I graduated in the top of my class from a good college. Somehow I expected a glamorous job with a $60 thousand salary. It's hard to get a job on earth when your head is in the clouds," she advised.

Nicole's interview clicked at Pitney Bowes for several reasons. First, two of her three interviewers were with women. "They were respectful to me, something I had not experienced on other, more male dominated, interviews," Nicole said. "More importantly, the people I spoke with were really passionate about working at Pitney Bowes. That helped me shift from a focus on glamorous products to a focus on working with committed people." In her first year, Nicole earned $35 thousand. "That's enough to pay my bills. Besides, in a year or two, $60 thousand is certainly in reach," Nicole concluded.

Mike Fortner
Account Supervisor
Great West Life

It was a cold day in Minnesota when I spoke with Mike Fortner, but he was as warm as can be when we discussed his job at Great West Life. Mike is an account supervisor in the employee benefits division. As Mike explained "benefits" to me, they are things other than salary that an employee gets from and through his/her employer. Examples include health insurance, 401K plans, Section 125 "cafeteria plans" and disability coverage. Benefits are critical issues to employers because they are the second highest expense (after payroll) and a factor in attracting good employees. Health insurance and 401K plans carry "stand alone status" and are Great West's biggest products. As "stand alones" an employer could contract with Great West for one of these products and nothing else. The other products, like disability, are available only when the health contract is already in place.

The core goal of Mike's job is to grow his "block of business" by finding employers who want Great West as their benefits carrier. To achieve this end, Mike works through brokers, (or consultants and agents as they might also be called). Mike establishes relationships with these brokers, who then may introduce Mike to their clients if they have confidence in both Mike and his products. The broker receives compensation, as does Mike, if a benefits contract is signed.

When Mike started at Great West in 1993 he spent most of his time in the field cultivating relationships with brokers and making joint visits to the broker's clients. As his block of business has grown, he spends more time in the office as he manages existing clients, exchanges new ideas with brokers, and "puts out fires" over the telephone.

If a company expresses an interest through a broker in exploring Great West as a carrier, Mike can't just run down to the employer carrying his basket of wares. It takes about a month for Mike to gather data, run a computer analysis and write a proposal. There is a lot to consider, including demographics and income levels on the employee side, along with operating expenses and insurance risks for Great West.

Although Mike enjoys his face to face meetings with brokers and employees, it is not all "hail fellow, and well met." There are often tense negotiations over price between Mike and/or the broker and the employer. In addition, there may be negotiations between the broker and Mike over commissions. As important as objective data are, a good deal of business judgment is involved.

Sometimes Mike may agree to certain terms largely to retain his overall relationship with a broker or to retain the employer's relationship with others, which benefits business. On the other hand, Mike has walked away from submitting proposals if the potential business lacks sufficient potential to bring in profits. "If I make a proposal, I want to win it. Otherwise, I risk losing business, which will cost me earnings and some respect from my peers."

One reason Mike loves his job is that he loves being in front of people. "People are different and they want different things," he told me. "That's an interesting challenge." Mike also enjoys being in control of his own schedule. That frequently means 10-12 hour days but Mike is home most evenings and weekends. He also enjoys the prestige of working with business owners and CFO's of Fortune 1000 Companies.

If you are considering a job like Mike's you need good interpersonal and communications skills. "That includes respecting the other person's point of view," Mike advises. He also recommends thinking in terms of annual goals and not being overly concerned about the daily battles. "Winning or losing a specific piece of business on any given day is less significant when viewed in the context of your goals for the year," Mike suggested.

Great West hires most of its employee benefit sales representatives right from the college campus and Mike was no exception. Mike came to Great West after graduating from the University of Minnesota with a degree in business. He had three other offers, but chose Great West because he felt most comfortable with their hiring manager. "I had no idea what a real world job would be like, and here he was offering me an opportunity to work with senior officers of major companies. That was an opportunity which frankly fit my ego." The average income at Great West Life is $53,000 for the first year; it jumps to $109,500 after the 5th year, and $146,000 after 10 years.

Brian Marsella
Director, International Sales for the Mid-West Region
CIGNA

Can an economics major that wanted to be a lawyer find professional success and happiness in the insurance industry? For 28-year-old Brian Marsella, who enjoys his job, makes a comfortable income, and has considerable autonomy in his work, the answer is yes.

Brian graduated from Holy Cross College in 1992. "I felt economics would be good preparation for law and I liked the analytical aspects," Brian told me. "But I decided to check out the job market and interviewed on campus for an underwriting position with CIGNA. Initially, I wasn't completely clear about what an underwriter did." Brian was attracted to the job because of his comfort with the recruiter, the understanding of underwriting as a financial position, which he gained at the interview and his attraction to working for a large, stable company. The attraction was mutual and Brian entered CIGNA'S 5½-month training program.

"One of the things I liked was that this company proved it values its employees. After all, CIGNA funded our training and our teachers are from revenue producing lines," Brian recalled. He also liked the fact that his underwriting training drew on both his analytical and interpersonal skills. "At Holy Cross, I was in student government, was the commissioner for some intramural sports and played rugby. I knew these experiences could pay-off professionally and they have," Brian noted.

The technical proficiency gained through the training program was tested in Brian's first assignment—working with the sales force on renewals. "My first role after training was analyzing rate structures and identifying any changes that were called for at clients' companies with at least 200 employees," Brian recalled. Rate structures reflect trends in medical claims, operating expenses and each client company's previous record for claims paid. In addition, to be an underwriter, you need to be an effective intermediary," Brian said. "For example, the actuaries might want to build in a 10% margin against unforeseen events, while the sales force wants a margin of zero to make their product more appealing on cost. We are a business, so we expect to make a profit, but at what percentage?" Packaging an acceptable proposal to bring to the client requires a good deal of negotiating. "By knowing your players, you can reach a successful agreement," Brian said.

Brian enjoyed his three years as an underwriter, in part because "It was like being the proprietor of a $100 million book of business and at a young age having considerable decision making authority." However, he decided to switch to the sales side because he liked "being on the hot seat, the real front line, in front of the client." Brian also enjoyed the increase in income. "I doubled my income in the first year and doubled it again in the second," he told me. Of course, my responsibilities increased as well. Ultimately the servicing of clients fell on Brian's shoulders. "We want to be known as 'number one' in good service, but you need good data from everyone to provide it. Tracking down that data can be very time consuming," Brian said. "But I enjoy making the client happy." He was especially pleased with his success in "turning around" some clients in his first assignment and learning about how companies integrate their differing business philosophies into their employee benefits.

Succeeding in the sales aspect of the business requires a number of skills. One, to use a CIGNA phrase, is "persistency", namely being in constant contact with existing business in order to retain it. A second is creative thinking to identify and pursue potential new clients. A third is self-motivation. "No one is setting a schedule for you," Brian observed.

In the spring of 1998, Brian moved to the international side of the business. "American companies are expanding globally, foreign governments are cutting back on social welfare or privatizing. This is creating a greater need overseas for our services," he reasoned. Brian now works on providing service, especially medical coverage, for Americans working overseas and key managers among the local nationals. "It costs a company an average of $1.2 million to send an American abroad for three years. A good health care policy is an important, relatively low cost, component of protecting that investment," Brian explained. Working with American multi-nationals based in the mid-West, Brian has three main approaches for connecting with potential clients. The first is entree through another CIGNA division, which has business with that client. Insurance brokers and consultants are the second; cold calling is the third. "I do a good deal of research on the Internet to identify multi-national companies," Brian said. "I make contacts through the Human Resources Association of Chicago. Sometimes I identify leads through international trade shows and seminars." Don't picture Brian as a globetrotter, however. His business traveling is mainly confined to the USA.

Brian advocates considering a career in insurance underwriting or sales because you are given considerable discretion early on, the compensation can be substantial and "the insurance industry will always be there." It is not necessary to enter the field straight from college. "If you have good people skills, are well organized and have an analytical thought process to bring with you, it's possible to transition to this business," Brian advised.

Brian is based in Chicago but CIGNA operates throughout the United States and 46 other jurisdictions. To read more about CIGNA, a company with assets of $111 billion, look at their Web site: http://www.CIGNA.com. Career information for both experienced workers and recent college graduates can also be found on the CIGNA Web site.

WHAT TO DO NOW

To help you prepare for a career in sales, the people interviewed for this chapter recommended organizations you can contact, as well as publications and Web sites that may prove useful in your search:

Organizations:

Association for Sales Force Management .... www.asfm.com

Customer Relationship
Management Association .... www.crma-saa.org

National Association of Sales Professionals .... www.nasp.org

Publications:

American Demographics .... www.demographics.com

Selling Power Magazine .... www.sellingpower.com

The Corporate Logo .... www.corporatelogo.com

Web Sites:

www.salesjobs.net

www.job-sites.com/intl/inlist.htm

www.jobs-careers.com

8

Finance & Accounting

No More Green Eyeshade

Sometimes when we think of financial services we think of only the stock market's gyrations or life insurance. In this chapter, financial service professionals talk about some jobs we may seldom think about.

Poise, professional presence and persistence are three qualities Robin Dunlap uses to sell her Citibank payroll service to corporate clients. Scott Schiele uses another "p" – patience – together with product knowledge and communication skills as a bank trust officer in Kansas City. Thinking out of the box, flexibility and long hours are helping Laura Kovach advance her career as an analyst in a regional brokerage firm.

There are also two interesting stories about accountants. We deliberately identified people from regional firms because the profession is not simply the "Big 5". There is a lot more to accounting than numbers and forms to fill out. Kent Beachy worked in manufacturing and a nonprofit environment before starting his career in public accounting. He enjoys working with small businesses while using both technical and client service skills. Darren Brewer's work in business valuations requires sharp analytical skills and the careful exercise of professional judgement.

Kent Beachy
Manager
Norman Jones Enlow & Co

Kent Beachy is a manager at Norman Jones Enlow & Co., a regional public accounting firm based in central Ohio. Many, perhaps most, people who build careers in public accounting start straight out of college. Kent took a different route.

After graduating with an associate's degree from a community college in Fort Wayne, Indiana, Kent spent two years as a staff accountant for a manufacturing firm in Chicago. There he reconciled the corporate cash accounts as well as various other general ledger accounts. Kent decided to return home to Indiana but was unsuccessful in obtaining a job in the accounting profession. However, he did contact a not-for-profit organization in Ohio and served there for three years as a controller and assistant treasurer. During that time, Kent earned a bachelor's degree in accounting and passed his CPA exam.

After seven years in the work force, Kent joined NJE as an entry level staff accountant. "Not having any public accounting experience, I didn't really think that much about starting at the bottom," Kent recalled, "although I can see where some people might." In a typical career progression Kent moved up to "senior" in 2 years or so, and in a similar amount of time, was promoted to supervisor and subsequently manager.

What does a manager in a public accounting firm do? Kent manages NJE's relations with a certain industry niche, in this case construction. He provides service in audit, tax and management consulting. "About 75% of what we do involves compliance; for example, developing financial statements for bank loans or construction performance bonding." Kent explained. "My job specifically is to manage the relationship. That involves planning for the engagement, including giving the client an assistance package so they can get materials in order before my staff arrives, making sure the client has communicated with their people about the engagement, preparing my own staff for special aspects of a specific engagement and budgeting staff hours. Once the engagement begins I monitor work in progress, review the staff's work papers and stay in touch with the client about any problems or concerns." Most of Kent's clients have been with NJE for 3 to 5 years. The relationships which have developed and the firm specific knowledge which has been gained makes the engagement both quicker and more effective.

When Kent interviews prospective new employees he looks for a number of attributes, "Technical knowledge is simply not enough," he offered. "You need to have a service attitude. After all, you are serving clients. You must be able to work well with people both here and at the client's offices. Using judgment when there is a conflict within the staff or with someone at the client's is essential."

Working with small businesses, many of which are family owned, is a challenge that Kent enjoys. He also likes the diversity of his work life and the opportunity to utilize both technical and client relationship skills.

Kent appreciates the opportunities for growth at NJE. The firm's management team includes three managers and three supervisors, so Kent does not need to wait until he obtains partnership to play a role in the firm's management.

Darren Brewer
Senior Accountant
Baird, Kurtz, Dobson (BKD)

Close your eyes and say the word "accountant." Do you picture someone with green eyeshades and sharp pencils? Is s/he sitting in a huge corporate tower in a large city or perhaps filling out tax forms in a strip mall? Now open your eyes and see Darren Brewer, a senior accountant at Baird, Kurtz & Dobson, a 900 person firm with 20 offices spread over seven states in the Midwest and Southwest.

Darren grew up in Van Buren, Arkansas, not far from where he now works in Fort Smith. Getting to BKD was hardly a straight line process, though. When Darren graduated high school in 1985, his first love was music. He played several instruments and was part of a jazz band. However, there was no living to be made in music, so he went to work in his family's small business. Darren started to take courses at a local community college, including a few in business. At the same time, Darren developed a relationship with a local CPA, who assisted Darren with the management of his family's business. The CPA impressed Darren with the scope of his knowledge and good business sense. That's when Darren realized he wanted to be a CPA. So, he joined the United States Air Force to work as an accountant and continue his education on a part-time basis.

The Air Force sent Darren to England for three years. "I was hoping to be based in the southern part of the U.S.," Darren told me, "but it worked out for the best. The University of Maryland offered bachelor's degree programs at my base in England. The Air Force even paid for 75% of my tuition." At the end of three years, including a stint serving in the Gulf War, Darren had earned a bachelor's degree and returned to Arkansas to earn a master of accountancy at the University of Arkansas.

The journey from high school through college degree wasn't easy. "When I joined the Air Force, I went from being a business owner supervising people twice my age to being low man on the totem pole," Darren remembered. "When I started at BKD, I went from experienced airman to entry level accountant. The other new accountants were younger than I and many of my supervisors were my age. That's quite an adjustment."

Most of the clients Darren works with are in three industries: construction, manufacturing, and wholesale distribution. After gaining some experience in "A & A" (accounting and auditing) and tax, Darren has started to specialize in business valuations and appraisals. These engagements are performed for many reasons including estate and gift tax planning and tax return preparation, conducting ESOP (Employee Stock Ownership Plan) transactions and mergers and acquisitions.

To do his job well, Darren gathers and analyzes large amounts of data including company, industry, local and national economic, and financial markets data. Even with all of this data, "valuation work is more of an art, than a science," Darren told me. "It involves using a great deal of professional judgment." When performing valuations, Darren works largely by himself, researching, interviewing company officers and inspecting facilities. Darren is a bit of a marketeer. He establishes good relationships with attorneys and other professionals which become a good source of referrals.

As Darren's career progresses, his job is changing in that he now has more client contact. "I enjoy being an advisor - like that CPA who helped me," Darren remarked. Although he still does "A & A" and tax work, Darren is trying to develop his valuation and consulting practice within BKD. Practice development skills are a must for anyone who desires to become a BKD partner.

"I have a great job" Darren told me. "I have autonomy over my work day and flexibility in scheduling. The pay is good and gets better every year. It's true that from January to April 15, I work long days but for the rest of the year things are pretty normal.

So Darren is back living very near his home town and very satisfied professionally. "I could have gone to a Big 6 firm—I had three other job offers before joining BKD. However I wanted to return to Fort Smith and work for a firm like BKD where I could gain experience in A & A, tax and consulting instead of only A & A as may have been the case with a Big 6 Firm." (Note: The Big 6 are now the Big 5. At one time, they were the Big 8.)

Robin Dunlap
Banker
Citibank

If you met Robin Dunlap at a party, you probably wouldn't guess her profession. She is pleasant and articulate. Do you want more clues? Robin is driven and persistent. Would you guess that Robin is a banker for Citibank?

Robin sells corporations on an interesting Citibank product. A large company will agree to a direct deposit of payroll checks in Citibank for employees who wish to participate. The depositor receives a waiver on all fees, has no minimum balance and is eligible for a lower interest rate on loans. The total savings can be $300 per employee per year. From the employing company's perspective, the plan is like a no cost fringe benefit. For Citibank, it provides a larger base of deposits and depositors.

Bringing a deal like this to fruition is not that easy. Robin spent her first ten months on the job building her credibility with Citibank's Corporate relationship managers. By building trust with these managers, Robin gained an introduction to a large corporation with 11,000 employees in New York. The relationship manager had to be certain that Robin's retail banking proposal would please the corporation. Otherwise he could lose a client. The corporation for its part needed to be assured that the program would work, including excellent service after the contract became operative.

Robin believes that she has the greatest job in the bank. She is gratified to sell a product which adds value for everyone involved. In addition, she enjoys the variety of working with a wide variety of corporate players, including foreign ones. (Yes, Citibank can deposit your New York employees payroll checks in New York and your Mexico City payroll checks "en Ciudad Mexico.")

Robin gets out of the office a lot as she calls on current and prospective clients. "It's a ten or twelve hour day and in many respects, I am a Lone Ranger. That's great for me because I wouldn't want to be behind a desk all day." However, when she is in the office, Robin is in frequent touch with the in-house bankers to make sure that her clients' needs are being served.

Many clients will not sign an exclusive contract with Citibank. Instead they agree to a fair where the various large banks can present their wares. Part of Robin's job is to arrange the fairs and perhaps be present herself. She likes the contact with the end-users, namely the individual employees.

A position like Robin's does require a degree of patience. Although her proposals are relatively simple and straight forward, it can take three months to close a deal. "It's critical to get the proper endorsements at the client site," Robin told me, "and some senior managers are concerned about complicating arrangements they have with other banks. In addition, Robin has to be able to make a deal acceptable to the prospective client and still profitable to Citibank. For example, Robin may need to negotiate a deeper discount on some consumer loans to seal the deal.

This is a position which requires a self-starter who manages time well. Robin needs poise and professional presence in addition to an appropriate degree of persistence. You don't have to know finance, but you need to enjoy selling and servicing your clients. Above all else you need confidence in yourself.

Robin showed some of those characteristics just getting into Citibank. Straight out of college, Robin worked for a consulting group which produced management training books. She had a marvelous manager, but was unhappy about the lack of people contact. In addition, Robin didn't really understand the value of the product she was helping to produce.

Looking for a change, Robin applied to the graduate program at the American School of International Management, also known as Thunderbird University in Arizona. She was rejected three times before being admitted *on probation*. During her second year she submitted a resume to Citibank which was interviewing on campus for three days. Unlike 75 of her classmates who were invited to interview, Robin was rejected. She waited for the recruiter between interviews and asked for five minutes to present her case. Response: negative. Robin tried on the second day. Response: negative. Third day, Robin tried again. The recruiter gave her "five minutes". Robin said that she was determined to have her name on a Citibank business card, come what may. The recruiter was impressed with Robin's moxie, offered her an interview in New York, leading to her great job at Citibank today.

Most banks, especially large commercial ones, sell lots of products to corporate or retail clients. To get a job like Robin's, you won't need a graduate degree, but you will need a focused determination.

Laura Kovach
Junior Analyst
McDonald & Co. Securities

Have you ever tried to figure out which way the financial markets are going or want some expert advice on specific stocks? Laura Kovach is building a career on answering just those questions.

Laura is a junior analyst at McDonald & Company Securities, a regional brokerage firm based in Cleveland. She supports analysts for three industries — steel, electrical equipment, telecommunications — in researching companies in any of those industry groups. This includes company specific research, investigating the broader industry, searching for news stories and crunching numbers. Most of the information is publicly available, but perhaps not easily accessible. Laura spends a good deal of time researching both prominent and arcane web sites. At times, she contacts a company she is following for clarification or information. The information Laura compiles for an analyst is used to forecast a company's expected profit picture two years in the future.

Laura enjoys surfing the Web, although "sometimes it can get tedious." Calling companies and visiting faculties, meeting with management (CFO's and CEO's) is especially interesting and Laura hopes to do more of that as her career advances.

Laura chose McDonald Securities in part for geographic reasons. "Analyst jobs tend to be in a company's headquarters, which often means New York or Chicago. I wanted Cleveland, and luckily McDonald is headquartered right here," Laura explained. Laura had been introduced to the idea of becoming an analyst through a guest speaker at her college, Bowling Green (Ohio). The speaker's subject was interesting and Laura sought a summer internship with McDonald Securities. In fact she spent two summers there before starting full time in 1995.

Laura started out in operations, "the behind the scenes stuff like balancing accounts," she explained, and moved over to investment consulting services. There she reviewed account performance and related issues for high net worth investors. A junior analyst position opened up when someone left; Laura applied and was accepted. While working full time, Laura earned an MBA, studying evenings at Cleveland State University.

There are many aspects Laura likes about her job, even with its twelve hour days and periods of unusual stress. "I know where I'm headed," she told me. "The career path is fairly clear. My next stop, if I am successful is becoming a regular analyst, then I hope to rise to Director of Research." Laura likes the analytical aspects of her job and the fact that she is constantly learning "Every case can be like a graduate school course," Laura said. "For example, I researched the input of Environmental Protection Agency proposed regulations on some machine tool stock we were following. You need to master a lot of facts and their implications in a hurry." Laura also likes the mixture of personalities she meets in the investment program.

Another attraction of McDonald Securities is its commitment to community service. Laura told me about proudly wearing her company tee shirt working with Habitat for Humanity, doing the March of Dimes Walk, and spending Mondays at a hunger center. In fact, Laura has become chairman of the company's Community Activity Committee.

If you are considering becoming a stock analyst, Laura recommends that you be able to think "out of the box," be flexible, and understand the needs of others. You will need a huge drive to succeed, to put in all the hours. You will also need a good understanding of spreadsheet software programs—such as Excel—and the capacity to handle several projects simultaneously. In addition, consider geography carefully, since an analyst's position will be found in a headquarters and not a branch brokerage office. In addition, be ready to get some good initials after your name. Laura is now doing a self study in order to pass the CFA (Certified Financial Analyst) exam.

Scott Schiele
Trust Officer
UMB Bank N.A.

Can three summers experience selling telephone book advertisements and one summer working in a trust department lay the groundwork for a career in banking? For Scott Schiele, a trust officer at UMB Bank in Kansas City, Missouri, it certainly did.

When he graduated in 1996 from Iowa State University (Ames) with a degree in finance, Scott returned to his job of two summers, selling ads. After a while, he realized that long term prospects with that company were not bright. Fortunately, Scott had a friend who was a commercial lender at UMB Bank and he helped arrange an interview for Scott. "Kansas City is one of the four Midwest cities that attract people from Iowa, so that was a plus for me," he recalled.

Scott was hired as a commercial banking trainee and spent some time in each division of the bank. He was particularly attracted to the trust department because he liked working with mutual funds and similar investments. "I don't give investment advice, but I get to really understand these products," Scott noted. "We handle a whole array of funds for both defined benefits and defined contribution pension plans. It's not a canned product, so what provides flexibility for the client provides variety for me." The main clients for Scott are companies with 50 or more employees. "The employee benefit division provides custody for pension assets, maintains records and generates reports for the company. Leads can come from our commercial lenders or can come in unsolicited. We solicit or simply receive an RFP or 'request for proposal'. I work on the request to determine what we can provide and at what price," he explained. "I have developed a data base with common questions and answers so I don't have to start from scratch each time."

Scott attends a Business Review Committee meeting each week. That committee will decide whether Scott can offer his proposal to a client or not. "I'll get a lot of good questions about whether the proposal is both feasible and profitable," Scott explained. "I need to be thoroughly prepared." Scott also needs to be patient. "The sales cycle for trust services can be one month to one year, depending on the size of the plan and the customer's internal decision process."

Scott enjoys meeting different people, each bringing their own perspective and issues to the table. "Some companies are more paternalistic and put all contributions into a general fund which the company directs. There is some legal risk for them if the fund underperforms, because employees could charge malfeasance. Other companies sponsor participant directed funds. That is permissible if the company is 404(C) compliant, meaning they have given the employees adequate investment information amongst other requirements," Scott explained.

Scott finds that his communication skills are critical to doing his job well. "Every client has their own learning curve and I need to adjust to that," he indicated. Since Scott is responsible for multiple clients and faces frequent deadlines, the ability to organize and manage his time well is essential. Scott is currently working on his designation of Certified Employee Benefit Specialist (CEBS), which will be quite helpful for his professional future. To accomplish this he has to pass 10 courses — mostly self-study — composed by the Institute of Employee Benefits in Wisconsin and the Wharton School in Philadelphia. "Keeping up in this profession is important," Scott said. "I attend seminars on employee benefit issues frequently and read in the field continuously." Included in Scott's reading are *401(K) Wire,* an online daily; *Deferred Contributions News,* a monthly; and *Benefits Quarterly.*

Ted Tobin
District Manager, Diversified Financial Concepts Division
Fortis Investers, Inc.

Ted Tobin works hard for himself by working hard for clients. As a manager of financial consultants, Ted works with small business owners, independent contractors and middle class families. His clients typically are planning for retirement, college costs and company pension plans. "I help them work towards higher yields or lower taxes on their investments," Ted explained. "If they purchase products I recommend, whether it be mutual funds, annuities or life insurance, I receive a commission." Ted must be careful that his clients invest with open eyes. "We start with their goals and then will help them meet their goals. They must understand that all investments involve risk, but all passbook savings accounts are sure losers when you measure their yield against inflation."

Ted described his compensation as "merit based," that is 100% commission. "I like it that way," Ted told me. "I get paid based on helping my clients. The more they benefit, the more I make. I had a salaried job once, but progress was slow and rewards were not commensurate with producing results.

Ted started at Fortis as a registered representative, having passed his product knowledge classes and earned his basic licenses (Like many financial consultants, Ted has licenses in life, accident and sickness, annuities, and a principal license which allows him to be a supervisor. Initially he has a series 6 and series 63 license). Ted moved up in the organization rapidly, becoming a district manager within a little over a year. "My main responsibility is to teach other representatives what experience taught me about this business, I hire, train and motivate them. In return I receive an override (percentage) of their commissions," Ted explained.

Ted graduated from the University of Rhode Island in 1993 with a major in Journalism. His first job was doing public relations work for a professional association of realtors. He enjoyed writing their newsletter, coordinating events, working in committees and generating ideas that were welcomed. But progress was slow there and when a friend offered Ted the opportunity to be a mortgage broker, he took it.

"There was a small salary. Most compensation was commission and I was really afraid of that," Ted recalled. "I enjoyed what I was doing, but it was difficult to break into the existing relationships among builders, brokers, and real estate agents. Ted moved to Atlanta in hopes of warmer weather and better prospects. "I read an advertisement for Fortis, applied and accepted a job offer. I was attracted by the chance to earn a large income. There is no glass ceiling and nobody is holding you back," Ted recalled. When Ted started to work at Fortis, he found an added satisfaction, "I help people achieve the American Dream," Ted said, "and that's a great feeling."

A typical week for Ted, who sets his own schedule, goes like this: On Mondays and Fridays he has district meetings in the morning, in the afternoon he works with representatives teaching them about financial products and role playing issues which arise with clients. Ted also does his administrative follow-up for the week. On Tuesdays, Wednesdays, and Thursdays, Ted is visiting clients or perhaps recruiting new representatives.

Sometimes Ted has a long day. "I can start at 7:30 AM in the office and end a meeting with a client in their office or home at 11:00 PM." I asked Ted how important sales skills are in his profession. "Eighty percent of my time with a client is educational. I learn about their needs and goals and they learn about our products and services." The rest is not sales so much as it is building a relationship of trust and bringing the client to a conclusion of some kind," Ted replied. Ted also distinguished between a financial consultant and a stock broker. "A stock broker holds a Series 7 license so s/he can sell individual securities (stocks and bonds). We can handle mutual funds but don't get involved in individual securities."

Ted estimates that a first year representative earns about $25,000. You can reach district manager in one to two years and earn between $40,000 and $60,000. The next step is to become a branch manager, with potential earnings of $60,000-$70,000 the first year "and six figures in two years."

Ted suggests that a person in his field needs to be committed to personal success through helping clients. S/he should have good leadership skills in order to advance to a managerial level and good communication skills at every step. "You need to keep things simple. Our training teaches the complexity of financial investments, but you need to boil things down so that the client can understand them."

In terms of Ted's own future, he hopes to have an office in Jacksonville, Florida as a regional manager. "Warmer weather and more money," Ted concluded.

Marc L. Wells
Account Executive
J.G. Wentworth

Imagine some great news, like winning the lottery jackpot or winning a large settlement in a civil suit. Now imagine that you have good reasons to receive a large sum of money now instead of receiving payments spread over a number of years. You could call J.G. Wentworth in Fort Lee, New Jersey and Marc Wells (or one of his colleagues) would explore with you the possibility of a structured buy-out.

"The first thing is to make sure that the person calling has sufficient reasons for wanting a structured buy-out. It's not the right approach for everyone," Marc told me. "If we can be helpful, I ask to see the terms of their settlement, lottery winnings, etc. Then I calculate the present dollar value of that settlement. The client would be getting fewer dollars, but getting them much sooner."

Of course there is some background work to be done. J.G. Wentworth must perform "due diligence " to make sure that the client's settlement is not encumbered by liens, taxes or judgments. "It is also critical to make sure that the client is exactly who he says he is. We need to guard against fraud," Marc explained. Due diligence is performed by J. G. Wentworth's underwriting department in Philadelphia. "I also make sure that the client's attorney reviews, understands and accepts our offer," Marc noted.

Marc didn't study finance or law in college. In fact, he majored in computer science and electrical engineering at the City College of New York. His first job was at a major computer firm working on the guidance system of submarine launched nuclear missiles. "The technical experience was great," Marc recalled. "You need all kinds of data and gadgets just to locate your own submarine relative to an enemy target. Then you calculate things like the sub's depth, the pitch of the sea and the height of the continental shelf. The problem was it just didn't feel good to be working on ways to incinerate people."

Marc decided to leave and start his own computer consulting firm. Unfortunately, it went "belly-up" after two years.

"Through a friend, I found a job factoring health care receivables in New York," Marc recounted. "It was an enjoyable job, but it lacked some of the interpersonal contact I wanted. In 1995, a friend who was a principal in the newly formed J.G. Wentworth invited Marc to become the seventh member of the company. Today there are over 400 members."

Marc told me that he has found a working home for himself. "This company is like a family. The principals care about every employee. They are down-to-earth folks who are open to input from anybody. There is nothing I would be afraid to ask of the company, and there is nothing the company couldn't ask of me," Marc said. He has enjoyed watching the company grow and his mentoring relationship with the newer employees. Marc also related to me stories of people who sent letters thanking him for his help in getting them a large pay-out when they needed it. "It is important to make a difference to people," Mark said. "For example one woman won a large injury settlement and shortly thereafter she was diagnosed with terminal cancer. She wanted money immediately to spend with and for her family while she was still alive to see them enjoy it. It made a great difference to her and that made a difference to me."

WHAT TO DO NOW

To help you prepare for a career in finance and accounting, the people interviewed for this chapter recommended organizations you can contact, as well as publications and Web sites that may prove useful in your search:

Organizations:

American Accounting Association	www.aaa-edu.org
American Institute of Certified Public Accountants	www.aicpa.org
American Society of Women Accountants (ASWA)	www.aswa.org
National Association of Tax Practitioners (NATP)	www.natptax.com
Associated Regional Accounting Firms	www.araf.com
American Financial Services Association	www.americanfinsvcs.com
American Bankers Association	www.aba.com

Publications:

Barrons	www.barrons.com
Financial Times	www.usa.ft.com
Journal of Accountancy	www.aicpa.org/pubs/jofa
Money Daily	www.money.comt
Wall Street Journal	www.wsj.com
401 (K) Wire	www.401kwire.com
Benefits Quarterly	www.ifebp.org/isbqsum.html
Management Accounting	www.mamag.com

Web Sites:

www.financialjobnet.com

9

Communications

Getting your Point of View Across

Communication skills are important in most professions, as the stories in this book attest. For some people communications is their profession.

What exactly do these folks do, how do they do it and how did they get into communications as a profession? In this chapter, we'll look at a path to University periodicals and a path from that specialty. We'll read about an ordained minister who initiated new businesses at a mature firm and a communications major who stayed with the field. There is a story about in-house public relations, the struggle to gain a position in a regional advertising firm and a former teacher who now directs publishing services for some 40 magazines.

There are some common themes in all these stories. Each person worked hard to develop skill sets they are currently using. Each is enthusiastic about their job and most tend to work a long day. All are aware of the needs of their audience and avoid the trap of viewing communications as merely a tool for self-expression.

Jay Cooperider
Assistant Director of University Periodicals
Purdue University

Let's say that you love to write, to delve into history, and to work in a team setting to publish. Would you pursue a position in university periodicals? Jay Cooperider did and has enjoyed his ten years at Purdue University immensely.

Jay is part of a team of writers, editor, photographers and designers responsible for two campus publications—the bimonthly newspaper *Inside Purdue* for faculty and staff and the quarterly magazine *Perspective*, which is distributed to 330,000 alumni, parents and contributors.

Inside Purdue is intended to inform and entertain. Informing includes news about awards won, campus events, etc. Entertainment includes providing a forum for ideas to be shared and to introduce people on campus. "This is a large university with twelve academic schools. It is important for people to have a sense of others whom they wouldn't typically meet in the course of daily business. *Perspective* was originally established as a 'friend raising' vehicle. Today it is a medium for creating a sense of pride and community among dispersed people with a Purdue connection," Jay told me.

Jay's role in part is to develop stories that people will want to read. "There is plenty of competition for people's time and attention," Jay noted. At the same time, Jay knows to leave the "shock" stories and scandal articles to the daily press. On the other hand, Jay doesn't avoid controversy; he just handles it carefully. "My first task, if the story involves controversy, is reaching an agreement with my administrators that it should be covered. Then we need to strike a balance. We don't want to simply be a shill for the university's administration or polarize issues into black and white. Subtleties and nuances are a serious part of most issues," Jay explained. As an example, he cited the case of a century-old building the administration contemplated tearing down. Traditionalists didn't want to lose a part of Purdue history, but the administration felt it was unwise to spend millions of dollars to repair the building and bring it up to modern codes and standards. "Tradition versus change is an interesting issue and I didn't want to present it as good guys versus bad guys" Jay noted.

Jay also delves into university history. "I can spend whole days going through university archives and handwritten letter files to find facts," Jay said with a lilt. "For me it's like a paid hobby." For example, Jay proved that the moniker "Boilermakers" in regard to Purdue athletic teams actually was started in 1891, and not 1889 as proclaimed by legend. A former newspaper reporter with a background in investigative reporting, Jay was challenged by the loose wording of the traditional origin of "Boilermakers". "No one had gone back to newspapers to check," he said. "It was right here in print."

Digging through dusty files and presenting balanced perspectives are only part of what Jay enjoys. He likes "planning, writing, rewriting, and editing" stories, writing headlines and laying out pages. In addition, he meets all kinds of interesting people in the course of his interviewing. He also works with printers and other businesses that help distribute *Inside Purdue* and *Perspective*. "I have variety and creative opportunity," Jay noted.

Jay graduated from the University of Cincinnati, where he had been editor of the student newspaper. He was also an intern for the *Cincinnati Enquirer*, a part of the Gannett chain. That led to a position as a reporter for the Gannett owned *Lafayette Journal* and *Courier* when Jay graduated in 1984. Within a year, he moved up to city editor. That was a mixed blessing. Gannett corporate managers told Jay he had a bright future, but that it would require a number of relocations. For family reasons, Jay didn't want to change geography, so he started to look for a job change instead. "Connections are a huge asset," Jay observed. A former staff reporter told Jay she was leaving her job at Purdue's School of Agriculture. Jay applied, was hired and started writing stories about farming and agricultural research. Two years after, he heard from a friend about an opening in university publications. His experience in writing and editing helped him get the job.

Jay identified a number of skills needed to do publications work well. One is "to think in the terms of reader and not yourself," Jay advised. "What is obvious to you may be brand new and obscure for others." You also need inquisitiveness that makes you continue to ask "why" when developing a story. Similarly, you need patience and perseverance to pursue your ideas. At the same time, you need to be a "quick study" and get a good grasp on news situations in a hurry. "It's helpful to have an eye for design, and you need good presentation skills in both writing and graphics," Jay added. Jay feels that anyone considering a job like his should have experience in journalism. "Although my work involves skills gained as a reporter and editor, I also work in public, alumni and staff relations," he said, noting that his work for a daily newspaper helped prepare him for his work at Purdue. "It's essential to be a member of the news and information consuming public to prepare you for public relations work."

Alex Hansen
Executive Vice President
JWT Specialized Communications

Can a philosophy major and ordained minister find happiness in the world of business communications? Will he investigate, innovate and initiate new businesses? The answer to both questions is "yes", if that person is Alex Hansen.

Alex is the Executive Vice President at JWT Specialized Communications, headquartered in Los Angeles. However he came to the company as its controller. At the time the core business at JWT Specialized Communications was helping business clients recruit employees by placing help wanted ads in the appropriate print media (e.g. newspapers; trade-journals). This service might include writing the ad itself (from three lines to a full page) in addition to the logistics of placing the ad.

"That business was significant, with 1,700 clients nationwide," Alex told me, "There was a lot of accounting and paper work, but not much creativity." JWTSC also wrote recruiting brochures for large companies and handled internal communications for clients, especially during times of mergers and similar dramatic changes.

One vulnerability of this business was its susceptibility to economic downturns. "In one recession, the company lost 30% of its revenue in two months," Alex recalled. He was appointed to his current position to diversify sources of revenue. In fact Alex helped moved the company from a traditional advertising agency with a staffing focus to a staffing communications company. "We moved in several directions," Alex told me. "First, we diversified our markets by adding services to the market for 'mature' Americans, the recruiting of students to educational institutions and business to business communications. Second, we broadened our services to recruiters. This included research for 'direct sourcing', Internet mining to uncover resumes, and diversity staffing. As part of that later effort, we identified 2,500 diversity focused organizations, from predominately minority churches to nation-wide groups, to receive job postings." We also initiated an on-line diversity job fair (www.diversityfair.com) with some 35 major company sponsors and extended want ad publication to minority-focused magazines.

The on-line diversity fair is an interesting mix of high touch and high technology approaches. Resumes are received from both Internet and print media sources and accepted in paper, fax or e-mail form. Then they are "cleaned up" if necessary and put into data base format to be maintained on line. The sponsoring companies, who have paid a fee of $450/month, can access the resumes on-line. About 600 new resumes are added daily. Alex even has his staff contact by phone, those who submit resumes to clarify their goals. At the same time, the staff asks "Do you know anybody else who might be looking for a new job?" That direct contact yields additional resumes.

Currently, Alex is planning the launch of another new business "We have eleven people in media planning getting us ready," Alex noted. "We will establish a service to help clients hire the right person the first time, and then retain them." This new service will include initial interviewing of potential candidates and providing the client with a candidate-specific interviewing guide identifying probing follow-up questions to ask.

Alex enjoys developing new business, "For one thing, these new projects could be extremely lucrative," he told me. "Second, it's interesting to work with people on the cutting edge of technology. Third, I will help change the way staffing is done in management America." Alex also likes the fact that people really like working with each other and that management gives material and moral support to innovative ideas.

A day in the office for Alex can be 10-12 hours, but "really I love this job so much I think about ways to do new things and do them better all the time." But this isn't the career Alex planned for.

Alex earned a degree in philosophy from Williams College in 1970 and entered Princeton Theological Seminary. "My first job was being an ordained minister," Alex told me, "but I soon found that having a pulpit was not my calling. I tried teaching at a boarding school and a private school. It was enjoyable, but when my kids were born, I decided not to be poor anymore. Alex had accumulated enough accounting credits to sit for his CPA (certified public accounting) exam and he went to work for a "Big Six" firm in their audit practice. JWT Specialized Communication was a client and they liked Alex's work. Soon he was invited to become their controller. When the company needed to push into new directions, Alex was the person for the job.

"My financial background helped me in strategic planning," Alex pointed out. "My teaching came in handy because I teach my staff how to help clients and teach clients how to take advantage of technology." Alex paused a moment and added "I suppose that I am really still preaching, too. It's important to pull people together into one team, each one coming with a different perspective and agenda. That's like gathering-in the disparate sheep and making them one flock." Alex also brought with him excellent writing and presentation skills.

For those considering a career like Alex's, he has some advice. If you are a career changer it is possible to break in because, in a sense, everybody and everything in this field is new. However, it would be important to bring a specific skill set, like marketing or staffing experience, that would add value quickly. For a college student, Alex recommends a classical marketing communications type of major and trying to start your career with a major advertising agency. In either case, Alex notes that the field is less secure than a typical corporation but more secure than a traditional, product centered, advertising agency.

Susan Newberry
Director in the Healthcare Practice
Burson-Marsteller

Let's say that you are a pharmaceutical company, Wonder Chem, which has just developed Rawknuck, a cure for raw knuckles. How could you bring your product to the attention of potential consumers? One way would be to hire an advertising agency, which would create a message and then buy media space or time to promote it. Burson-Marsteller, as a perception management firm, would take a different approach. When it comes to generating media attention, their goal is to get the reporters (print, radio and television) to run news stories about this remarkable medical breakthrough. The person in charge of the effort (if Burson-Marsteller is hired by Wonder Chem), is Susan Newberry, a Director in the Healthcare Practice, located in Washington, D.C.

Susan has been in public relations since graduating from UCLA in 1986, and joined Burson-Marsteller in 1998. How does she get stories about Rawknuck and/or Wonder Chem into the media? Susan develops press releases, which focus on aspects of the story, which she believes news journalists will find news*worthy*. The emphasis is on "worthy". "The journalist could be my brother-in-law and he won't cover the story unless he believes it news*worthy*. It's the story which sells the decision, not my personal relationship to the journalist," Susan explained. If one medium does pick up the story, others may do so as well. This ripple effect, or "pack journalism" as it is called, can multiply the dispersion of what started as a single story. "Our goal is to ensure that the perceptions which surround our clients and influence our stakeholders are consistent in their business objectives," Susan explains.

Susan's public relations work is also carried out through relationships with professional associations. For example, if a client develops a product to help mitigate strokes, Susan may arrange a symposium through an association of neurosurgeons. I asked Susan if there was any danger of tainting a scientific presentation when linking it to a commercial product. "The danger is there, but steps are taken to prevent that occurrence," Susan told me. "For one thing, the professional association controls the content, and they won't allow anything which isn't scientifically sound. Second, a scientist stakes his/her reputation on the validity of their procedure and findings."

Another potential vehicle for Susan is trade publications, of which there are two types. Some are peer reviews journals, which publish carefully screened reports on scientific studies. There is little role for public relations in those cases. On the other hand, newsletters directed to professional groups would be open in press releases about products of interest or the fact that a client company is sponsoring a certain type of research.

Irrespective of venue, the goal of public relations work is to get people to act. That could mean writing in support of specific legislation if the client has concerns in the government policy area or considering a specific drug if the client is in pharmaceuticals.

Susan graduated from UCLA as a Communications major in 1986. While there, she interned in the college public relations department, and had outside internships at CBS and Paramount. In addition, she worked as a clerk in the biomedical library, which gave her the opportunity to read a large number of articles on that field. Straight out of college, Susan joined a small public relations firm as a junior account executive. Her first client was in health, specifically an organization of optometrists. Susan wrote press releases regarding studies which showed an increased danger in night driving as people get older. This wasn't simply a public service. Instead, the news stories indirectly encouraged people to have their eyes examined.

A year later, Susan moved to a larger firm with more national clients. She enjoyed the latitude she was given, including the chance to write a newsletter for a client's franchisees.

Susan moved to the East Coast and found a position with a national firm handling bio-tech accounts. "I had to come up to speed pretty quickly, learning to understand our clients products chemical fertilizer and pesticides," Susan recalled. "I enjoyed organizing agriculture round tables to bring our people and farmers together. There is a lot more to bringing food to people than just filling a shopping cart."

Several of Susan's colleagues started their own firm in Washington and asked her to join them. She was sent to London "for a few months" and ended up staying for two-and-a-half years. "I was doing things like organizing press conferences for people from 15 different countries," Susan remarked. When Susan returned to the U.S. she was attracted to a major New York public relations firm, where she worked for two years before coming to Burson-Marsteller.

Despite the long hours and frequent stress, Susan thinks that she has "the best job in the world — at least for me." I am always challenged intellectually to learn new subjects and develop new strategies. Even though I have developed expertise in my craft, I am still always learning," Susan said. She enjoys mentoring and developing her twelve member staff something "many public relations firms neglect because the immediate need to generate revenue is so pressing." Susan told me, "in my opinion the wider the base of the company's talent pyramid, the higher each of us can go."

There are some difficult aspects to a career like Susan's. "It's a 25 hour day in a highly competitive business. We seldom have exclusive agreements with clients. There are outrageous deadlines, and losing a potential client after making a great pitch can be disappointing," Susan told me. "In addition, sometimes clients work very slowly but in public relations we need to move quickly."

If you are considering a career in public relations you should have a voracious appetite for public affairs, markets and marketing. "Your ideas are critical in this field, so you need a lot of content, context and intellectual stimulation to find ways to reach your public," Susan explained. She also recommended being a "visionary with the guts to pursue your ideas tenaciously." It's critical to be a good time manager, in part because of short deadlines and in part because you need to handle multiple tasks concurrently. Of course writing and speaking are essential and an understanding of journalism is very helpful.

Cheryl Flohr
Manager, Communication Services
Parker Aerospace, Parker Hannifin Corporation

"I'll sweep the floor for you, make photocopies, dump the trash. Anything! I just want some experience in writing." Cheryl Flohr wanted to improve the skills she had already developed as a writer, then assistant editor, for her college newspaper. With enthusiasm like that, Cheryl was hired, full time, to work in Biola College's public relations department during her senior year. "I wrote news releases and articles for the alumni publication, rather than sweeping the floor. I always liked both the analytical and creative aspects of writing," Cheryl told me. "This position let me apply those skills to assure that the content and perception the college wanted to communicate was in fact conveyed to our public."

Cheryl worked for Biola an additional six years. When she left, she was responsible for a staff of 11, including writers, graphic designers and support personnel. "I attended a meeting of a small communications group in southern California, where some one mentioned an opening at Pepperdine University," Cheryl told me. "It was time for a new challenge, so I applied for the position and was hired." At Pepperdine, Cheryl was responsible for the editorial content of all University sponsored publications, including the annual report, a four-color alumni magazine and the college catalogues.

"Editorial work requires a lot of planning. Each story is part of a public representation of the client, in that case Pepperdine," Cheryl explained. "Every story has to be reviewed for length, content, style and consistency. Every page has to be reviewed and proof read. Photographs and illustrations have to be created. With all of that, you still have to scramble to accommodate any number of last minute changes," she continued with a laugh.

After two years at Pepperdine, Cheryl went to work for a newspaper chain, then a group of medical centers. In 1988, she came to Parker in employee communications, working on employee newsletters. But she seized the chance to do other things as well.

"In most companies, even some very large ones like Parker, the communications department is small and everyone wears lots of hats," Cheryl explained. "Now I spend 75 percent of my time on international trade shows, something we are learning about as we do it. A few years ago, I did mostly "marketing collateral", like brochures and advertising. When it's time to host financial analysts at Parker, I spend 75% of my time on that, when we're compiling Parker's annual report, I will spend 75% of my time working on our section of the report. You need to be flexible and volunteer to try different things if you want to progress in this profession." Flexible she is. Cheryl is also responsible for production of the company's employee communications efforts, including human resources literature, handbooks and internal newsletters.

Cheryl wasn't kidding when she said "small". She has the assistance of one full time and one half-time staff member. "We share resources," Cheryl noted. "For example, I share responsibility with the graphics area and can rely on those folks for support when I need it. We also use many outside professionals, including a superb ad agency."

What is the purpose of communications services? As Cheryl explained it, "You are the in-house public relations or advertising agency for your company. Your goal is to serve the client in an honest and ethical way. For example, when you speak to a media reporter, you want to give accurate and timely information but still represent the company. To do that well, you need to have your client's agenda in mind and make sure you get it in."

Cheryl clearly needs excellent writing and communications skills, but they alone would not be sufficient. The ability to understand every aspect of the organization and facilitate cooperation among units of the company is critical. In addition, she needs to be well-organized to help projects move forward in a productive and timely fashion.

Engaging her sense of presence and communication skills to properly represent her client is something Cheryl enjoys. More broadly she believes that these are the skills which differentiate those who succeed best in organizations from those who work hard but don't advance. Cheryl also enjoys the work environment at Parker. "We want to be the employer of choice, so Parker encourages two way communication and a culture of doing what is right—not what is merely expedient. That gives me a great sense of pride in the company and energizes me to represent it well. At the more personal level, I am given creative freedom. No one tries to micro manage me."

What's next professionally for Cheryl? "Those steps would have to be created," she noted. Luckily, Parker is a creative company.

Cheryl is accredited by the Public Relations Society of America, based in New York City, and is a member of the International Association of Business Communicators, headquartered in San Francisco. She chairs the communication council of the Aerospace Industries Association. Parker Aerospace designs, manufactures, and services hydraulic, fuel, and pneumatic components, systems, and related electronic controls for aerospace and other high-technology markets. Based in Irvine, California, it is an operating segment of Parker Hannifin Corporation, a global producer of motion-control components and systems for a wide range of aerospace, industrial, and automotive markets. Parker Hannifin sales in fiscal 1998 were $4.6 billion.

Laura Sutherland
Account Executive
The Martin Agency

Getting to her job at The Martin Agency requires an early morning start to the agency's Richmond, Virginia office headquarters. Landing her position in the first place was a more difficult trip, so let's start Laura Sutherland's story there.

Laura was an honors student at the University of Virginia, graduating in 1994. She created her own major in Political and Social Thought and wrote a thesis about creativity, business and ethics. She gained her first exposure to advertising during her career planning class. Laura attended a workshop at The Martin Agency, where she worked with a team of students from across the country developing a case study strategy. Together, they created and presented an advertising campaign for an existing client. "When choosing my career, I wanted to match my strengths with my passion and this was it," Laura told me.

Laura whole-heartedly pursued a position in advertising. She made a portfolio of her work to demonstrate her research and strategy skills. She met as many advertising people as she could, showing them her portfolio and sending them articles of interest as a means of staying visible. Even The Martin Agency's chairman made time to meet with her and share valuable professional insight. Laura went to an advertising career fair, entered a creative resume contest — and won.

There should be a happy ending here, but not yet. Graduating with no job, Laura found a position through a colleague of her father's. "It wasn't exactly what I was looking for but it was a good opportunity to learn in a small public relations firm. I made $200 per week working out of the president's home," Laura recalled.

But Laura had earned a break — of sorts. Her prize for winning the creative resume contest was an interview at The Martin Agency. They knew her, she knew them. There should be a job offer now, right? Not quite! After an extensive interview process and passing a long writing test, Laura was offered the opportunity to work for two weeks on a trial basis. The trial was extended for several months. Only then was Laura hired on a regular basis.

Laura's first assignment was in the public relations side of the business as an assistant account executive. She coordinated press events designed to bring favorable publicity to clients. For example, with her client as a sponsor, Laura coordinated a special drive around the track in a racing car for children with a terminal illness. Laura's job was to sell the story to reporters by sending photos and videos of this event to newspapers, racing magazines and TV news programs. Her display book of media coverage demonstrated that the client's donation to a good cause had contributed to a favorable public image.

Laura believed that the future trend in advertising agencies would be integrated communications, so after two years she moved into advertising within the agency. "It was a lateral move," Laura observed, "but I was quickly promoted to account executive."

Now, her core responsibilities included making print, radio, TV and direct marketing recommendations to her client. "My job is to develop strategy and work with our creative teams to develop a product that drives sales for our client. Our creative executions must not only be done well but also on time and within budget." Laura explained that "developing impactful advertising involves listening to our client, understanding the consumer, and focusing on a single message."

A recent example is the case of seven telecommunications companies, which together wanted to convince consumers to use the Yellow Pages telephone directories more. "Our challenge is to change current perceptions about the Yellow Pages. Traditionally, the Yellow Pages has been used reactively, like when your sink leaks and you need a plumber," Laura noted. "The strategy behind our new campaign is get consumers to think about the Yellow Pages proactively—as an 'idea source'. In a nutshell, it's a place to go to get ideas for travel, beauty needs and more." To sell the idea to the Yellow Pages Publishers Association, Laura helped pull together the presentation for her chairman. The presentation highlighted market research, outlined the strategy and displayed the creative concepts. Upon approval of the campaign, she will manage the production process. "I will work with the client as well as creative and production teams until the ads are in the public. That means making sure the end product is always in mind during photo shoots and in layout and copy stages."

Laura feels that "her passion for creativity fits with The Martin Agency's goal to be ranked consistently as one of the three best creative agencies in America." She relishes the variety of her work, which includes listening to focus groups, attending photo shoots, brainstorming and developing communication plans. "It's a long day, but that's O.K. The people are great and it's a fun and challenging business," Laura said. "I'm in the office by 7:30 AM and finish at 6:30 PM. Then there may be dinner with clients. Before we make a presentation, I could be working at 1 AM. But we are in the image business, and there can't be mistakes."

To succeed in this business, you need to have a passion for it. But passion is not enough. "Communications skills, both written and oral, are essential. You need excellent interpersonal skills to develop trust with clients and be an effective motivator for the creative teams. Sometimes you need to be a diplomat mediating between the client and your agency teams," Laura noted. "Constant flexibility is key in this business because we switch quickly between detail work and the big picture."

Laura provided several tips for job seekers such as: starting salaries at advertising agencies are pretty low, but if you're talented, it can be a rocket ride to the top. Join professional organizations like The American Marketing Association. Lend your skills to the non-profit realm; it rounds out your experience and makes you feel good about contributing to the community. Agencies like ours do pro bono work for charities. Finally, because business is integrated with world affairs, stay current with news, by reading *USA Today*, *The New York Times*, and *The Wall Street Journal*. Other good publications include *Advertising Age*, *Ad Week* and *Creativity*.

Linda Wright
Director of Publishing Services
Penn Well

Linda Wright is the Director of Publishing Services for Penn Well, a publisher of some 40 magazines and trade publications. To understand why this is a great job for Linda, we should probably go back 21 years.

Linda was trained to be a teacher, but couldn't find a job when she returned to her native Massachusetts in the late 1970's. She walked in the door of *Computer Design* magazine, without an appointment, to talk about a job—any job. As luck would have it, the person in charge of advertising traffic had just announced her departure. After a three hour interview, Linda was hired.

What was great for Linda as a single parent was drawing a paycheck and being close to home. Her employer was also very flexible about letting Linda work at home when her child was sick. "There was very much a family atmosphere," Linda told me. "It was like having a second family, especially during special occasions, whether happy or sad."

Two years after Linda started, Penn Well corporation purchased Computer Design. For Linda, this meant a change from an organization of 25 employees to a larger, corporate structure which had a its headquarters 2,000 miles away. Overall, the change worked out well for Linda. She now had more career opportunities, but a flexible, family friendly atmosphere still prevailed.

Linda was promoted to Product Manager in a unit which provided services to all of Penn Well's magazines. Next Linda was put in charge of Buyers Guides—business to business directories. Subsequently Linda became the first business manager for her unit of Penn Well. She created budgets, made projections, a host of business skills she had never been taught. "Because of my experience from the ground-up, I knew the pragmatic realities behind the numbers I saw," Linda told me. "Penn Well doesn't stop you from trying new areas if you are a hard worker who has produced results. You aren't precluded from an interesting position tomorrow just because you didn't have a similar position yesterday."

Today, Linda is the Director of Publishing Services. Five departments comprising 55 employees report to her. Linda reports to the head of a division and hopes to become Penn Well's second woman vice-president. Linda finds her position very satisfying partly because she has a great deal of freedom to set her own work agenda and to establish goals for a big part of her company. She has no specific operating model to follow. In fact, she doesn't even have a job description, although Linda does have corporate goals to meet. She also finds constant challenge in meeting those corporate goals and experiencing new situations.

How did Linda Wright get such a great job? Of course, it started with a piece of fortuitous timing. On the other hand, timing would have meant nothing without Linda's own initiative and daring. Linda worked long days—12-13 hours—and served on a variety of corporate committees. By showing interest and contributing to the committees' goals, Linda made herself known as a "can-do" person with the potential for doing even more.

WHAT TO DO NOW

To help you prepare for a career in communications, the people interviewed for this chapter recommended organizations you can contact, as well as publications and Web sites that may prove useful in your search:

Organizations:

Public Relations Society of America .... www.prsa.org
Society of Professional Journalists .... www.spj.org
Inet Communications Network .... www.cabe.com
International Association of
Business Communicators .... www.iabc.com

Publications:

Ad Week .... www.adweek.com
Advertising Age .... www.adage.com
American Journalism Review .... www.ajr.org

Web Sites:

www.profnet.com

www.copydesk.org

www.prweb.com

www.publicity.com

www.ragan.com

10

Sports

You Don't Have To Be A Professional Athlete

Many of us had fantasies at some point in our lives of being professional athletes. Although very few people actually make a living on the playing field, there are other professions associated with sports, like promotions, coaching, stadium operations and agent. In the next four stories, sports professionals tell us what they do and how they got there. It was never easy and not always lucrative.

Three of our stories are about people who entered sports from another field: hospitality, banking or marketing. Skills developed outside of sports management can be transferred to this field. Those who do try to start out in sports management still don't start at the top, as Missy Bequette reminds us. If you're looking for glamour, it's not always there. Fifteen minutes before entering the broadcast booth, Bill Fagerson may be cleaning up bird droppings.

An underlying theme in these stories is the skill of patience, whether working with players, clients or staff. Another is being prepared to do a good job, continuously, so you will be prepared when your break comes.

This chapter is not about "show me the money." It is about "show me the reality"

Missy Bequette
Assistant Coach
The Portland Power

She had no intention of becoming involved with professional athletics. She intended to be "pre-med". True, her father and two brothers had been on their varsity college football teams. True, she loved sports and played in high school. But she wasn't going to get that involved with athletics in college. Well, OK, so she volunteered to be the "team manager" for the University of Missouri's women's basketball team, a position which involved taking care of the players.

It seems that for Missy Bequette, any conflicts she felt about committing herself to sports were resolved in favor of a deep involvement. In fact, she remained as the team manager for four years and decided to major in physical education. Upon graduation, in 1985 she entered a graduate program in sports management at the University of Arkansas and volunteered again, this time as an assistant coach for women's basketball. Missy also considered a legal education for its usefulness in sports management. However, after a year she decided that "law school just didn't agree with her." Fortunately, Missy was invited back to the University of Missouri as an assistant coach, and served in that capacity for nine years.

Finding her position with the Portland Power was a case of preparation and opportunity coming together. Missy was aware of the opening at the Power from a friend and from a colleague who knew the team's general manager. She knew and respected the head coach, Lin Dunn, from crossing paths at summer basketball camps and at the Olympic Festival's northern trials. Missy handed Lin a resume when they met at the annual conference of the Women's Basketball Coaches Association in 1997. Missy had a well-established reputation and ultimately Lin offered her the job.

It's a job which isn't easy. In the American Basketball League, there is only one Assistant Coach, whereas in college there could be three. During the playing season, Missy is preparing for games by scouting the opposition through game tapes or watching the game on TV. Missy also consults with the strength coach about each player's program and progress, takes care of the equipment and works with the players in practice. Once the game starts, Missy is observing the other team, deciphering their strategy, anticipating substitutions which might cause a mismatch and thinking about possible adjustments by Power players. She also keeps game management statistics like personal fouls and time outs. "We can return to Portland from another city at midnight and I may be back by 6:00 AM looking at game films to prepare a shoot-around practice," Missy noted, "or to make breakdown tapes for individual players and for the team."

Even in the off season, Missy is busy. She may be checking on the well being of newly hired ballplayers, participating in promotional appearances, organizing youth camps or preparing logistics for the next season. "I try to get to know the players so they can be settled when they get here and be ready to develop further as professionals," Missy told me.

One of the skills Missy needs is to be a great communicator with different types of people. "Our players come from different backgrounds growing-up and in terms of basketball experience. Some are fresh out of college and some have played in Europe or other leagues. In each case, it's someone's career and I have to understand them if I'm going to help." Missy reflected. Patience in working with others is important, but so is being able to make a quick decision during a game if the head coach wants her input. "Since there are lots of activities to coordinate and volumes of information to access, it also pays to be well organized," Missy reflected.

Missy has been blessed by the great role models her coaches have been. "Coaches are always teachers, so take advantage of every chance to learn," she said. Ultimately, Missy would like to become a head coach herself.

If coaching appeals to you there are many opportunities to get a start and develop a reputation. "High schools need coaches, and you don't have to be into physical education. I know coaches who were history teachers." Students could volunteer, as Missy did. "One key is to demonstrate a deep commitment," she told me, "Loving sports is not enough and nobody starts at the top."

As we were preparing fo rpublication, the American Basketball League folded. By further developing her skills and reputation with the Power, Missy has probably laid the foundation for a great job with another team.

Mike Fagerson
Director of Stadium Operations
Portland Sea Dogs

How many jobs combine maintaining a sports stadium, counseling employees, and being a "color commentator" for a sports broadcast? Actually, if you are interested in the non-player side of professional (but not major league) sports, there may be quite a few of them.

Mike Fagerson starts a typical day during the baseball season at 9 AM. When he goes home depends on where the Sea Dogs, a Class AA minor league affiliate of the Florida Marlins, are playing. If it's a home game, Mike leaves the stadium at 11 PM — if he's lucky. It's a good thing that Mike likes variety. His first stop of the day may be with the food service director to make sure that there are enough hot-dogs and drinks for the fans who may fill this 6,800 seat stadium. Then he will check the two club houses (team locker rooms) to make sure they are in proper shape for the players. Next it's a check for cleanliness. The team leases the stadium from the City of Portland, which is also paid for providing clean-up and daily repairs. "If there's a problem, there may be a need to cajole and finesse folks at city hall. They have a lot of responsibilities on their agenda, but I need my place to be ready for receiving fans by batting practice time," Mike told me. "Then I have got to see if the radio broadcasters need anything. Taking care of the puzzle pieces is interesting, but time consuming." If the Sea Dogs are out of town, it's like a mini vacation, that is, Mike can leave at 5 PM.

Mike's personnel role revolves around the 300 part time and full time employees at the stadium. He gets the full time employees signed-up for the organization's health insurance and 401(K) retirement programs. Mike is also counselor, mentor and conflict resolution master should the need arise. This one-on-one contact is what Mike likes most about his job.

Mike's background is not typical for people in his field. After earning a degree in Hotel, Restaurant, and Travel Administration, Mike took at job at Kennedy Airport working in Food Services in the building of international arrivals. From there, he took a position in auxiliary service at a large university, while studying full time for a Master's degree in Industrial Labor Relations. While there, a friend of Mike's became the General Manager of the newly formed Portland Sea Dogs and asked if Mike would be interested in becoming Director of Stadium Operations. Mike was intrigued by the opportunity and grabbed it.

"There are a few things to remember about my situation," Mike told me. "One is that I was very fortunate to get a position like this. A more typical approach is to start out as an intern, especially from a sports management degree program, and work your way up. We help our interns by trying to make connections for them when the internship is over, and most other organizations do as well. Two, this is not an especially well paying position at the pre-major league level. I was able to parlay my work experience into a lateral move to the Sea Dogs, without a cut in pay. Someone else coming in as a career switcher could see their income cut in half, if that. Three, there is not a lot of turnover in the better jobs. We have replaced three full-timers in five years. Four, don't think this is a glamour field. Fifteen minutes before getting into the TV booth, I may be cleaning up bird droppings."

Mike identified several skills he needs to do his job well. One is patience, whether dealing with municipal maintenance issues or under-performing employees. A second is being well organized "No work day is long enough if you are not," Mike told me. Third, you need to sincerely care about your personnel and be a good listener. Fourth, it helps to be flexible. "You could be getting a broken toilet fixed, and the next thing you'll be finding a new player a place to live or go golfing," Mike said, by way of example.

Ironically, Mike doesn't get a chance to watch many games unless he is in the TV broadcast booth. Managing the stadium can take him away from the ball game.

Most sports have a trade association which can be somewhat helpful. For example, all minor league baseball teams belong to the National Association of Professional Baseball Leagues. They sponsor an annual winter meeting and some people find jobs there. Be current with the field. For example Mike reads *Baseball America* magazine, which also publishes a directory of every major and minor league team in the country.

Steve Freyer
Agent
Freyer Management Associates

Imagine that you are at a party and playing "What's my Line of Work". Steve Freyer tells you the following about his job: people often think of me as a contract negotiator, but that is really only a part of my job. I manage finances, tax planning and retirement preparation for my clients. Sometimes I deal with personal issues, like marital tension. What kind of job do I have?

Would you guess that Steve is an agent, primarily for professional baseball and hockey players? Steve entered this profession indirectly. After an extremely brief stint as a professional football player, Steve became a sales representative for a company that made vinyl sports surfaces, such as those that can be used on tennis courts. As part of the job, Steve met with a large number of tennis professionals. These contacts brought Steve to the attention of Lamar Hunt, who was developing World Championship Tennis. The innovative concept of the WCT was to put tennis players under personal service contracts and then promote tennis tournaments in which these players would be the main draw. Steve enjoyed his association with WCT, but after a few years left to pursue a career in commercial banking.

Eight years into his banking career, Steve met a sports agent at a cocktail party. They became engrossed in an extended conversation and Steve was soon invited to join his new friend's small practice as an agent for major league baseball players. After eight years, Steve and his partner agreed that Steve would establish his own practice. "By that point, I had a long track record which established my credibility with clients," Steve recalled. "A prospective client can look at the quality and length of my relationship with others, and that helps him feel comfortable with me." Both the Major League Baseball Players Association and the National Hockey League Players Association have also certified Steve as an agent.

Banking has been a major asset for Steve. "A large part of my responsibility is paying attention to my clients finances," Steve emphasized. "What I don't do myself, I refer to attorneys, insurance experts, money managers and tax people in whom I have complete confidence. Steve is also a good negotiator when it comes to contracts. "Representing a superstar is actually easier than representing a marginal player," Steve noted. "The superstar's talent and fan recognition are well established, so it becomes a matter of salary. I develop a comparison pool of players and use their compensation packages as a reference point." More marginal players, are harder to assess and easier to replace, so the agent is negotiating with fewer strong cards in his hand. Similarly, if a client needs to find a new team to play for, it is easier to find a new team for an established player. Steve's practice also includes minor leaguers, a big change from previous years. "The minor leaguers are actually money losers for us, but this business is so competitive agents now try to lock them up in the hope that some will make it really big," Steve explained.

Steve also represents broadcasters, including non-sports personalities like talk show hosts. "I get involved in everything from elocution lessons to career management," he remarked. Steve noted that there is not the wealth of statistical data in broadcasting as there is in big time sports. However, as his own broadcasting client base has grown, Steve has developed his own in-house database which helps in having a fuller understanding of the industry's workings.

In some respects, Steve's work life has a seasonality. About 80% of July and August are absorbed by hockey. Baseball negotiations occupy most of November and December. But Steve is at his clients' service at any time. "I tell them I am always available, but if it's after 9 PM, it should be really important," Steve remarked. "Important" clearly includes a midnight call from a player upset about a trade. "I try to help the client see events in the most positive light possible; the situation can be stressful for the player. Trades can be personally disruptive and professionally threatening."

Steve identified several skills, which have been valuable to him. One is his financial experience. "A lot of other agents are lawyers, but I don't think that is necessary," he observed. Understanding the negotiating process, being patient—"Let things evolve, slow down your client, don't force things—and working towards a win-win solution is helpful in reaching contract agreements." In addition, Steve maintains a low public profile. "Be discrete and stay in the background. The agent is not more important than the athlete," he remarked. On a more subjective level, Steve believes that really caring about a client is critical in what is, after all, a personal services business.

As much as Steve loves his job, he wanted to add that this is a very tough profession to enter and there is a high potential for burnout when you're in it. You are never really "after work" or "on vacation" since you are always available to your clients. Also, there are some disreputable people in this profession, just as in others.

When he interviews potential employees, those with a Sports Management college degree have only a very slight advantage, assuming all other qualifications are equal.

John Brazer
Promotion Manager
Philadelphia Phillies

How do you get a baseball to homeplate? The sports purist would expect to see a pitcher wind up and deliver. Fans at Philadelphia's Veteran's Stadium saw the Phillie Phanatic, the team's clown mascot, slide down several hundred feet of wire, baseball in hand. That's one way to get kids to say "take me out to the ballgame", an experience which includes a lot more than what goes on between the white chalk lines.

John Brazer is the promotions manager for the Philadelphia Phillies major league baseball team. He describes his position as a combination of marketing and public relations designed to garner interest in the Phillies by multiple means. This may include arranging for a celebrity like Luke Perry to throw out the first ball, having a famous entertainer sing the national anthem or developing human interest stories about the ball players. John also arranges for media coverage at low or no expense. Sliding Phanatics are a part of his promotion mix.

Let's take a look at what a day for John might be like. By 6:15 AM, he is visiting the first of six radio stations with Phillies gold glove third baseman, Scott Rolen, plugging the Phillies current home stand. Then John goes to the office and negotiates a barter deal with a local newspaper: a print space advertisement for the Phillies in exchange for a radio ad for the newspaper. A breath later, John is making arrangements for Meat Loaf to rehearse at the stadium before playing the national anthem. No time to rest. John is off to the Art Museum where the Phillie Phanatic will help open a Cezanne exhibit.

Cezanne, the famous French post impressionist, and baseball? "Promoting baseball is a very creative enterprise," John told me. The Phanatic gave away Cezanne baseballs and tickets to the stadium. The media loved it, which promoted both the museum and the Phillies.

Back at the stadium, John checked out the details for that night's between innings "extreme games" event. Tonight it will be two fans racing to the top of the outfield stands. One wears a red hat, the other blue. The public address announcer will encourage the 25,000 fans to cheer on their favorite "running dot". You won't feel left out if you don't like the amateur races. Earlier in the game, John will have the Phanatic shoot hot dogs into the stands from a special launcher.

John loves the creativity of his job and its fluidity. "You never know what tomorrow will bring and that's great." He also enjoys being the main contact to the Phillies for people throughout the area from local TV and radio people to the Governor to entertainment stars.

I asked John about some of his most memorable experiences. He told me about the Free Agent Fan, a man who felt betrayed when his favorite players left his favorite team. This fan attracted national media attention by announcing that he was available to root for the team which gave him a good reason to do so. John sent the fan a five page letter describing the Phillies rebuilding plans and asking for support while the team improved. Because of John's letter, the fan announced on a network morning news program that he would henceforth root for the Phillies, then a last place team. John felt huge satisfaction in gaining favorable publicity for the Phillies when it was sorely needed.

On a more personal level, John recounted the story of a woman from Nebraska who was a life-long fan of Nebraska's own Richie Ashburn, the Hall of Fame Centerfielder who, prior to his death, was a TV and radio announcer for the Phillies. This eighty-year-old woman had collected a scrap book of Ashburn's athletic accomplishments going back to his high school days. John brought her to the Veteran's Stadium to meet her long-time hero. The woman was so moved by the experience that she said, "This is the greatest day of my life. There is nothing more I want to accomplish." For his part, Richie Ashburn was so much taken by the Nebraska woman and her scrapbook that he couldn't bring himself back to the broadcast booth until the game had already started. Did this charming story of two elderly Nebraskans generate good media coverage? No, but that's not the point. "Baseball," John told me "is a sport and a business, but it never stops being very human. It's nice helping someone achieve their dreams."

Typically, a person holding a job like John's starts out as an intern and (if they are very fortunate) remains with the organization in a paid position. John's route was different. When he graduated from the University of Virginia in 1987 with a liberal arts degree, he went to England for a year to play professional lacrosse. When John realized that he wouldn't have a long career as either a player or a coach, he took a job in the U.S. selling corporate health plans. From there, he became an insurance consultant. But it wasn't insurance which led to the Phillies, it was love.

At a friend's wedding, John was introduced to the Phillies' Marketing Vice President, Dennis Mannion. John and Dennis became involved in a spirited discussion about baseball and marketing. "You have the greatest job in the world," said John. "I think the Phillies can use a person like you," said Dennis. John and Dennis stayed in touch and four months later Dennis had an opening which he thought was a great fit for John. John took a pay cut to join the Phillies and has never regretted it. "You could offer me four times my salary to work in a bank and I wouldn't even consider it," John told me.

Jobs like John's are extremely difficult to get. The supply of people wanting to be near professional sports far exceeds the available opportunities. To have a shot, the best approach is to get a low pay or no pay internship with a professional sports team. As a known entity, you have a chance to move to a paid position. Another possibility would be working in a related field, like selling television advertising time, and apply that skill for the sports organization. On the bright side, there are a huge number of professional sports organizations to consider.

WHAT TO DO NOW

To help you prepare for a career in sports, the people interviewed for this chapter recommended organizations you can contact, as well as publications and Web sites that may prove useful in your search:

Organizations:

Women's Basketball Coaches
Association .... www.wbca.org

National Association Of
Professional Baseball Leagues .... (727) 822-6937

National Association of Basketball Coaches .... www.nabc.com

National Association of
Sports Commissions .... www.sportscommissions.org

National Association of Sports Officials .... http://naso.org

Publications:

Baseball America .... www.baseballamerica.com

The Sports Business Directory (E. J. Krause and Associates)

Professional Sports Directory-4D Publishers (ed. Douglas E. Morris)

Sports Illustrated .... www.sportsillustrated.com

Web Sites:

www.coachesedge.com
www.onlinesports.com

11

Human Resources

More Than Just Completing Your Dental Forms

At one time, human resource , or personnel, professionals were not held in the highest esteem. That is hardly the case today. Bringing in the right employees, motivating them and compensating them fairly are central to the success of any enterprise.

This chapter presents stories about people facilitating transitions in new acquisitions, creating a drug-free workplace, developing compensation plans, identifying the best benefit packages, training employees and having senior level responsibility for a number of functions.

In the stories you are about to read, five people came to human resources from other fields, including flight attendant, secretary, accountant, sales and commercial art. In each of these cases they developed skills which they were able to apply to their current field. Although human resource people tend to be compassionate, as Charles Liebenauer put it, they exercise compassion and good business sense simultaneously. Other common threads are excellent analytical, communication and multitasking skills supporting an inclination to be proactive.

What are some of the satisfactions for the human resource professional? Brian Paley identified working with cutting edge issues. Denise White enjoys her high degree of responsibility. Sid Scott spoke about variety and the technical aspects of his job.

Denise White
Director, Human Resources and New Ventures
Microsoft

Denise White has a complex role that requires her to wear two hats. Let's start with the more unique hat, one that Denise herself designed.

The first hat is Director of the New Ventures HR team. This role entails evaluating pending acquisitions, developing an effective strategy and communication plan around the "people assets," and leading a HR team to successfully migrate the people to Microsoft. The ultimate goal is to retain key talent and ensure return on investment on the people assets of the deal, by making this a compelling opportunity and positive experience for the newly acquired employees.

When her employer, Microsoft, acquires another business, it is important to "align the acquisition and its intellectual capital with the purchase of the company." That means focusing on people as the very basis of the acquisition—although computer code and licenses are involved, too. You learn most from bringing in an intact team, so it's important to put people in the forefront of an acquisition. As Denise explained it, most acquisitions evaluate market worth, negotiate a price and then worry about the people involved last. By contrast, Denise steps in "as soon as an acquisition is a glimmer in management's eye." "We start a discussion about the processes that need to be involved. For example, we need to build trust with the principals (owners) of the company so we can understand better the company they built and the people they hired," Denise told me. "The principals are very concerned about the welfare of their employees, people who worked so hard to make their start-up a success. They may feel very loyal to their customers as well." Once a Letter of Intent (LOI) is signed, the principles feel vulnerable themselves since their best people could just walkout before the sale is complete, upset the acquisition plans, and leave the company substantially weaker.

To minimize those problems, Denise creates a communication plan to address employee feelings, respond to questions and mitigate concerns. "The impediments would be material, like benefit packages or communication. We need to deal with both parts," Denise explained. "If someone might lose their job, we need to be up-front about it and develop a good exit plan."

"When the acquisition is completed in the legal sense, the next phase is a successful integration. We need to make sure that we hand the situation to Human Resources appropriately, including a carefully designed compensation package, logistics (e-mail, parking) and new employee orientation. After each acquisition, we do an evaluation," Denise said. "We've had 35 acquisitions, and there is a different report card on different areas of the process each time. We're constantly learning to do things better."

Denise likes the high degree of responsibility involved. "I want to make sure that we spent the right amount of money in the right way," she noted "and I want to assure that we treated the employees of the acquired company the right way."

Denise's other HR hat involves the Interactive Media Group (IMG), where she has a more traditional role. "People are your greatest asset and greatest expense. It makes sense to align your people and your business practices as closely as possible," Denise said. In that regard, she is involved with traditional HR roles like compensation review, employee relations and coaching managers on difficult staff issues. On the less traditional side, Denise determines ways to pick top talent and keep them connected to Microsoft.

Denise studied neither computers nor human resources in college. Instead she majored in Kinesiology (the science of movement) and education at the University of Washington. When Denise graduated in 1976, her first job was teaching, largely in junior high. After three years, she became a flight attendant. After four years in the air, her company put her on special assignment where she traveled all over the world opening or closing airline bases. This included training managers on the service ethic of her company, hiring local nationals, and streamlining and localizing processes for the staff, it was her first real exposure to HR type work. After eleven years with the airline, Denise started her own management consulting business. A few years later, she closed shop to move to Dallas with her husband. There she became a Regional HR Manager for Microsoft. "It was a real start-up environment," Denise recalled. "I learned three things, which have helped me ever since: get comfortable with ambiguity, move quickly, and come to meetings with your options ready." A few years later, Denise moved to Microsoft headquarters in Seattle. There she was asked to consult on an acquisition negotiation. Her positive impact on that acquisition was just the beginning, and led to the job Denise has today.

Denise attributes her success to an ability to look across different aspects of a business and identify appropriate links between them. She also learned to "filter out noise which doesn't create value and focus on the issues which have an impact." When she recruits for her own HR staff, Denise looks for people with business experience, not necessarily HR training.

Brian Daly
Affiliate
Florida Power & Light

Florida Power & Light is a $6 billion company with 10,000 employees serving about half of Florida. A relatively new employee is Brian Daly, who entered FPL through its Affiliates Program. When I spoke with Brian he was completing an eight month human resource rotation. In this rotation, Brian coordinates FPL's Alcohol and Controlled Substance Program, part of the company's rigorous commitment to a drug free work place. Brian manages three different types of substance testing situations: the first is random testing, through which about 25% of FPL's population will be tested annually. The testing is done by a third party under contract and Brian's research played a key role in identifying this new vendor. A second is post accident testing, which is mandated in part by the Federal Department of Transportation. The third is probable cause. These tests could be generated by work history situations, absenteeism, or the smell of alcohol on a person's breathe. Brian serves as a source of expertise when questions arise about the need for testing, in post accident and probable cause situations. "*Consistency* is key," Brian told me. "If people are treated differently in similar cases, FPL could be in legal trouble."

The substance abuse testing program is not a source of praise for Brian, but it is a source of pride. Some employees object to what they consider an invasion of privacy. Others feel that they are being earmarked for observation if their name is called more than once in four years, even though the random testing is intended to be exactly that. Still, Brian feels that it is important to enforce the substance abuse policy strictly. "It is a documented fact," Brian told me "that those who are under the influence are a danger to others."

Brian loves his job for several reasons. One is that he finds himself working with a cutting-edge issue. The need for a drug free work place is increasingly accepted by senior executives and the rise in youth substance abuse suggests increased need for vigilance in the future.

Second, Brian loves working with people, which is often not very easy. He has built a constructive relationship with the union at FPL, something Brian says is based on giving respect. "When the union guys saw me, they wondered what this 'kid' thought he could do. But we worked through several problems, and now there's a lot less head knocking than there used to be," Brian related.

Brian also enjoys the challenge. He told me about a change in policy which Brian was instrumental in bringing to fruition. At one time, an employee involved in an accident could not return to work until a negative drug test result was received. This policy angered many managers because it could deprive them of an entire work crew for several days. Brian was tasked with the responsibility of convincing the union, managers and top executives (who were concerned about liability issues) to support an immediate return to work, pending test results. Through written and face to face communication, Brian gathered enough support to effect a change.

Brian also spoke with enthusiasm about FPL as an employer. The facility is beautiful (it's located right on the water) and the company encourages a balance between work life and self. For example, there is a wellness center which includes health screening and tips on healthy cooking in addition to exercise equipment. Brian is also confident in the company management which "is supremely prepared to prosper in the new environment of a re-regulated power industry." Brian told me. "It's great to work for people who know their business."

Brian came to FPL after earning an MBA at the University of Florida. An MBA is not a requirement, but it does help in understanding the business side of issues. Brian had worked in human resources in a Philadelphia refinery after earning his bachelor's degree, but left for graduate school when he felt that further advancement would require it.

Human resources is not only a job to love—it is a job to keep. Many of Brian's friends went into finance, where opportunities were more numerous and lucrative. "There are fewer human resources jobs," Brian reasoned, "but there are fewer people trained for them. It kind of evens out. Besides, I am well paid and reasonably secure."

To succeed in a job like Brian's, you need good business sense, the ability to build, not manipulate relationships, and the patience to wait for your hard work to show results. It could be worth it. As Brian pointed out, "human resources should be a part of every company's strategic plan, and it has to be. A work place which helps new workers become productive quickly, which assures a safe environment and which generates a sense of trust is a key to business success tomorrow."

Brian has some recommendations for those considering a human resources career. First, don't get discouraged. Human resource jobs are difficult but not impossible to get. Second, academic excellence is an asset. Third, develop a portfolio of accomplishments to show prospective employers, for example: Bring something unique to the interview. If you have a panel interview, while one person is asking the questions, the other can, at their discretion, look at the portfolio. Talk about a particular experience/skill and then go to the portfolio ("Let me show you something I worked on"). The portfolio helps you explain and support your accomplishments and increases your chances to land that perfect job!

Zanita Hawkins
Compensation Analyst
Crown Vantage

Picture yourself in northern New Hampshire. The scenery is great, but jobs are not plentiful. Zanita Hawkins had been holding part-time jobs with the typical double downer—low pay and no benefits. Zanita wanted better pay and insurance benefits in case her husband lost his. That brought her to James River Corporation, a huge paper products company and the largest private employer in Northern New Hampshire. Zanita started as a secretary in the Human Resources Department. That was 16 years ago. Today she is an influential and well-paid Compensation Analyst.

That original job opened the door to better opportunities for Zanita. For one thing, her company believed in helping people develop their potential. The company paid for Zanita's college education through the Life Long Learning program at the University of New Hampshire. In additional, the company paid for Zanita to become a Certified Compensation Professional. This required passing an extensive nine course program sponsored by the American Compensation Association.

A second good thing was that Zanita's mill was spun off and became a part of Crown Vantage. The new company didn't have any corporate compensation people, so there was opportunity for Zanita's upward movement.

Working as a compensation manager in a paper mill may not be one of the great jobs you have dreamed about, but for Zanita it is exactly that. A good part of Zanita's job involves doing compensation surveys. An independent organization (in this case, the Paper Industry Compensation Association) collects data from membership companies. These companies cannot share compensation data directly with each other, but they can provide it to an independent service, like PICA. Zanita has to do a lot of research of computerized data to find the requested data for her company. She must make sure to gather all relevant data, including bonuses.

Companies participate in compensation surveys because they want to be competitive in the labor market without paying more than necessary. An accurate compensation survey can save thousands of dollars in salaries without jeopardizing a company's competitive position in the labor market.

Zanita enjoys the survey work for many reasons. One is that she has a hand in evaluating positions as they evolve. She assess what the new position or responsibility is worth on a labor market basis, keeping in mind the needs of internal equity. Second, Zanita is in a position of quiet power. After all, she is the one who controls the data. "Speaking with the data is a powerful tool," Zanita told me.

Zanita also enjoys exercising her judgment, something she couldn't do very much in previous jobs. It was scary at first, but Zanita's "safety network" of professional counterparts in other firms have been an invaluable resource.

The social environment of her workplace is important to Zanita. She likes being close to the people she serves. What's more, she has earned their respect. One way Zanita earns respect is to give people information about the decision she makes. Another way she has earned respect is by gaining a thorough understanding of the industry. "Even disappointing decisions are easier to take if you provide a reasoned explanation," Zanita told me. Zanita has "been through the mill", literally and figuratively. She requested and received permission to take a seven month course in pulp and paper making. Whenever she visits another mill, Zanita asks to take a walk through their production process. As a result, she is no less conversant with the terminology of the industry than the people whose jobs she evaluates.

Zanita voluntarily comes in to work on weekends. One reason is that she loves her job. It makes her feel important to know that others rely on her and that she is making an important contribution. Further, the company was sensitive to her need for flexible scheduling when her children were young and remains sensitive even now. For example, Zanita was able to take time out to plan a funeral for a great aunt who had no children. By being sensitive to Zanita's personal needs, Crown Vantage has been able to retain a talented professional.

I asked Zanita what she likes least about her job. "Exit interviews," she told me. "You can have grown men cry when they are terminated either for individual performance issues or because of the mill's economic requirements. No matter what the cause, they bitterly wonder, 'why me?'" Zanita remarked. Still Zanita has a chance to use her compassionate side. Just being there to listen helps. In addition she can offer severance pay, career counseling and out-placement service advice. On the other hand, Zanita remarked that having other managers refer to human resources as "overhead" is a bit of a downer.

Zanita's job has evolved in recent years. That is because she volunteered for new areas or expressed an interest in specific issues. Speaking with Zanita , you do not sense that she had to fit her professional foot into a pre-existing shoe.

If you are interested in a job like Zanita's (which pays $50,000+) you should have compassion, be self confident, be well organized and analytical. You would do well to earn the title Certified Compensation Professional from the American Compensation Association. To learn more about Crown Vantage, contact Katie Cutler, Senior V.P. of Corporate Communications or check out their Web site: www.crownvantage.com

Charles Liebenauer
Employee Benefits Manager
Forest City Enterprises

Sometimes people take an indirect road to finding the right career home. That was the case with Chuck Liebenauer, who is the employee benefits manager for Forest City Enterprises (FCE)

in Cleveland, Ohio. FCE, a national company, owns or manages a significant amount of commercial and residential real estate, including, 12 malls and 34,000 apartments. Chuck's job is to develop and manage medical care, disability and pension programs for 2,300+ employees located throughout the United States.

Chuck's job is not to tell you how to fill out a dental claims form, although he will answer calls about that. Instead Chuck tries to find the plans which will provide high quality coverage for FCE employees while being prudent about costs to the company.

Part of these efforts requires a good deal of research. Chuck uses the Internet, trade journals, health care journals and the *Wall Street Journal* as sources of new ideas. On the more interpersonal side, Chuck belongs to several organizations in Cleveland whose members meet monthly to share ideas, including suggestions about programs which produce high quality benefits at reasonable costs. Chuck's network of professional friends also deals with good ways to educate employees about their benefits. Sometimes these organizations lead to the formation of a purchasing consortium designed to drive down costs. Chuck gave an example of a dental insurance program which provided poor service at high cost. Through the consortium, he was able to provide better care, while cutting costs by 25%.

If part of Chuck's job is research, planning and doing cost benefit analysis, the other part is helping employees. Chuck believes in being proactive, involved and helpful for everyone's benefit. "If your child is sick, you will not really be a productive worker if you have to worry about health care issues," Chuck explained. "We want to make sure that people have choices which work for them." I asked Chuck about any conflict between high quality and reasonable cost. Chuck said a conflict could exist, but he is determined to make sure this doesn't happen. He does this by showing compassion and good business sense simultaneously.

Chuck provided an example which I found interesting. An employee contacted him for advice on her medical insurance. She was happy to have become pregnant, but was concerned about a history of premature, low-birth weight babies in her family. Chuck made sure she took full advantage of her insurance coverage and helped her enroll in a pre-natal nutrition and education program. Chuck's extra effort did cost FCE time and several thousand dollars upfront, but the employee was less stressed and there were fewer birth complications. As a result of avoiding serious birth complications, the company saved $100,000 in insurance claims. "Everybody was a winner and that's what I want," Chuck told me. "I do my best to make everything a win-win situation." On another occasion, Chuck fought to get an employee extended coverage for a complex problem, therefore providing him with 24 instead of 12 medical visits. "Yes, it cost us more, but the company got something back from a healthier and happier employee," Chuck remembered. "For me personally cases like this bring a huge amount of satisfaction."

Chuck actually started his career as an accountant. He earned a bachelor's degree at Cleveland State University, working half time and studying half time, "I chose accounting for job security," Chuck remarked. "I came from a low income family and having at least a basic income was priority number one." His first accounting job led to a job in the payroll department of a bank. In this job he worked closely with the bank's Human Resources Department. Chuck found a new job managing three departments and 120 people for a car rental agency which downsized. Luckily, Chuck was invited back to his former bank, this time to handle the benefits area for 9,000 employees. Another downsizing led Chuck to seek another job. He became the controller for a sales and distribution company, but stayed in touch with his friends in the benefits area. Through one of these friends, Chuck was referred to his current boss as a potential replacement for a long time employee.

"The accounting background gave me a good understanding of financial issues in areas like health care. That's helped me do the research and evaluations on various benefits vendors. My car rental position gave me some good experience in managing personnel. I can do my job better because of where I have been," Chuck told me. "In addition, I found my exposure to computers, which I love, comes in very handy."

Chuck had been at FCE for 19 months when we spoke "What I really love is making a difference for people—knowing that someone's life is better because of something I did," Chuck said. "Sure, sometimes you can get discouraged, but I have learned to see the bright side when things get tough."

To do Chuck's job requires good analytical skills, the ability to ask good questions, intellectual curiosity and a solid network of colleagues. "Not every day is pleasant or even interesting," Chuck told me. "But the worst day at FCE is better than my best day anywhere else."

Mark Werner
Implementation Specialist
Towers Perrin

There is a saying in the market place, "Try before you buy". Mark Werner did that twice while still in college and thanks his lucky stars for it.

Mark started his college program at Temple University in the Pharmacy School. For the first two academic years, he worked part time as a pharmacy technician for a local drug store chain. "It was an important experience for me because I hated it," Mark recalled. His friends suggested he study finance and "I liked numbers, so it seemed a good idea." Mark choose to add a second major, Risk Management and Insurance, because friends told him it was an up and coming field that was constantly changing. "Sometimes friends give you good advice," Mark observed.

Mark applied for a summer internship with Towers Perrin "to try out another field." His first summer, Mark worked on defined contribution pension plans and subsequently moved to defined benefit plans. "I enjoyed the benefits field in general. When the company let me work on more than one kind of plan, I was able to find the best of the best for me," Mark said. He returned for a second summer, and worked part-time at Towers Perrin during the academic year as well. With a proven track record, Mark was offered a full-time job before he even graduated.

Mark works with a team to design computer software for the administration of client pension programs. "Our clients want a system that will calculate pension obligations 25 years in advance," Mark explained. "We take the company's specifications to design the software and their demographic data to run it. My specific function is to test the software to assure that it's producing the correct figures." Mark tests hundreds of potential scenarios. "For example, what if there is a change from normal to late retirement for an employee?" The computer should match the results which Mark derives from more tedious calculator and matrix computations. If not, the software needs to be checked against the client's specifications. "You need to know your way around a computer," Mark told me, "but knowing the applicable laws and having an analytical mind are more important tools for me." Communication skills are also essential to specify exactly where problems lie to other members of the team. "Good communication saves time and time is money," he noted.

Mark enjoys the analytical challenges his job provides and "the day-to-day satisfaction of solving problems." He also finds his managers open-minded and extremely helpful which is equally important early in my career."

His college coursework was completed in 1998, but "studying and keeping up goes on forever." Mark is current with professional journals like *Benefits Quarterly* and is studying for his CEBS (Certified Employee Benefits Specialist) certification.

Emily Brazukas
Recruiter
Lutron Electronics Co., Inc.

Have you ever dreamed of writing your own job description? Emily Brazukas actually wrote the proposal which created her current job at Lutron Electronics Company, a Pennsylvania based, multinational company which has been a major player in lighting controls since 1961. Lighting controls could include everything from your living room dimmer to a computerized lighting control system for an office tower building.

Emily started out at Lutron in 1995 in a sales capacity. At Lutron, sales involves generating demand for their dimming products among end users. For example, Emily trained distributors in product knowledge and sales techniques to encourage greater promotion of Lutron products. In a similar vein, Emily explained Lutron products to engineers, and architects, hoping that they would choose Lutron for their projects, while visiting large corporations and small business as well. "You move the product by creating awareness and comfort with them. I didn't actually sign procurement contracts," Emily explained.

It was precisely this training aspect which Emily enjoyed most. In addition, she wanted to cut back on her travel, which took her through six states in the Midwest and occupied 50-70% of her time.

Emily now recruits new sales people annually, largely straight out of college. About half are engineers, while the others might be liberal arts majors or hold MBAs. She visits college campuses, conducts interviews and decides whom to invite for 1½ days of on-site, activity-based interviewing at Lutron. Emily is part of the team which jointly decides on extending job offers to qualified candidates and identifies the best person to share the good news. "If the candidate really clicked with someone during the interview process, it helps to have that person extend the offer." Emily explained.

After hiring comes training. Emily meets with each new salesperson. She wants to understand how they learn and their specific interests to help guide them through Lutron's six month rotational training program.

Emily enjoys helping people grow. "I liked that in sales and I like that in training," she indicated. "It's hard to explain why. Why do teachers like to teach?" Emily also develops the training curriculum and identifies the best people, inside Lutron or from the outside, for the once-a-week classroom part of the training.

When she graduated from Princeton University in 1995, with a degree in Politics, Emily had four job offers. She chose Lutron in part because of its rotational sales training program which would allow her to explore different parts of the company and discover her strengths. Even more important though, was that Emily liked the "smart, fast paced, driven people" she met at Lutron. "I played field hockey and lacrosse at Princeton and I am very competitive. Lutron felt like home to me," Emily remarked.

When I asked Emily about her next career step, she told me that Lutron likes well- rounded people. "There is no flow chart as to where you will go. Maybe I will focus more on sales operations," Emily suggested.

If you want a job like Emily's, she suggests having high energy and being able to work independently. You should be a good listener with a desire to help and guide others. Writing skills are useful and you will need to juggle a multitude of tasks simultaneously. For sales recruiting and training specifically, sales experience is an enormous plus.

Sid Scott
Vice President - Human Resources
Woodward Communications Incorporated

Sid Scott is the Vice President - Human Resources at Woodward Communications, Inc., which is headquartered in Dubuque, Iowa. WCI is owned 70% by the Woodward family and 30% by the employees. The company concentrates on the information/ communication field through its four divisions (newspaper, broadcast, weekly publications, commercial printing) and serves customers in Iowa, Wisconsin and Illinois. Recently, it has also ventured into Internet services.

Sid is responsible for functions of employment, compensation, benefits, training, safety and internal communications, as well as serving as part of the top management team. Sid has been at WCI for fourteen years. When I asked him about his proudest achievements, Sid mentioned two. The first was a management training program which brings current and prospective managers to Dubuque every other month to enhance the knowledge and skills needed to become better leaders. The second accomplishment is the establishment and implementation of an Employee Stock Option Program (ESOP). Through this program, WCI employees have accumulated 30% of the company's stock. Although their shares are "non-voting," the ESOP program helps extend the family concept from the Woodwards, who have owned WCI for 100 years, to all of the employees. This is both a great motivator to participation in moving the company forward and a form of auxiliary pension for the employee-owners.

Like many human resource professionals, Sid started his career in another specialty. Sid graduated from Illinois State University with a major in commercial art. His first job was doing promotion and public relations for a newspaper in Peoria. Sid's responsibilities were developing ad designs, advertisements, writing copy and working with printers. After eight years, Sid moved to another newspaper as manager of circulation and promotion. While there, Sid earned an MBA at Bradley University.

Sid started his own consultancy which he managed for 6 years. It was interesting, but not as rewarding as Sid had hoped. An opportunity arose to return to the newspaper business, when a former co-worker invited him to take a new post in human resources.

Part of Sid's strength flows from the fact that he has worked in many different areas of the newspaper business, so he understands many line situations from his own experiences. He also has a good staff, comprised of both human resource specialists and former line employees.

Sid enjoys the variety of his responsibilities, but he finds working with people more appealing than the numbers and technical aspects. He strongly encourages good communication skills, under which he includes three parts: listening, writing and speaking, with the emphasis on listening. To succeed, you will also need to balance a number of projects at the same time and be able to shift from one to the other quickly.

Doug Pelino
Vice President, Human Resource Operations and Consulting
Xerox

When we mean "Photocopy", we often say "Xerox" and at Xerox when they need expertise on human resource issues, they often say Doug Pelino. Xerox has around 90,000 employees and about half work in the United States. The largest of several divisions is called US Customer Operations, with 22,000 employees, mostly in sales and service roles. Doug's role is to implement Human Resources programs to support his division's line managers and employees.

Doug could be called upon for his expertise in a number of areas, including employee satisfaction and morale, staffing, compensation and affirmative action. Typically, Doug meets with a line manager in his/her office to coach and counsel (not preach; not mandate) the manager on ways to handle HR issues and opportunities in the best way possible. Sometimes Doug is called in to deal with a problem which has already begun to fester. Preferably, Doug can educate managers to avoid problems by following Xerox's human resources process discipline. An example might be a morale problem.

"An employee's feelings about his/her job are often based in large measure on how they feel about their direct manager," Doug told me. "Couple that with the fact that people generally would prefer to hear important information directly from their boss, and not second hand or from a general newsletter. One way to head off a morale problem is to let the employee know that s/he is respected, professionally and personally, by their manager. Part of that respect comes from direct, timely communication. You can avoid many morale problems just by acting on these principles."

Doug spoke about a paradigm shift, at least at Xerox. "Early in my career," Doug recalled "the operating attitude was 'human resources will handle it'. Now it's the responsibility of the line manager, with guidance and assistance from human resources."

Part of this shift results from an operational reality: There are far fewer HR people in the company than there used to be. That has limited the "process capacity" of the HR professionals. Second, line managers now have access to information that used to be kept in "Personnel." Between coaching and computer data, the line manager now has the tools to do more of the functions which were previously done by HR. Another shift has been in the area of efficiency and productivity. "I used to win praise for delivering on requests before deadline, with extra material. Now that's considered a potential waste of time and resources. Therefore, today I deliver only *what* is requested *when* the manager needs it," said Doug describing the new approach. "In other words, I meet my internal customer requirements by delivering what they want, when they want it. If I can't, I negotiate with them to reach a reasonable compromise."

Doug has some long-term projects to oversee as well. For example, he recently managed the Voluntary Reduction Program (early retirement, voluntary separation) for his division, a process that can take months to plan and implement properly.

Doug graduated from the Rochester Institute of Technology with a degree in business and earned an MBA at Syracuse University. In his last semester, Doug interviewed with Xerox and was offered a position — in sales. The University's Placement Director stopped Doug in the hallway and suggested that he "check out an opportunity at Xerox in HR." To keep the Director happy, if nothing else, Doug signed-up for an interview. "I was impressed by the man interviewing me. He was compelling, persuasive and sharp," Doug recalled. "Somewhat to my surprise, I took the job in HR instead of sales. As a foot note, the man who interviewed me eventually became my boss, my mentor, rose to Vice President and still meets with me for coffee once a week, even though he has retired."

The first several years of Doug's career were spent in staffing — interviewing and hiring new employees. "I loved it. We were hiring people at a great pace and it was very exciting. But staying so long in one role so early can be a mistake." A friendly manager suggested that Doug needed experience outside of staffing. When an opening developed in training, Doug grabbed it. From there he took assignments in compensation and then employee relations. As college recruiting grew in importance, he became Xerox's College Relations Manager for several years before becoming a division personnel manager. "I had to make a lot of moves from Rochester, to Dallas to Stamford, Connecticut. But it was an important enabler to gain the scope of experience I needed to become the human resources generalist that I am today," Doug told me.

Doug has enjoyed his thirty plus years at Xerox in part because "this company really cares a lot about its people." In addition, Doug knows that he is making a difference not only in corporate productivity but also in individual lives. Further, "I am empowered to make a lot of decisions and I have always worked for and with people I could respect," Doug noted.

Doug told me that he is successful primarily because of his soft skills. "This job requires maturity, common sense and persuasive communications. You need to build relationships of credibility quickly and of trust over the long haul. In regard to trust, I have always delivered in the past, so the managers who are my customers trust that I will deliver in the future." Doug said, describing his own skills. "In a way, those are the same intangible skills you need in sales." Doug said with a laugh, "Maybe my two job offers from Xerox weren't that different after all."

Doug offered some very down to earth advice for anyone looking to advance a career. First, be proactive. Don't wait for the opportunities to come to you; seek them out. Second, careers don't always develop in a linear fashion. Sometimes what might appear to be a lateral move or a zig-zag turns out to broaden the base of your skills. Third, every business function deals with people in some measure. If you say that you want to go into HR because you want to work with people, that tells me that you don't understand the contemporary work world. Further, not everything in any field, including HR, is fun by a long shot. Headaches come with every job. Finally, "don't get locked into a narrow area by staying with it too long. Take risks and experiment. If I hadn't taken the advice to move out of staffing, I probably wouldn't be a vice president today," Doug concluded.

Doug advises that joining organizations like SHRM and ASTD can be helpful for two reasons. One is they help you stay current with your professional knowledge base. Second, networking is very important to success in HR.

Susan Clark
Manager of Recruiting Services
DataStudy, Inc.

Observing Susan Clark doing her job, you might assume that she had been in human resources forever, but it's not so. Or you might think that Susan made a lateral move within the organization to fill a vacancy, but that's not right, either. Let's take a look at what Susan does and then trace her less than conventional route to getting there.

Susan is the Manager of Recruiting Services for DataStudy, a 250 person consulting firm which provides "expert guidance in the evaluation and implementation of Human Resource, payroll and financial software packages." In a nutshell, Susan's current job is to bring new people on board.

Susan is given a budget and a hiring plan tied to the company's anticipated growth. "An early step is to allocate the budget to the various modalities which attract job applicants," Susan told me. "Our single most successful approach is referrals from current employees. We pay the current employee $1,500 for every hire resulting from their referral." Newspaper classifieds account for attracting another 40% of the applicants who are ultimately hired. "I write the ads and decide where and when to place them. One classified ad can cost as much as $8,000," Susan explained. I enjoy the creativity of writing a text people will respond to and then analyzing the causes for the ad's success or failure." Susan has increased her use of the Internet as the number of hires from this source continues to rise.

When Susan receives resumes, she reviews them for a potential interview. Each resume is scanned for depth of knowledge in the subject matter, related implementation experience and practical business experience. "The applicant has two opportunities to persuade us to consider them for the open position. We will bring an applicant in for consideration if their resume demonstrates a strong match with the requirements for a position. We will also bring an applicant in if they provide a convincing argument in a cover letter which illustrates how they would utilize experience that is not an exact match."

The next step for Susan is to conduct a pre-qualifying telephone interview. During this interchange, Susan is evaluating not only their qualifications for the position, but also their interpersonal skills. "We expect an applicant to communicate effectively and enthusiastically why they should be brought in for an interview." If the applicant makes a favorable impression, an interview is set with the hiring manager.

Susan enjoys her job for several reasons. "The challenge of meeting our projected recruiting goals while keeping the cost per hire down and the quality of hire up, in a tight labor market, is invigorating. I am always analyzing which applicant sources are working and researching new sources to test." DataStudy's employee base has grown from 6, when Susan joined them nine years ago, to 250. "It's a special pleasure to know that I've played a major role in attracting and selecting our new employees. I'm especially proud that our turnover is less than 5% in an industry that averages 25%-35%."

It took Susan a while to get where she is today. Sixteen years after graduating high school, Susan went to Smith College and earned a degree in Government in 1981. She moved to New Jersey and did "temp work" for a year before working for an employment agency. While there, she read a "how-to-get-a-job" book and took a position in telemarketing for a computer systems software development company. After 3½ years, Susan moved to a full, outside sales position, but lost her job when that company was sold. She joined a small consulting firm in a sales capacity, but didn't succeed after her mentor left.

Needing a job, Susan found a telemarketing position at DataStudy. As the company began to grow, the need for additional consultants increased and Susan added a recruiting element to her telemarketing effort. When a telemarketing call would prove futile for the potential sale of services, Susan would ask the prospect if they had ever considered becoming a consultant. That would initiate an interesting conversation, which would frequently lead to Susan's attracting an experienced person to work for DataStudy. This dual approach (prospecting for clients and sourcing future consultants) began to occupy a sixteen-hour day. Acknowledging Susan's ability as a recruiter as the solution to a staffing bottleneck, the company decided to let her focus on recruiting.

Susan suggested that her story carries a general lesson, not just for human resource positions. "Seek a position with a growing firm. Be attentive to the company's business direction so that you can anticipate its future needs. Don't be afraid to identify and create a job which brings you joy while adding value to your employer.

WHAT TO DO NOW

To help you prepare for a career in human resources, the people interviewed for this chapter recommended organizations you can contact, as well as publications and Web sites that may prove useful in your search:

Organizations:

ASTD (American Society for
Training & Development) .... www.astd.org

American Compensation Association 602-951-9191
.... www.acaonline.org

SHRM Society for Human
Resource Management .... www.shrm.org

National Association of Personnel Services .... www.napsweb.org

Publications:

Benefits Quarterly .... www.ifebp.org/isbqsum.html

HR News .... www.shrm.org/hrnews

Human Resource Management www.ipmaac.org/journals/hrm.html

HR Magazine .... www.shrm.org/hrmagazine

Benefits & Compensation Solutions .... www.bcsolutionsmag.com

Training and
Development .... www.astd.org/virtual_community/td_magazine

Web Sites:

www.hrworld.com

www.hrimmall.com

12

![graduation cap icon]

Education

Three R's and More

Education and teachers. Professional educators today can be found in child care and corporations in addition to traditional classrooms. They can help you find the meaning of life or help you find the means to make a living.

In this chapter, seven educators tell us what they do and what drives them to build careers in the field. On the more traditional side, Joan Janicelli has been teaching elementary school for over twenty-five years and is still learning from experience. David Griffith left government work to become a special education teacher. There is also a business component to education, albeit one which is driven by a special kind of commitment. Tammy Marquez started her career as a teacher and now sells an educational service. Robyn Milbury left the practice of law and now builds connections between businesses and classrooms for the benefit of both. Paul Leverington helps students parlay their college education by developing a career.

Two former classroom teachers reappear as educators in a different way. Mary Lane has become a trainer of teachers who could be twice her age. Penny Porter became discouraged with traditional teaching, but applied her skills as a trainer in occupational safety and health.

Tammy Marquez
Regional Sales Manager
ARAMARK Educational Resources

As a teenager, Tammy Marquez thought she would like to become an elementary school teacher. Tammy still follows her calling "to make a difference in the life of a child," but she does so in a broader capacity.

Tammy married while still in college and subsequently left school to be with her first child full time. When she and her husband looked for a good pre-school, they found Children's World near their California home. "I thought it was a wonderful, creative environment for kids," Tammy recalled. "Since I had earned my associate's degree in Early Childhood, I also mentioned my availability to be a substitute, if needed." The school did in fact call upon Tammy to be a substitute and liked her work so much that she was asked to become assistant director. Partially because of her skills, and partly because Children's World was a rapidly growing division of ARAMARK Educational Resources, Tammy was asked to be the Center Director for a brand new facility. "They saw that I had talent and tenacity and I wanted to work with children. Within two years, I went from making a difference to one child, my own, to making a difference for thirty and then 144." In addition to the children, Tammy also became responsible for a staff of 28.

One of Tammy's personal concerns was the difficulty working families had in finding affordable, quality child care. "I read whatever I could on work/life issues and came-up with an idea which should help everyone," she recounted. On her own initiative, she started visiting local employers with an idea for employer supported child care. "If they would assist employees in enrolling their children in our center, I would lower the tuition by 10%," she explained. This project turned out to be a winner for everyone. "The children received good care, the parents could be mentally at ease, employers had employees who were less distracted and Children's World had full enrollment," Tammy noted.

Children's World took note that Tammy's teaching ability and zeal for child care were also a benefit from the business perspective. In 1989, Tammy was appointed to develop corporate accounts with larger corporations within the western region.

Today Tammy, with the assistance of six direct reports, has responsibility within the Western region for two main areas of "direct reports". The first is on-site child care at corporations. Key elements here are feasibility and commitment. "The demographics need to show employees with children they would like in a center and a commitment from the employer to support the effort in terms of space and publicity," Tammy explained. A second area is public/private partnership, such as an after school program in an elementary school. "I work with the school board, the principle and parents' groups to see if we can design a program that benefits everyone," Tammy said.

"I was a latch key child myself and I took care of my younger sisters. Quality child care is more like a mission than a job for me," Tammy explained. "Some people ask about the fact that I work for a 'for-profit' corporation. In my opinion, how my employer files their taxes is not the issue. In any organizational structure, if you don't meet your expenses, you can't provide the service."

Tammy told me that she likes having her autonomy in daily work life and the entrepreneurial aspects of her job. She also likes the variety implicit in working with complex school districts and diverse issues like contracts, licensing and liability. In addition there is the challenge of handling multiple tasks simultaneously and "getting into someone else's shoes" to foster a mutually satisfying agreement. On the other hand, the politics of working with people who have conflicting agendas can be draining, as is frequent travel.

Tammy is now finishing her bachelor's degree and looks forward to further professional growth. "This job is a good fit for me because I worked hard to make it that way. I fulfill my commitment to children and experience the 'creative refreshment' of new challenges," Tammy remarked.

Children's World, a division of ARAMARK Educational Resources, contracts for a variety of services for children from ages six weeks to twelve years. AER is a subsidiary of Aramark, Inc.

Joan Janicelli
First Grade Teacher
Floyd Bell Elementary School

It's nine o'clock at night and Joan Janicelli is still reviewing her work plans. "I have got to see if the weekly plans I developed over the weekend really worked out as anticipated today," Joan thinks to herself. Is this a highly placed corporate official working through the night? No! It is an elementary school teacher preparing for the next day, just as she has done for twenty-seven years.

"I always wanted to be a teacher," Joan told me. "I wish I were younger so I could teach another twenty-seven years." Joan has spent most of her career with first graders. She considers first grade critical since it is there that children build their foundation in reading and writing.

Joan typically arrives in her classroom at 8:00 AM to prepare for the 8:45 AM start of classroom activities. Students often start with a "tiny task" like making vocabulary words out of clay. It gets them involved immediately, they learn something and they enjoy it, Joan explained. "It's important for children to *want* to learn. That's one reason we move around a lot, sit on the rug and maybe play a game, if the students get wiggly," Joan explained. "But even that is educational. For example, when we play the copy cat game it helps the students with listening skills and word sounds." As in many schools, Joan's students enter first grade with different levels of language art skills. "Some are already reading while others are unfamiliar with the alphabet," Joan noted. She takes a balanced approach, doing a whole group language arts activity at one point in the morning and then working with small groups at their own instructional level at other times. "I make a point of saying that we all learn differently and give examples from my own life. That way kids are less likely to feel superior or inferior to other kids," Joan noted. "In addition, if someone has trouble reading, I praise them for something in which they excel like art or sports."

The afternoon is dedicated to math, science, social studies. Sometimes there are special classes (gym, library, music) and time for learning projects. The day ends with a closing meeting where the first graders can discuss their day. After the children leave, Joan may meet with parents or discuss educational issues with colleagues before leaving at 5 PM or so.

Having 22 kids in a classroom is a lot of work, but Joan enjoys it. "The kids are terrific and I love to watch them progress," she related. "I change too. Every child is different, so they need different approaches. In addition, I never stop learning from experience. Besides, today's students are more worldly than those of twenty years ago. They travel more and have a broader sense of the world from television—it's not completely a bad thing—and computers."

Joan came to her school district after graduating from Mansfield University, a state teacher's college in Pennsylvania. She still lives in that state and commutes to the Windsor School District in New York. "I love this district, so it's worth the commute," Joan noted. "Besides, they offered a better salary than I could get in Pennsylvania." After a moment's pause, Joan laughed and qualified her comment: "My salary was $6,200 dollars to start. Teachers are better paid today, but salary was always a marginal issue for me."

Joan feels that patience, flexibility, understanding of curriculum and an understanding of how children learn are essential ingredients in teaching. In addition, good people skills with adults are very useful. "You need to be honest but sensitive when discussing a child with his/her parent," she noted.

Joan advises people interested in teaching to observe various grade levels in action: Primary, Intermediate, Middle School, High School. Each group has commonalties but still is unique. This should help someone decide which group he/she could best work with. Also, she feels that a person needs to ask himself/herself,

"Am I patient?" "Am I flexible?" before going into teaching. These two characteristics are a must for a good teacher. Finally, be ready to spend time learning specific curriculum and a variety of teaching strategies to help all students succeed!

Robyn Glazer Milbury
Schools to Career Director
Chelsea, MA Public Schools

Robyn was raised in the wooden tenements of Chelsea, Massachusetts. She "escaped" through the vehicle of higher education to become a practicing lawyer. Today, Robyn is back in Chelsea.

As Director of Chelsea's School to Career Program, Robyn has designed and implemented an initiative to give students basic skills through school based and work based experiences. "These experiences range from an informational interview through a hands-on apprenticeship," Robyn explained. "I recruit business partners to work with our teachers to add an 'outside world' dimension to education. For example, local business people have helped establish a student run credit union, a store and a GIS (Geographic Information Systems) Program." Some business people even co-teach in the classroom, to enhance understanding the importance of communication skills, including vocabulary, presentation and interviewing. "Our goal is to motivate students to stay in school and even attend college by adding a learning and earning dimension to their experience," Robyn noted.

Robyn spends a good deal of her time developing new relationships in the business community and maintaining old ones. "The presence of local business people in the school is especially helpful because it demonstrates the existence of good opportunities in an recognizable context," Robyn noted. She also spends time with teachers exploring ways to assist them achieve their educational goals through some outside support. "It's important to me that I am understood as a resource which is part of the school's mission, and not some independent activity," Robyn observed.

Robyn also works with individual students. "Sometimes I show people the tenement I grew-up in. That lends extra credibility when I tell students 'No excuses! Your family situation or ethnic group aren't going to hold you back if you work hard and have the right attitude.'"

Of course, it wasn't supposed to work out this way. When Robyn graduated from Northeastern University Law School in 1982, she joined a small firm and was instrumental in building up its real estate practice, representing tenants in Housing Court. In a twist of fortune, Robyn was then recruited by a firm representing commercial real estate interests. "I tried to sensitize them to tenant concerns," she remembered.

1992 was the year of Robyn's mid-life crisis. She left the law firm and worked part time for some nonprofit organizations. "I said, OK, you've been a lawyer for ten years, now what do you *really* want to do?" Fate seems to have had an answer waiting. A member of the Chelsea School Committee suggested that Robyn interview for a program for older, at-risk students. Robyn got especially involved with developing the work component of the program. "I enjoyed that job so much, I felt guilty getting paid for it," Robyn told me. When Chelsea was awarded a federal grant for a school-to-work initiative in 1995, Robyn was the natural candidate for that job. "The Chelsea School Board retained the position even after the grant expired. That's how committed this community is," Robyn observed.

Robyn enjoys seeing the fruits of her labors: "When I see a student I helped standing on their own, that's reward enough for me. One of the first students I worked with is going to graduate from a top University this year and we still stay in touch. What more could you want?"

Mary Lane
Point Trainer
Success for All Foundation

Picture someone with red hair, freckles, 5 feet 3 inches in height. Is this Annie, from the Broadway play? Actually it's Mary Lane, and she is training teachers who could be twice her age.

Mary is a "point trainer" for the Success for All Foundation, a nonprofit organization. Mary spends 80-100 days a year on the road training elementary school teachers in her organization's reading and learning methods. "The first day we talk about cooperative learning," Mary explained, "since that's fundamental to our approach. On the second and third days, I train teachers in our 'Reading Roots' component, which shows young children how to begin to read. For kindergarten teachers, I work on Early Learning, which is the component that prepares the youngsters to read. We also have a 'Reading Wings' program for students reading on a 2nd grade level and higher component, but I don't teach that component yet."

As Mary explained the program to me, if Success for All Foundation is contacted by a school, the Foundation sends a trainer make an "awareness presentation". The faculty votes on a proposal to adopt Success for All for a three year period. Eighty percent of the faculty must vote in the affirmative for the contract to be signed. "This is a serious commitment," Mary explained. "Our approach is a total school restructuring program involving not only academics but family support as well. Children work in groups based on their reading ability for 90 minutes a day. Since the groups are determined by reading level, not grade, the whole group works with the teacher for the full ninety minutes. "In traditional classes, the teacher has children at, let's say three different reading levels, the teacher may then have two groups doing busy work while she works directly with one group at a time," Mary said, contrasting teaching methods. "We assess the children every eight weeks to see if they are making progress."

I asked Mary if it might be a bit awkward to train people who were teaching before she was even born. Mary laughed in response but painted a realistic picture. "When you are younger, the issue of credibility is a greater challenge. What I do is dress professionally. But fundamentally anyone coming in from the outside has to build credibility and a relationship with an audience which might be, at the least, skeptical. It helps that I was a teacher for two years before joining the Foundation. In addition, I constantly stay current with the field and I come with a great deal of self confidence."

Typically, training is in the summer more often than not, because schools want to minimize disruptions to the classroom. Mary returns to each school two or three times a year to provide support for the teachers and administration.

One of the things Mary likes about her job is that every day is different. "When I do the initial training, I am in different schools and different states working with different people. During the academic year, I could be in a different school everyday," Mary told me.

Mary has had a long-standing interest in education. "I taught my brother how to read when I was seven years old," she recalled. On a more formal basis, Mary attended Loyola College in Baltimore and studied elementary education. "At Loyola, in our freshman year, we already spent one day a week in a school. Each year, we spent more time in actual classrooms. By the time I graduated, I had worked in public, parochial and independent private schools," Mary recounted. When Mary started teaching her own 2nd grade class, only a few students were able to read — many were at a Kindergarten reading level. Mary looked into ways to help her pupils, and discovered the Success for All Foundation, whose approach she began to use her second year of teaching. The school received the Foundation's newsletter, and Mary noticed an invitation to explore becoming a facilitator. Mary applied and was offered a position.

"I accepted the offer for a number of reasons," Mary recalled. "I knew that I could always go back to teaching, so I wasn't closing that career door. There would be a lot of travel, and I was excited by that. In addition, I was working on a master's degree in Educational Administration at Johns Hopkins, so I had an interest in seeing different school systems and having contact with district level administrators," Mary explained.

"It was a good decision for me," Mary continued. "I am still working with children and indirectly I can help several thousand a year. For me, that's fulfilling." Mary is well compensated: "More than a second year teacher in Baltimore, less than a Master Teacher in the New York City Public School System," she told me.

There is a career progression at the Success for All Foundation. Everyone starts as a facilitator, learning the Foundation's teaching approach and how to work with schools. The second step is becoming a point trainer, like Mary, who is the primary contact for a number of schools. In two or three years, you may become a senior trainer, which means you can train in every component of the Foundation's system. The next step is regional manager, who will be in charge of 10 - 15 trainers.

Teaching experience is almost a requirement at the Foundation. In addition, Mary recommends an outgoing personality, good presentation skills, thinking on your feet and a sense of humor. "Whether it's lost luggage or a difficult school, you're going to need that humor," Mary said with a laugh.

David W. Griffith
Special Education Teacher
Mary Hoge Academy

Some friends are highly paid lawyers, but David made another choice. Some friends are involved with high profile federal antitrust suits, but David made another choice. So, how did a bright young man from Ohio, with the potential for a prominent career in law, find a job he loves as a special education teacher in the Rio Grande Valley of Texas?

David Griffith visited Washington, D.C. as a junior in high school. "I fell in love with the place, its history, grandeur and tempo. When it came time for college, I accepted an offer of admission from American University and studied political science, justice and law," David recalled. Motivated by his goal of attending a top law school, he excelled academically. David also became active in organizations concerned with the environment and human rights.

"Senior year, my peers were all applying to law school. I didn't even take the LSAT (the law school admissions test). I just wasn't ready to make that commitment," David explained. Instead David pursued a position in the United States Department of Justice, Outstanding Scholar Program. While there, David researched materials for several high profile antitrust investigations. -"It was important work, and I enjoyed being around highly energized people," David related, "But the importance of the work was too distanced from those who were actually benefiting."

David decided to reflect on life, in search of what was truly "important." He recalled being happiest when working with and helping other people, specifically kids. "While driving to New Jersey for a vacation, a good friend listened to the story of my career unease. I explained how I felt disheartened by the conventional definition of 'success.' I wanted to do something important, something lasting. My friend recommended teaching."

The pressing issue was how a person with a political science degree could get involved in teaching. David considered several possible scenarios. "I had traveled through South America. The idea of teaching English in a foreign country appealed to me. Teaching at a private school was an option, too. Ultimately, I wanted to get involved in teaching where there was real need. My friend recommended Teach for America."

Teach for America places recent graduates, of all academic backgrounds, in "under-resourced" rural and urban communities. It is similar to a domestic "Peace Corps" with a focus on teaching. When David heard about TFA through his friend, he applied immediately. "On the application, I indicated a preference for working in Washington, DC, San Francisco, or the Rio Grande Valley. In order to appear flexible, I indicated a willingness to teach special education." Upon being accepted into TFA, David, like all TFA corps members, was trained at an intensive six-week summer program in Houston. "It was valuable, but nothing substitutes for experience," David noted. Subsequent to successfully completing the program, David moved down to the Rio Grande Valley and was hired as a special education teacher in Weslaco, Texas. He teaches ninth grade English to "students who have varying disabilities." "It requires a huge amount of patience," David observed, "And a deep belief that all students can learn."

David's first four months were "overwhelming," he told me. "I didn't feel sufficiently equipped to teach, let alone teach students with disabilities." But David persisted. "I had never given up before, so I wasn't going to start now. Also, my job was truly important—I just couldn't give up on my kids," David told me.

Today, David teaches in three types of class settings. He co-teaches in an "inclusive" class of both regular and special education students. He teaches a "self-contained" English class exclusive to students with disabilities, and he tutors students who are having difficulty with their regular classes.

David describes himself as a fair teacher, but not yet the solid teacher he strives to be. "I live, eat, and even dream teaching," he said. "My weekends are devoted to lesson planning, grading and contacting parents." David emphasizes the importance of involving parents in the educational process. "If a parent is involved in his or her child's education, that validates the importance of education. Education and learning shouldn't stop when a kid leaves school," David stressed.

David is committed to special education, in some capacity, as a career and plans to earn a master's degree in the field. "Teaching is one of the most important jobs you can ever do," David addressed. "Don't shy away because you are paid relatively less than other fields. Maybe I could have a six-figure salary or be involved in news making events, but nothing is more rewarding and important than positively influencing the life of a young person. Teach!"

Penny Porter
Safety & Health Training Instructor
Bailey Controls

Penny Porter works for Bailey Controls, a world wide corporation that designs and manufactures systems to control industrial processes. These processes include those found in chemical plants, pulp and paper, oil and gas, utilities, food and beverage, pharmaceutical, mining, cement, steel and waste water facilities. As Penny explained it, "The control system is a network of computers that are engineered to control flow rates and levels, temperature, pH, and pressure to name a few. Alarms are built in to notify operators of any change in process." Would you suspect that Penny started her career in a high school classroom or imagine that she still regards herself as a teacher?

Before coming to Bailey Controls, Penny taught high school chemistry and physics for twenty years in many different types of school systems. To supplement her income she also worked part time and during the summers at an environmental consulting firm. "We were liaisons to both companies that hired us and governmental agencies such as EPA and OSHA. While working there, I assisted them in filling out governmental forms, air sampling for contaminants, measuring noise, decontaminating plants, HAZMAT services, providing lab packs to landfill hazardous chemicals, environmental site assessments and provided training in safety," Penny recalled.

Penny became discouraged with teaching and decided to apply elsewhere for a position. "I looked at my resume and thought I would try training in the field of occupational safety and health. I was hired after my first interview," Penny explained, "because I had had experience teaching as well as in the safety field."

"I became as an OSHA training instructor, to train employees and customers in the many safety training courses required by the Department of Labor's Occupational Safety & Health Administration Federal regulations. These include such courses as 'Lockout/Tagout,' 'Confined Space Entry,' and 'Hazardous Materials Handling'," Penny said.

Penny described her work week this way:

"A typical week is determined by whether I will be teaching, preparing to teach, working on curriculum or taking a class. When teaching, the week begins Friday afternoon while the classroom is prepared for the students. This entails checking the equipment, setting up the textbook, tablets, pens and name tags for each student. Material used during lecture is checked such as projectors, power point presentations, and overheads. Monday morning I greet the customers (students) and begin to immediately build a rapport with them. We begin class, which runs from 8:30 until 4:30 through Thursday and Friday, 8:30 until approximately 11:30. (Lunch and several breaks are included.) Not only must I be able to teach the technical material within the course, but I must also be a "tour guide" for the customers who may come to Cleveland from anywhere in the country or world! It is fun telling them places to visit such as the Rock and Roll Hall of Fame, the sports facilities, the Flats, and Playhouse Square!"

"If preparing for a course, the week is spent researching the material, practicing the labs, discussing procedures with others who have taught the course before. If working on curriculum, it means researching the material and discussing needs with other teachers on staff, polling customers and doing desk work. If I am taking a course, it means actually sitting in with customers and taking the course! Much learning is accomplished when you know you may have to teach it one day!"

Communication skills, written as well as verbal, are central for Penny in developing her courses and instructing employees or clients. Social skills are essential to cooperate as a team member or to serve as leader. In addition Penny needs to be "prepared, prompt and flexible."

"This job is demanding and time consuming, but I still enjoy helping people learn, researching new materials and writing curriculum for my courses," Penny noted. She also enjoys the travel connected to her job. "This is typically for one or two weeks and can be located anywhere in the world. Our training center is always filled with students from all over the world which makes it very interesting and educational," Penny told me.

Penny has a B.S. degree in Education from Bowling Green State University in Ohio. Her major was "science comprehensive," which means that she is certified to teach any science course in grades 7 through 12. "The caveat is that I am 'jack of all trades, master of none'!" Penny observed. "I have taken many workshops and computer courses throughout my career, but I never could choose one program to concentrate on for a master's degree," she concluded.

Paul Leverington
Interim Director of Career Opportunity Center
University of North Texas

Can a culmination also be a coming home? The story of Paul Leverington suggests that sometimes it might. Paul is the Interim Director of the Career Opportunity Center at the University of North Texas, the same institution from which Paul first graduated over 20 years ago.

Paul's office is responsible for the career development of UNT's 26,000 students and any alumni who seek his assistance. The undergraduates, who comprise 75% of the students visiting Paul, come from any of 88 separate programs. Paul helps students in several ways. One is his job search strategy workshops, which include interviewing, resume writing, interpersonal networking and utilizing the Internet. Paul also sees students and alums individually for about 50 minutes per visit. Another of Paul's tools in helping others is his own career journey, so let's take a look at that.

Paul graduated UNT in the early 1970's with a major in physical education and a minor in biology. For three years, he was an athletic trainer for the Dallas Independent School District. "Trainer in a sports context means preventing injuries if possible and rehabilitating athletes if necessary," Paul explained "It does not mean teaching someone how to play the game." This was a large undertaking. Paul was responsible for six high schools, five middle schools and 125 games per year in each of the three major sports. "The sports stadium became a home for me," Paul remarked. The district invited Paul to become a classroom teacher as well as athletic trainer in one of the high schools. He accepted, and enjoyed the new position for about two years.

Paul began to ask himself if he wanted to be dealing with sprained ankles at age 50 and decided that he did not. He had been selling insurance and financial securities on the side, so he decided to try that full time. "Bad timing," Paul recalls. "With the unemployment and inflation of the early 1980's, who had the extra money to invest?" The arrival of a new child made Paul's desire for some financial stability more urgent.

Leveraging his previous part-time work in a grocery store, Paul became a management trainee in a discount drug chain. Within a year, he was managing his own store. After turning the sales profits around at one store he was sent to another store where he accomplished a turn around again. Unfortunately, Paul had a serious car accident and was not permitted to return to work without proving a 100% recovery. Given the medical reality, Paul was out of work.

"I set myself up as a business consultant," Paul recalled "business cards and everything. There is no definition for 'business consultant' so with my experience managing the store, I fit the bill." Paul's first client was in the wholesale silk flowers business. "I knew nothing about either wholesale or silk flowers," Paul admitted, "but I knew a lot about people." Within a month, Paul was hired as the company's business manager and helped produce the three most profitable wholesale sales markets in the company's three decade history. As Paul remembered it, the company's owner seemed to feel more threatened than appreciative. Paul was out of work for the second time.

Wherever Paul turned for his next job, he heard a consistent refrain "we are looking for business degrees." At age 37, he decided to pursue an MBA degree, but was encouraged by a business professor to get his degree in Applied Economics with an emphasis in personnel and industrial labor relations. While earning his degree, Paul started to work part time for a government funded employment center working with people who had been laid off and those with personal difficulties which interfered with holding a job. Upon graduation, Paul assumed a full time position at the center. Paul developed a computer based research center, utilizing existing software to help his clients research prospective employers and/or raise their educational skill levels if needed. "I realized from my two experiences with being unemployed that it wasn't easy to find career research information, so I put in place employer research software to help my clients research four areas about themselves: abilities, interests, values and temperament," Paul noted. "You really need a better understanding of yourself before you can be truly successful in the job market."

While working in the employment center, Paul was among those who read a notice from UNT about an opening in their career service office. "I knew as soon as I read that job description, that it was the culmination of all my life and work experiences," Paul told me. Despite not having an education or direct experience in this field. The admiration was mutual and Paul started at UNT.

One of Paul's duties at UNT, involves overseeing the student/alumni recruiting program which attracts 150 employers to the campus each semester. In addition, UNT is part of a consortium of 35 universities in Texas which holds two huge career fairs in Dallas every year. But Paul spends less than 10% of his time on those efforts.

Most of Paul's time is spent directly working with students and alumni. "A first job can be a life changing event; so is your next job after a lay-off," Paul said, in explaining his motivation for such intense work with individuals. "I want to be the person who makes that change possible. The best advice I can give to job seekers is for them to show/tell an employer what they can do for the employer today, instead of focusing on what they did yesterday. I'm living proof," Paul stated, "that job searching today is only two questions: 'What do they want?' and 'What do you offer?'

Education and experience are enhancements; the keys are your skills, abilities and characteristics."

Paul has also built an extensive Web site for career guidance and job search purposes. It has links to a huge volume of resources, arranged in a logical manner which makes them relatively easy to access. This guide provides the complete career search process from career exploration to employer research to networking and job search. "I want my UNT clients and other job seekers on the World Wide Web. "I developed the career guide with others like me in mind because I had no idea where to find these resources when I needed them," Paul remarked. "I want my students and alums to utilize this as a resource without getting mired in it. Going out and meeting people, building your network of human contacts is still the way to go," Paul added.

WHAT TO DO NOW

To help you prepare for a career in education, the people interviewed for this chapter recommended organizations you can contact, as well as publications and Web sites that may prove useful in your search:

Organizations:

National Association of Educators of
Young Children (NAEYC) Washington, DC .... www.naeyc.org

National Education Association .... www.nea.org

American Federation of Teachers .... www.aft.org

Corporation for Business,Work, and Learning .... www.cbwl.org

Teach for America, ... 1-800/832-1230, x 225
.... www.teachforamerica.org

The National School to Work Learning & 1-800/251-7236
Information Center, ... www.stw.ed.gov

Corporation for Business, Work, ... 1-617-727-8158
and Learning, ... www.chwl.org

School to Work Training and Technical Assistance .. 1-617/287-7054
Clearinghouse, ... www.stw-clearinghouse.org

Publications:

Teach Magazine .... www.teachmag.com
Education Week
Education Daily .... www.eddaily.com
Vocational Training News

Web Sites:

www.unt.edu/coc
www.studentaffairs.com
www.hire-ed.org
www.stw.clearinghouse.com
http://web66.coled.umn.edu/schools.html
www.asd.com
www.jobweb.org/search/schools
www.schools.com
www.teachersatwork.com
www.nationsjob.com/education
www.teachforamerica.org/
www.academploy.com
www.usjobnet.com
www.privateschooljobs.com

13

♥

Nonprofit

Some No-nonsense Ways of Doing Good

Does a career in the nonprofit sector mean that you are soft hearted and soft headed? Reading these stories, we find people who are deeply concerned about others but quite pragmatic in achieving their goals.

We will read about building grass roots organizations, managing hospital volunteers, public health, resources for women in need and leading a well known network of social service agencies.

All of these roles require a substantial set of skills. For example, Paula Barvin speaks about the need to focus intently on what she is doing while being able to shift quickly from one issue to another. Deb Schroeder found that being gregarious and highly extroverted helps, as does the ability to set priorities.

There are also powerful satisfactions which can compensate for less than robust paychecks. Gail Price spoke about the creativity of her grant writing and knowing that she has contributed to improved health domestically and abroad. Lara Sladick savors the appreciation of her clients. For Brent Stewart, there is a powerful picture of a little boy in his mind.

Paula Barvin
Regional Director
Progressive Action Network

How do you build an effective, democratic public interest organization that will influence government legislation and regulations? The Progressive Action Network (PAN) has a grass roots answer for organizations interested in either environmental or consumer issues. PAN conducts door to door canvassing to help enlist new members. "The idea is to touch base with everyone in a community, not just the leaders," explained Paula Barvin, a PAN Regional Director based in New Jersey.

The goal of PAN is to increase the number of people who will do three things in support of a client's cause: sign a statement of support, write a letter to the appropriate public official and contribute funds to support the client's organization. The client organization, for example the New Jersey Environmental Federation, pays dues to PAN for this service.

At first I was taken aback that those friendly people knocking on my door "to protect our neighborhood groundwater," weren't volunteers. As Paula explained, being a good canvasser requires training and experience coupled with the ability to deal with rejection. You usually need paid staff to do the job right.

Paula herself started out as a canvasser, raising funds to support ERA (Equal Rights Amendment) ratification after graduating from Barnard College in 1978. "I was actually planning to go to law school, but my canvassing convinced me how important organizers and fund raisers can be," Paula recalled. "I never left the field and never regretted it."

Paula moved from canvasser to canvass manager to canvass director in about one year. Someone starting in canvasser's position today would make about $15-18 thousand at entry level, $18-20 thousand as a manager and between $22-34 thousand as a canvass director. "You can't get rich, but you can have a middle class life style," Paula reflected.

As regional director, Paula has a supervisory role giving advice, solving problems and making sure that goals are met. "The canvass directors need to meet program demands," Paula told me. "They should be generating a certain number of letters, raising funds and managing their budget. If they need advice, I can give it. If they need a carrot, in the form of a bonus, I can give or withhold that too."

Paula's clients are not limited to New Jersey. She played a large role in helping Wisconsin pass a mining moratorium which a PAN affiliate supported for the purpose of preventing toxic discharge into the Wolf River.

To do her job well, Paula needs to focus intently on what she is doing while being able to shift quickly from one issue to another. She listens carefully and trains others to do the same. Paula also needs to enforce clear communication throughout the organization. "Canvass directors need to be both clear and firm: 'We are what we say', so we have to say it right," Paula said with conviction.

Paula thinks her job is great for several reasons. "What I do relates to what is going on in the world," she remarked "It is clearly relevant. In addition it's like a small business. You have a concrete input and you can see quantifiable results." Paula also likes the people intensive aspect of her position, especially developing leadership skills in others and the fact that she respects the people with whom she works.

There are some downsides to this profession. One is that Paula could make more money doing something else. Second, she feels the strain of working with financially stressed organizations. For entry level canvassers, there may be a problem with evening hours, typically 2 PM to 10 PM. "Those hours don't mesh with everybody's outside life," Paula remarked.

Some people who go into grass roots organizing start straight out of college or high school. Others come from more lucrative professions in business because they find organizing or public interest more fulfilling.

If you are interested in considering this type of career Paula has this advice: Examine and prioritize your goals in life. Decide what's most important to you at this time. Is doing work that is meaningful more important to you than making as much money as you can? Evaluate your own skills. What additional skills would you like to learn? How could you best use the skills you have and develop new skills to reach your goals? Recognize that because nonprofit organizations have "to do a lot with a little," staff are encouraged to develop and take on more responsibilities quickly. You can gain valuable experience by working with a nonprofit.

Remember that you make a living by what you earn, but you make a life by what you do.

Feel free to contact the following people to learn more about job opportunities in our network: On the East Coast: Paula Barvin, Progressive Action, 556 Haddon Ave., Collingswood, NJ 08108, 609-869-0007, email Pbarvin@aol.com. In the Midwest: Marjie Henry, Wisconsin Citizen Action, 152 W. Wisconsin Lave. #308, Milwaukee, WI 53203, 414-272-2562. On the West Coast: Lori Schroyer, Washington Citizen Action, 100 s. King St. #240, Seattle, WA. 98104, 206-389-0050, Web site: www.eskimo.com/~WCA.

Deb Schroeder
Director of Volunteer Services
St. Joseph's Mercy of Macomb Health Services

What do community workers, teenagers, "pre-med" students, senior citizens, and court-ordered referrals have in common? They all might be among the 900 active volunteers at St. Joseph's Mercy Hospital in Macomb County, Michigan. Deb Schroeder is responsible for each one of them.

"We have volunteers in over 70 departments and they help us in important ways ranging from clerical functions to patient liaison in the emergency room," Deb told me. "They might be fulfilling a course requirement, wanting to get the feel of a hospital or just doing a good deed. Some want to contribute a skill they developed outside the hospital and some want to try something completely unrelated to their professional experience." Whatever brings an applicant in, Deb interviews them to determine if they have a clear sense of purpose, can stand the stress of a hospital and are likely to observe guidelines on confidentiality. Deb tries to find the best match between the volunteer's schedule and goals on the one hand, and a master schedule reflecting the hospital's needs on the other. "A good match is to everyone's advantage," Deb noted. Court referrals for community service require a stricter screening process, but Deb is willing to give such people a chance if they are truly well motivated to change.

Then Deb's work can take her and some volunteers outside the hospital walls. "Our real mission is to keep the community healthy, not just to heal the sick," she said. Community activities may include handing out healthy snacks at a health fair or supporting a fund raising event.

Although volunteers may work at any time during the week and any hour of the day, Deb's position is a more standard five-day week, eight hour day. Deb is paid as a professional and supervises a small staff. "The day really flies by," Deb noted. "I work with people who want to be here and it really feels like a large family of people who care for each other. The fact that my manager, a hospital vice president, gives me a lot of leeway to try out new ideas also helps a lot."

Deb started at the hospital 20 years ago. Her first position was being a unit coordinator taking care of clerical work at a nursing station. After seven years of part-time work there, Deb became the staffing coordinator for nurses, scheduling nurses for appropriate assignments. "I held that position for three years. It was very stressful and included working alternate weekends and holidays," Deb recalled. She applied for a position as Volunteer Coordinator and was accepted. When the director left, Deb moved into her current position.

To succeed in her field, Deb has found that being gregarious and highly extroverted helps. She also is extremely well organized, can set priorities and juggle multiple tasks. Deb has used her listening skills to evaluate situations, and counsel volunteers in need of correction. She also manages educational sessions for volunteers on customer service, confidentiality and approaches to speaking with patients. Sometimes Deb also needs to educate staff members about the value of volunteers—how to motivate them and keep them coming back.

Although some directors of volunteers have earned a college degree, Deb has not. However, she did earn an associate degree in "medical assisting" at Ferris State University, has continuously taken courses at Macomb Community College and often attends health care conferences which relate to her job. "This education helps me do my job better. My goal is to continue to offer quality volunteer programs and help the volunteers meet their personal goals," Deb said.

When she leaves work, Deb spends a good deal of time volunteering. She serves in the Macomb County Advisory Board the Housing Commission of Macomb County, and school activities in addition to being active in the St. Joseph's Auxiliary.

For those interested in pursuing a career in volunteer management, Deb suggests "becoming a volunteer yourself." "Find out what your community needs are and help to meet them. Once you're in an organization, you may have the chance to make your avocation into a profession," she suggested. "Remember that this job is about being there for the volunteers, hospital staff, and the community," Deb added.

Chris Sullivan
MIS Director
Minnesota Council of Nonprofits

Why is a bright, hard working computer whiz working in a nonprofit organization instead of pulling down a Silicone Valley type income? He didn't plan it that way.

After graduating from the University of Minnesota with a major in English, Chris Sullivan took a job in California with an information retrieval firm. While there, he developed the idea of pairing Computer Science with Library Science. "That way I could be a real expert in information research," Chris told me. But it didn't work out that way. Chris had already worked for several years after high school to pay for his college expenses and "there just wasn't a lot of money available to support the kind of studying I wanted to do." Chris returned to the University of Minnesota to study Computer Science. "I took a job as a grant accountant because that would waive my tuition. However, in order to enter the graduate program, I had to fulfill all the undergraduate requirements in computer science, and that would take about four years. So I decided to earn a second undergraduate degree, this time in computer science."

One day in class, a fellow student, probably several years younger than Chris, mentioned that a nonprofit organization desperately needed a MIS person. "I knew very little about nonprofits at the time," Chris recalled, "and my classmates were prone to discuss very attractive, corporate opportunities. I went to the interview, we hit it off and I got hired. Five years later, I am still here and I have never regretted it."

Chris' employer is an association of charities in Minnesota. It provides research and education functions, public policy and advocacy, public information about the nonprofit sector and certain member services, such as group purchasing. Its members are other nonprofit organizations. Chris started out building a database of nonprofit organizations and supported staff members who needed technical help.

"But my job grew as I asked for more responsibility and more people came to me for a wider variety of help," Chris recalled.

Today, Chris directs both technical functions, like databases and a local area network (LAN), and managerial functions, such as budget and purchasing. He is also responsible for two external areas. The first is working within Minnesota as the voice of nonprofit organizations among info/tech professionals when policy issues are under discussion. The second is national. Chris chairs a committee of the OMB Watch Nonprofits' Policy and Technology Project, which funds nonprofit organizations in pilot projects combining the Internet and public policy.

For Chris, there is a lot to love for his job. "I have the opportunity the use my communication skills, both listening to others and interpreting technical issues into layman's terms. Also, I am a fairly quick read, which is especially helpful in managerial situations. I like the fact that I can draw on different skill sets in different situations, so I don't fall into the rut of cookie cutter solutions," he told me. Chris also enjoys his co-workers and his Executive Director, whom Chris described "as a man of vision." There is something else. Chris now knows how important nonprofit organizations can be. " I am on the board of two organizations and I contribute to causes which are important to me," Chris noted.

Like many computer people, Chris reads publications like *Info World* and other computer magazines regularly. He also reads the *Chronicle of Philanthropy*. His job has brought two worlds he loves together.

Gail Price
Coordinator for Domestic Activities
Management Sciences for Health

Management Sciences for Health is a nonprofit organization whose focus is "helping managers and policy-makers narrow the gap between what is known about, and what is done to solve, the major problems of public health that still separate advantaged and disadvantaged populations." Although most of MSH work is in developing countries, Gail Price is the coordinator for domestic activities for MSH and her route to this position helps explain why she loves it.

Gail began her career as a physical therapist in a hospital. One thing Gail enjoyed enormously was speaking with patients and staff who had an international background. The thought entered her mind that there was little communication between American health officials and those overseas, especially in regard to what the United States could both teach and learn. Gail left her job to study at the Harvard School of Public Health, and became more familiar with international health issues through some of her course work.

After graduating from Harvard, Gail took an residency position at Beth Israel Hospital in Boston and moved from there to the Massachusetts Hospital Association because that job was more involved in policy issues. Gail's next stop was working for the Commissioner of Boston's Health and Hospital Department (DH&H) where Gail developed commonly based health services utilizing ideas she had gained from her experience in Columbia, South America. The Commissioner was interested in international health issues which might affect Boston, so Gail had an opportunity to pursue her interest in that area. In fact, when MSH approached the Commissioner to propose a consulting role for that organization, Gail was put in charge of the relationship.

In the course of one of her projects, Gail arranged for MSH to participate in management training for the DH&H and attended a training course herself. She also discussed a number of other possible projects. Gail got to know many people at MSH. Convinced that MSH might offer a chance to combine her passion with her profession, Gail suggested herself as a candidate for several open positions at MSH. Knowing the high quality of Gail's work and her deep commitment, MSH offered her a job in 1994 and she eagerly accepted.

But Gail is not merely an employee, she is a pioneer. She redesigned her position to deal with domestic, United States activities. This is in an organization which does 99% of its work in Asia, Africa and Latin America! Part of Gail's job is to write proposals for funding to private foundations or government agencies like the US Agency for International Development. "This is a highly competitive process," Gail told me." There are many organizations interested in public health." Gail also works with organizations like the National Association for Community Health Centers to educate Americans about international health issues.

Why should an American even care about international health? Gail told me several reasons. "There is the sheer brotherhood of it, a kind of global citizenship," Gail suggested. "But there are purely pragmatic reasons as well. First, we in America can learn a great deal from people overseas. For example, many developing countries have a better track record on immunization of poor children under the age of two than we do in the U.S. Second, there are thousands of immigrants and refugees coming to the U.S., and it makes sense to have good contacts with the home countries. Third, there is no such thing as an isolated disease anymore. Public health overseas can help protect Americans from highly mobile diseases. Fourth, on a commercial level, healthy people make better markets for American products than sick ones."

As part of her educational effort, Gail brings people who manage successful public health programs to make presentations in the U.S. Just to surface the names of people to contact can require hours of work on the telephone. "I had to get one of those operator type head sets because all those phone calls were hurting my neck," Gail told me. Then Gail needs to carefully screen the potential presenters. "They have got to be passionate and charismatic to make an impact," Gail observed. With speakers coming into place, Gail needs to identify whom to invite. She looks for the commonality and linkage between speakers, topics and potential conference attendees.

The payoff of all these efforts is expanded health issue education for MSH, and "sheer bliss" for Gail. "I love to see people who start out cynical about the value of someone else's experience develop bonds with those people based on mutual respect and learning," Gail told me.

There are other things Gail enjoys about her job. "It's like starting a new company. I love the creativity involved in writing competitive grants and developing new products — new educational conferences." At the same time, there is some downside for Gail, "Seeking funds can be exciting, but it's also stressful, especially when deadlines draw near. There is also a great deal of pressure, from MSH and self-imposed, to bring in the dollars. Without funding, we can't carry out our mission. In addition, I really feel uncomfortable competing with other organizations which are also dedicated to public health," Gail acknowledged.

Gail offered some advice to those who might like a job like her's. "First, start with a principle, feel that you are doing something of value. When you find something you believe in, it softens the aggravation that any job entails. Second, make sure that you really understand the field. If you don't have a degree in public health, it is especially important to get immersed in the issues through professional conferences and periodicals. Joining a good professional association like the American Public Health Association or the National Council for International Health would be a good way to do that," Gail concluded.

♥

Lara Sladick
Career Counselor
Women's Resource Center of Sarasota, Inc.

When we picture Sarasota, Florida, we probably think of balmy weather, beautiful palm trees and golf-playing retirees. But like so many places, Sarasota also has a large service industry which forces many divorced, separated and widowed women into low paying jobs. These women can come to the not-for-profit Women's Resource Center of Sarasota for a variety of help, including assistance in returning to the work place.

Lara Sladick is there to provide career counseling. "The first thing is to determine where the client is in the job search process," Lara told me. "If she's still in distress, I will focus on being warm and supportive. I would refer her for assistance in dealing with personal issues. For example, there is the Challenge/Action Program where women in transition receive help with self-esteem building and determining steps for setting career/life goals. On the other hand, if she is ready to pursue job leads in an identified field, we can get to that pretty quickly." Most of the women who come to the center are over 35, and have at least some post-high school education or training. Only 10% are on welfare. "Women are not forced to come to the center by a judge or welfare office. They are usually self motivated," Lara observed.

As an example, Lara told about a woman who was out of the work force for six years with a serious illness. When she went into remission, the woman wanted to return to work. Lara helped her develop a resume which focused on her transferable skills, not just a history of previous jobs. Then they worked on interviewing, with Lara giving constructive feedback. Prepared with refurbished job search skills, the woman followed-up on leads Lara had given her and landed a good job.

Through her previous experience in human resources, Lara understands the employment process. She has also developed a large base of contacts through active involvement in the local chapter of the Society for Human Resource Management. "My experience in the hiring process has definitely allowed me to help these women better," Lara told me. Having a balanced approach to counseling is also important. "On the one hand you need the ability to listen and be patient. On the other hand you need to set boundaries and make it clear that you won't do somebody's search for them," Lara noted. Lara refrains from the temptation of giving advice. Instead, she presents facts on both sides of an issue, leaving the choice to the women who come to see her.

Lara graduated from the University of Florida (Gainesville) in 1989, with a bachelor's degree in human resources. Her first job was screening and hiring non-instructional staff for a local school board. Lara also gained exposure to employee relations by working on the day-to-day management of a newly instituted union contract.

After four years, Lara became a human resource generalist for a 100 employee environmental consulting group in Florida. "The people were nice, and I had a chance to work with commercial business issues like billable hours and strengthening the bottom line," Lara recalled. "But the company was in financial trouble, so I decided to pursue further education. I was accepted into the University of Florida's accelerated MBA program and completed my degree, with an HR concentration, in eleven months."

MBA in hand, Lara became the human resource director for a physicians' practice group. Unfortunately, after three months, her position was eliminated in a downsizing. After some time off for travel and some temporary jobs, Lara came to the Women's Resource Center. "The fact that I have had the experience of being downsized helps me understand what it's like to be a single woman without an income," Lara said. "It also made the objectives of not-for-profit, helping organizations more appealing and the risks of for-profit employment less attractive."

Not-for-profit pay prospects are typically less than corporate, Lara noted, but she is better compensated in terms of the appreciation she receives from clients and colleagues. In addition, Lara enjoys the teaching, networking and program development aspects of her position.

If you are still in college, Lara suggests trying out a profession like hers through internship experiences. "Make sure you know this is for you before getting started," she suggested. For prospective career changers, consider how much less salary you are really ready to accept. "Good intentions are hard to fulfill on a daily basis if you are unhappy about a shrunken pay check," Lara noted.

Since 1979, the Women's Resource Center of Sarasota has been dedicated to fostering the pursuit of individual excellence through education and service. Programs are designed to help women achieve independence through personal growth, life skills and career planning. The Center offers support and guidance during distressful situations such as divorce, widowhood, career change, marriage, parenting, physical or financial limitations.

A note about Lara: Lara enjoyed her position at the Women's Resource Center. However, as we went to press, Lara accepted a new position as the Human Resource Director for the Shannon Hotel Group in Longboat Key, Florida. "My new position better utilizes my MBA and experience. In addition, it almost doubles my salary," Lara said.

Brent Stewart
President and Chief Professional Officer
United Way of Greater Battle Creek

Brent Stewart is a man with a picture in his mind. Whenever the long days and working weekends begin to wear on him, he focuses on that image and his energy returns. What he sees in his mind's eye is a widowed mother holding the hand of her youngster. They walk up a set of stairs toward a big building, hoping that the people there might offer help.

From his adult life, we might not guess that Brent was that little boy. Brent graduated from Howard University in 1981 and enlisted in the Army, in part because of a government program designed to help Army veterans pay for graduate education. With financing earned through the Army, Brent studied Regional Planning at Pennsylvania State University. While there, he accepted an internship with the United Way in nearby Lancaster. "It was a great match," said Brent with a smile. "They were looking to pay a person to do some planning, and I needed some money."

He came to realize that the United Way network of social service agencies was making a very positive difference in the lives of local people, and that Brent was part of it. "Helping others is a great feeling. Within two months of working for United Way, I was hooked. I knew than that I wanted to remain with the 'helping' profession," Brent told me.

Nearing graduation from his master's program, Brent began to distribute his resume through a number of United Way agencies. One of the responses came from White Plains, New York. "The United Way there hired me to work in its campaign division," he said. "Campaigning is another word for fundraising. Campaigners are sales types and extroverted. A person with a 'planning' background is thought of as being more introverted." Landing the job in White Plains was an opportunity to broaden abilities and develop the additional needed skills to sustain a successful career in the nonprofit sector.

In the course of working with a large number of charitable agencies in White Plains, Brent was recruited to run an employment and training program at the local Urban League. It was a difficult decision to leave United Way, but ultimately he took that position because it gave him a new opportunity to help others more directly. "At United Way, we provided support to agencies, who in turn worked with clients in person; that is what I wanted to try." His new job was helping low-income adults who needed assistance make themselves more marketable in the work force.

"It was extremely rewarding when these folks succeeded and their self-esteem soared. I will never forget the expressions of pride on their faces when they came in to tell me that they had landed a job," Brent recounted.

Two years later, Brent was sought out again by his former employer at the United Way in New York. He accepted their offer as vice president. "I worked there five more years honing my leadership skills and learning a great deal about the added value United Ways bring to local communities. Then, I said to my family, I think it is time to try putting my training into action in another part of the world, so I began another job search." An opportunity presented itself in the Cereal Capital of the World, Battle Creek, Michigan, and Brent pursued it.

A typical day for Brent often begins at 7 AM with his own volunteering at a nonprofit agency. Then he heads to work. He leads a staff of seven who help him coordinate hundreds of volunteers working to raise more than $3.3 million annually. These funds are distributed to 45 local health and human care programs. "It is hard work," added Brent. "But it's worth it when you see the impact you are having on others. Our funded agencies provide clothing for needy children and adults and other basic needs like food and health care."

There is always administrative work that needs doing. When I spoke with Brent, he was preparing reports for his volunteer board of directors. "Our board wants to know that we are investing our money wisely in local programs," he said. "We are proud that more than 90 cents of every dollar contributed goes toward the health and human care programming. That is far better than the national average for charitable organizations."

When not in the office, his weekends are often spent attending United Way-funded program events. "This is not a 9 to 5, Monday through Friday job," he continued. "I believe it is important that I am both accessible and visible in the community."

Brent considers himself fortunate that his family is so supportive of his hectic schedule. "It does put a burden on the family but they have certainly been understanding of my career. They share my picture of the youngster walking up to the big building seeking help. He is hoping that the people at that Salvation Army may have a toy or two for him to put under the Christmas tree. After all, that little boy was me."

WHAT TO DO NOW

To help you prepare for a career in the nonprofit sector, the people interviewed for this chapter recommended organizations you can contact, as well as publications and Web sites that may prove useful in your search:

Organizations:

The Peter F. Drucker Foundation
for Nonprofit Management .... www.pfdf.org
National Society of
Fund Raising Executives .... www.nsfre.org
National Council of Nonprofit Associations .... www.ncna.org
Council on Foundations .... www.cof.org
The Society for Nonprofit
Organizations .... http://danenet.wicip.org/snpo
American Society of
Directors of Volunteer Services .... www.asdvs.org
American Public Health Association .... www.apha.org
National Council of International
Health .... www.ncih.org

Publications:

Chronicle of Philanthopy .... www.philanthropy.com
Philanthropy Journal .... www.philanthropy-journal.org
Nonprofit Times .... www.nptimes.com

Web Sites:

www.access.org
www.idealist.org
www.nonprofit.gov
www.jobsinnonprofit.com
www.opportunitynocs.org
www.essential.org
www.impactonline.com

yahoo.com/societyandculture/issuesandcauses/philanthropy/community

www.independentsector.org

www.nonprofits.org

14

Government

When it Really Is a Public Service

The people in this chapter provide a variety of services through our local, state or federal government. These include fixing roads, rehabilitating the injured, the Peace Corps, weapons design, firefighting, the FBI and military service.

Many of these positions require a significant amount of technical skill, whether Julie Crego's Geographic Information systems for identifying road repairs or Mary Beth Morris' knowledge of Computational Fluid Dynamics to design ways for protecting US Navy vessels.

Charlene Davis draws on her knowledge of psychology, neurology and educational theory to help individuals return to work after sustaining a serious injury. Leslie Dominguez needed a knowledge of farming, environment and local culture to work with villagers through the Peace Corps.

Some government employees use their skills while putting their very lives on the line. Jim Timoch rushes into burning buildings . As an FBI agent, Peter Ginieres loves fighting crime in a wide variety of cases. Staff Sargent Sedric Wade enjoys the physical and mental conditioning the Army requires and has exercised his leadership ability from Kentucky to Desert Storm.

Julie Crego
GIS Software Support
Department of Transportation (DOT), State of Wisconsin

Did you ever hit a pot hole or get lost driving to your second cousin's house at night? Then you can appreciate the work of Julie Crego, especially if you live in Wisconsin.

Julie works in software support for Geographic Information Systems (GIS) at the State of Wisconsin Department of Transportation. The GIS is a tool which incorporates graphics and location into traditional computer programming and mapping. "A GIS system gives you the ability to ask questions and to perform complex analysis to solve problems like identifying road conditions and determining which of the trouble spots should be fixed first," Julie explained. "With an application that uses GIS tools, you can find the answers you need quickly and see the results displayed on a map or computer screen. A picture is worth a thousand words. For instance, an easy to understand GIS system is the on-board mapping systems in some newer cars," Julie said by way of explanation.

Julie was a "late bloomer," to use her phrase. She started college in her early 30's, earning a two-year associate degree in computer programming from Madison Area Technical College. "Getting to Madison, Wisconsin, at all was a bit of a trip," Julie recalled. "I grew-up in Michigan, but when the economy there took a dive in the late 1970's, my husband and I moved to the Sunbelt. First we went to Florida, then to Texas," she continued, "Our job situation was still not great and we actually missed the four-season climate we grew up with. Friends of ours lived in Madison and loved it, so we decided to move there."

Move they did, without a job. However, within two weeks Julie started work as a "limited term employee" for the State of Wisconsin, and her husband found a job as well. When Julie completed her computer programming degree, she transferred to a data processing position with the Wisconsin Department of Transportation. In 1989, a fortuitous bolt of lightening struck. Her department was establishing a new unit for GIS purposes, and had to fill a position there immediately or lose it altogether. Julie was available and chosen for the job.

In the beginning, Julie did a good deal of hands on learning from her supervisor and colleagues. In addition she took technical classes which were vendor specific.

A work week for Julie can be very diverse. She is now so expert in Arc-View, a software package produced by ESRI, that she provides "product support" — assistance and good counsel — to colleagues who need it. Julie also maintains a manual for location control and has put it on the GIS unit intranet. In fact, Julie is the web author of the GIS support intranet for the DOT. Julie also coordinates a bi-annual Arc view user group for the department, which has over 200 licenses. Over the week, "small fires" arise, caused by computer glitches and data errors, which Julie must work extinguish.

Julie loves doing this type of work, in part because she is "drawn to mysteries and figuring things out, and [she] likes being creative." Computing is ever changing, and Julie enjoys learning new things. People are another great plus for Julie. " Our unit works together very well, care about what we build, how well it works and how well it solves the problem. We spend time together socially as well," Julie told me. Her job puts her on a cutting edge of her field. "Our unit has always been involved in pushing the envelope. This allows you to set the pace and determine directions as well," Julie commented.

There is no clear path for someone interested in entering the GIS field, as GIS's come from many different vocational backgrounds. However, understanding spatial data is a critical skill and cartography (map making) is very useful because it involves the skill of taking geographic features and displaying them on a surface. Julie came from a programming background but others come from different fields, with "earth sciences" being very prominent. That would include surveying, cartography and geography.

Charlene Davis
Vocational Evaluator
State of Vermont

To understand what Charlene Davis does professionally, seek out someone who returned to work after experiencing a traumatic injury or suffering a debilitating disease. Ask them what it took to put them sufficiently together, body and soul, to become productive employees. Part of the answer will always be someone like Charlene.

Charlene works with individuals having cognitive, physical or mental disabilities with the goal of assisting them in making job choices in order to become productive employees. "This is a very vocationally driven situation. My satisfaction comes when I can help disabled people maximize their abilities at work," Charlene told me. Her "consumers", to use the State of Vermont term, have an initial 2-3 hour session with Charlene in which she will start to evaluate their transferable skills. The evaluation may flow from a combination of testing and discussion. Charlene gave me this example. "Let's say I have an engineer who has sustained a traumatic brain injury. Using computer software, I can get feedback on the aptitudes an engineer typically needs to be successful. Through observation, testing or discussion, I can assess the consumer's current range of abilities. Then I can identify steps s/he could take to work at their maximum level. If the consumer's disability has prevented them from ever working, my focus will be more on basic work preparation and identifying interests."

The consumer's initial session will be followed by 2-3 more. In between, there may be 'homework' like practicing interview questions or observing someone doing the kind of job Charlene believes may work out for her consumer.

Charlene has been working with individuals with disabilities for most of her 25 year career. She graduated from the College of St. Joseph in Rutland, Vermont with a degree in Special Education in 1973. For three years, she taught children with learning disabilities in two New Hampshire public schools. Many of us would consider that draining, but Charlene thought "it was fun." Still Charlene wanted to pursue a graduate degree "because it would open me to more variety, including work with good assessment and evaluation instruments." To save money, Charlene moved back in with her parents for a year before starting an intensive twelve month program at Keene State College. It emphasized education for special needs children.

Master's degree in hand, Charlene went to work in a "self-contained" classroom for two years. "All my children were emotionally disturbed or developmentally disabled. They were not well integrated in those days," she recalled. Unfortunately, funds for teacher aides were drying-up and Charlene "started to feel more like a class-monitor than a teacher."

The mother of a colleague knew about an opening for a police and ambulance emergency dispatcher. "I stay calm and take initiative in emergencies, so I took the job," Charlene recounted. After three years, the night shifts and weekend work were wearing on Charlene. " I didn't mind the nature of the work, but I missed working with disabled people. I explored my options, and found a job in a sheltered workshop as a rehabilitation counselor. "My main functions were dealing with behavioral issues and coordinating services with other concerned people, whether professionals or relatives."

A co-worker at the sheltered workshop took a job in Vocational Rehabilitation for the State of New Hampshire and alerted Charlene about a position there in vocational assessment. Charlene passed the interview process, but after three years her position was eliminated through budget cuts. Undeterred, Charlene passed the State rehabilitation counselor examination. She was hired to help people develop a plan for getting back to work by the same agency which had just cut her from the payroll.

A desire to come home to Vermont to help care for her ailing mother led Charlene to the job she currently holds. "There's lots of variety here and I enjoy it. I work with neurological deficits, back injuries and schizophrenia in a single week." Charlene pursues continuing education and updated assessment techniques.

She is also studying for national certification as a CVE (Certified Vocational Evaluator). "The CVE would be especially helpful if my field is privatized or if I decide to pursue employment part-time." Charlene reasoned.

To do her job well, Charlene must draw on the knowledge base in psychology, neurology and educational theory she has developed through college course work. The right characteristics are also essential. While Charlene needs to be a keen observer and listener, she also needs to be open-minded and non-judgmental. It is also important to be empathetic without being paternalistic. "My consumers need expert assistance, not misguided sympathy," she noted.

"I got a lucky break," Charlene told me. "In college, I was invited to work at a Christmas party for children with Downs Syndrome. Certain that it would freak me out, I was reluctant to go. But when I met those children, I fell in love with them. That party wasn't fun in the usual sense, but it helped shape my life."

Leslie Dominguez
Volunteer
Peace Corps

Life can be full of interesting and valuable experiences. For example, some people have the good fortune to come from a privileged family and attend an elite college. Others experience life from an isolated village in a poor country. As a Peace Corps volunteer, Leslie Dominguez has experienced both.

Leslie graduated from Oberlin College in Ohio in 1994, with a major in Chinese. To facilitate opportunities to speak Chinese, she moved to California and found a job in a YMCA after school program. She enjoyed working with children and did get to practice Chinese. After two years, she felt it was time to move on, but doing what? "I didn't feel that I wanted to start a formal teaching career," Leslie told me. "On the other hand, I did want the experience of working abroad, I wanted to work with a population in need and I wanted to learn Spanish. The Peace Corps seemed a perfect fit," Leslie recounted.

Leslie applied to the Peace Corps in October, 1995, was accepted four months later, and by July 1996 she was in the Dominican Republic for training. For Spanish language training, the volunteers were taught by Dominican teachers. Her agricultural training consisted of two parts. First was basic agriculture, including planting, spacing, insect control and crop compatibility. Second, Leslie and the other volunteers were trained in how to consult. "You can't just say I am going to teach you how to farm," Leslie observed, "No one will listen and frankly my experience in the soil was as a gardener, not a farmer. Instead I say 'I know some helpful techniques which will improve what you are already doing. Do you want to learn about them?' "

Leslie lives in a small community, or *campo* of about 150 people. It is about 45 minutes by foot (the only transportation) to the next campo. The campo does not have electricity, potable water or plumbing. Therefore, Leslie reads by an oil lamp, boils her water and uses a latrine. She has an excellent blanket and a fleece winter coat from the U.S., so she is warmer in the winter than other members of her community.

On the agricultural side of Leslie's service, she focuses on conservation farming. This includes erecting barriers (rocks, logs, oregano) to inhibit erosion, and planting leguminous crops which help fertility. "I have a small demonstration plot," Leslie explained, "so I do the same things I might suggest to others." This campo owns the land through a co-op (an uprising 50 years ago established that fact) and has an irrigation system. However, the land is not really fertile and is located on a steep hill. Leslie is trying to encourage a shift to organic or at least sustainable agriculture, in part because the campo is expending much more than it can afford on pesticides and fertilizers.

Leslie also has teaching responsibilities. She teaches environmental issues in the elementary school and English to 6th graders. "That's as far as formal education goes," Leslie explained. She also teaches English to interested adults and an adult literacy course in Spanish to those who want it. To help the campo's families generate a little extra income, Leslie has helped the local women's association in small business projects.

Leslie likes the people of her campo enormously. "They are a very social people," she said, "If I close my door in the evening, someone will bring me soup because they are afraid I might be sick." The experience of a different culture and life situation is also a big plus, although Leslie doesn't expect to live without potable water or electricity when her two year Peace Corps stint is over.

"One potential negative is that this job can get lonely," Leslie said, "As friendly as the Dominicans are, sometimes you just want to speak with people who think the way you do." Volunteers do try and stay in touch with each other, but this can be difficult. "You can walk for an hour to another campo and your friend's not home. So you just leave a note and walk on home," Leslie explained. Leslie has had the opportunity to date, but keeps her social life separate from the campo.

Leslie has some thoughts about the skills needed in a Peace Corps volunteer. "For me, the ability to teach and to present things in front of others has been the most important," Leslie said. "You need to be friendly and to love talking to others. It's important that you know how to take care of yourself in terms of both creature comforts and diversions," she concluded.

Thinking about the Peace Corps?

You should apply to the Peace Corps within one year of when you are available to serve. On average it takes 9 to 12 months to meet all the screening requirements and leave for an assignment— depending on the demand for your particular skills. Placing married couples may take longer.

Peace Corps programs have evolved as the world has changed. While the need has remained for volunteers to work in agriculture, education, forestry, health, water sanitation and skilled trades, countries are increasingly requesting help in new areas: business, the environment, urban planning, youth development, and the teaching of English for education, commerce and technology.

Because the Peace Corps places volunteers in response to specific requirements from countries requesting assistance, the host country representatives — together with Peace Corps staff — establish the specific professional and educational requirement for each assignment. In general, most assignments require a bachelor's degree. Some assignments may require three-five years related work experience instead of, or in addition to, a bachelor's degree. Others may require a master's degree.

Contrary to popular belief, liberal arts majors are competitive for Peach Corps assignments. However, liberal arts majors should show a demonstrated interest in a particular program area e.g. tutoring experience for English Teaching assignments, gardening/farming experience for agricultural programs. In addition to meeting the skill qualifications for a program area, you must be a US citizen, at least 18 years old and in good health. There is no upper age limit.

Mary Beth Morris
Mechanical Engineer
Naval Surface Warfare Center

If you walk into the Naval Surface Warfare Center in Dahlgren, Virginia, you are liable to see Mary Beth Morris sitting behind a computer. That's where she spends most of her working hours. It may look as though she is playing some very sophisticated computer game, but her work is deadly serious.

Mary Beth predicts air flow patterns in or around naval vessels, utilizing her training in Computational Fluid Dynamics (CFD). Her specific project is to determine the impact of chemical/biological agents if they were deployed against US ships. This is a long term project; Mary Beth has already worked on it for several years. "This job is always a bit different since I am constantly drawing on different data bases. Further, I change assumptions and scenarios to see how they might impact the outcome," Mary Beth explained. Although some people at NSWC develop their own modeling software, Mary Beth uses what is termed COTS (commercial, off-the-shelf). "I am a team of one," Mary Beth remarked "but that's OK. Besides, my office mates are great and everyone at NSWC is always available to help. My software vendor gives me excellent technical assistance and my boss trusts my judgment when I request new or upgraded equipment."

Mary Beth finds a lot to like in her job. "I like to work by myself and at my own pace," she told me. "I am very self disciplined and conscientious but I like the fact that my deadlines are not hard and fast. I am doing what I enjoyed in college and NSWC will support outside education if I request it. This job gives me both flexibility and freedom. What more could I want?" Mary Beth is also pleased to be on the cutting edge of her field, and to have access to the latest computers. She enjoys building data bases and developing 3-D graphics "so you can see the ship in every detail without going blind looking at endless rows of grids."

Mary Beth earned both her bachelor's and master's degrees in mechanical engineering at Virginia Tech, receiving her graduate degree in 1992. She especially enjoyed her fluid dynamics classes because they were so mathematical. "I didn't want to go to work straight out of college, although many of my classmates did. I wanted an R&D (Research and Development) job, and a master's degree is very important for that," Mary Beth recalled. "I did get some practical experience though, working on some contracted projects for my professors."

When Mary was ready for the work world, her resume was made available to employers by the Virginia Tech career center. NSWC saw that her objective was very targeted and explicit. "I knew I wanted to work in 'fluid dynamics' and I said so on my resume" Mary recounted. "NSWC invited me to stop by their booth at a career expo. From there, they set me up with an on-site interview. I was offered a job over lunch, and accepted it a month and a half later. NSWC met Mary Beth's interest in fluid dynamics, suited her well in terms of location and provided an atmosphere in which she felt comfortable.

For Mary Beth, mechanical engineering was perfect training for what she wanted to do. Others at NSWC studied physics, aerospace technology, mathematics, chemical engineering, computer science and electrical engineering. To learn more about the NSWC, contact Mary Thorsted, 540/653-8041 or mthorst@nswc.navy.mil.

James Timoch
Firefighter/Medic
Akron, Ohio

Most of us have been taught to leave a building threatened by fire as quickly as possible. Jim Timoch has been trained to enter the fire scene to protect life and property.

This is a career which literally gives its baptism by fire. The tip man is the firefighter who "hauls in the nozzle" to the burning building. That assignment is usually given to a rookie. "You crawl in, hauling the fire hose by the nozzle. Usually you don't know exactly where the fire is because there's so much smoke," Jim explained. "When you find the source, you spray it with copious amounts of water. That should do it." Fire-fighting requires team-work, and Jim could also be the hydrant man, attaching the hose to a water-source, or the driver who also operates the pumps. "Fighting a fire can give you an adrenaline rush, but you are completely drained when it's over," he noted.

Like the others in his unit, Jim works a 24 hour shift and then has 48 hours off. There isn't a serious fire call every day, but fire-fighting begins before the alarm goes off. "Typically, I arrive at 7 AM and check out my equipment and my SCBA (self-contained breathing apparatus). Then there's firehouse clean-up, training and drill. We do training exercises twice a day. It might be practicing cutting off the roof on a junk yard car or studying new paramedic equipment. We are always practicing a plan," Jim told me. "When I started in this career I wondered how I would ever do it. But by practice, practice, practice you put yourself on auto-pilot when an actual situation arises."

Those situations aren't often very pretty. "Once, I was the tip man at an accident scene. I was ordered to bring the nozzle up to the car window in case it started to smoke. Inside was the body of a woman. She was obviously dead and I had never seen a corpse before. I so much wanted to help her in some way, but I stood there with the nozzle. Otherwise I would have been putting the lives of my fellow fire-fighters in jeopardy if the car started to burn," Jim recalled. "You need to get used to seeing people in their worst situation, whether it's a family that has lost its home or a mother grieving over a child with gunshot wounds."

Car accidents, gunshot injuries, heart attacks. Jim had already seen them all in his first three months on the job. "In this fire house, we can expect maybe ten ambulance calls a day, so we're hopping even when there isn't a fire," Jim noted.

Jim lovingly remembers his grandfather, who was a lieutenant in the Cleveland fire department. "I used to spend weekends in the firehouse with him, watching the guys work and listening to the stories they told," he recalled. But Grandfather told Jim he should go to college, and Jim graduated from the University of Akron in 1990, with a degree in marketing. "I was a fraternity president, a resident assistant, a section editor on the yearbook. It just seemed natural to go into sales," Jim said. For eight years he was a pharmaceutical sales representative in places like Chicago and San Francisco. On his 30th birthday, Jim had a serious discussion with himself. "The money is great, but who am I helping besides myself?" he pondered. "Also, I'm spending too much time on the road. I wish I could be as satisfied with my job as Grandfather was with his."

Jim set a goal of passing the required fire-fighter test. He studied every spare moment for the six hour exam which tested math, reading comprehension, memory and psychological profile. "I took that exam and one other, since every jurisdiction has its own hiring process. Some people take the exam many times for that reason," Jim explained. After four months, Jim was notified that he had passed the written exam and was now eligible to take a grueling physical test. "I walked with ladders, dragged a hose up a three story tower, found my way while wearing a black-out mask, among other things," said Jim. "I'm in great shape, so I passed that too." The next step was a round of personal interviews, after which Jim started his three month training at the Akron Fire Academy. "We were well trained in the nuts and bolts of fire-fighting and medical emergencies," Jim recalled, "but only experience really makes you a professional. I thought I would be bothered by the sight of blood and gore, but I have seen it all and I can do what I need to," Jim continued. "After every run, whether it's fire or EMT, we go back to the station and discuss the lessons we can learn for the next time."

One of the things Jim loves about his job is the intense camaraderie in the fire house. "We live together and we depend on each other for our very lives," he noted. There is good natured but intense competition with other fire houses. "We compete to see who can unroll the hose faster, for example. That kind of constant striving to be best also helps bring us closer together," Jim observed. The sense of duty and service is also essential for Jim: "I want to know that I am making a difference for people, and not just making a living for myself."

Jim suggests that people interested in pursuing a firefighter/medic career be in excellent physical shape to chop a hole in a roof or carry someone from a flaming building, know how to take orders and function in a team and are self-motivated. For example, no one should have to tell you to clean equipment or have your fire suit ready for rapid dressing.

Each jurisdiction has its own process for screening applicants. Find out what you need to do from the human resource people. Sometimes exams are given once a month, sometimes only once a year. You need to know the specifics. There may be credit given for military experience, having a college degree or obtaining EMT certification. The testing process is highly competitive, so get every advantage you can.

Peter Ginieres
Special Agent
Federal Bureau of Investigation (FBI)

Peter Ginieres has been a special agent at the FBI since 1972, and has been the media coordinator in the Boston office since 1995. The FBI "is the principle investigative arm of the US Department of Justice. At present, the FBI has investigative jurisdiction over violations of more than 200 categories of federal crimes."

Pete loves two aspects of his job. First, he is performing a public service by fighting crime. Second, being an FBI agent requires handling a wide variety of cases. For example, in a single day, Pete might investigate domestic terrorism, an armed bank robbery and a bank president suspected of laundering drug money.

After serving as an army officer in Vietnam, Peter came to the FBI through its diversified hiring program, which includes a military to FBI option. He has never regretted that decision. Today, however, a majority of new recruits are people in their 20's and 30's who are changing careers — and often taking a pay-cut in the process. These new recruits are attracted in part by the lore surrounding the FBI and in part by the agency's new investigative programs.

Many of today's recruits are computer specialists or people with business experience like stock brokers and accountants. These people develop a mutual attraction with the FBI which is deeply involved in fighting white collar crimes like securities fraud. In fact, many people apply to the FBI after attending agency sponsored seminars at their work place designed to detect and prevent business crime. "When they see how interesting and sophisticated our work is, it can put a real bee in their bonnet," Peter told me. A number of teachers have also joined the FBI and are especially sought after if they have strong language skills.

The FBI's budget has been increased in recent years as Congress identifies more crimes for the FBI to confront. Fighting parental kidnapping and kiddie porn adds variety and an additional sense of mission in addition to budget security.

There are two main paths into the FBI: agent and support. The agents are the folks with the badge and gun. To be accepted as a trainee, you must pass both written and oral tests as well as a stringent physical. New recruits spend 15 weeks of intellectual and physical training in Quantico, Virginia, which includes training in fire arms, martial arts, and investigative methods. Those who successfully complete the training can indicate their geographic preferences from a list. Their initial compensation is at GS-10 level ($34,000) plus 25% for built-in overtime. A typical day for an agent is 10 ½ hours.

"A good agent needs to be dedicated and have a love of public service," Pete told me. "She or he needs to have the persistence to stay with 20 or 30 of their own cases at any one time, while being a team player when needed for activities of their squad." Agents also need to be comfortable in two different environments. "There aren't many jobs where they give you both a bullet-proof vest and a lap top computer," Pete remarked. A comfort with people from all social backgrounds and "occupations" is essential. "After all," Pete explained, "informants are a critical source of information. Some get their education in graduate school and some grew up in the streets."

The second entry point to the FBI is support staff like mail room, computer operators and administration officers. These people are the "backbone and lifeblood" of the FBI's law enforcement effort. In contrast to agents who may relocate frequently, support staff tend to stay with a specific local office.

In terms of job satisfaction, consider this: The FBI has a very low attrition ratio. "Other than retirements, almost all the agents I have ever worked with are still with the FBI."

Individuals interested in the FBI should contact the nearest FBI district office—there are 56 of them—c/o the appropriate Applicant Coordinator.

Sedric Wade
Staff Sergeant
United States Army

It is 1989. Picture an eighteen-year-old straight out of high school. He wants challenge, adventure, travel and a chance to continue his education. He decides to enlist in the U.S. Army and is accepted into the Airborne Infantry. Was this really a good choice for him?

"I loved the Army from day one, even in basic training. There were new people to meet from lots of cultures and we learned to rely on each other as members of a team. In addition, I enjoyed weapons training, although it was a challenge to identify, employ, assemble or dissemble a variety of weapons. The obstacle and confidence courses were tough, but I got into the best physical shape I have ever been in," Staff Sergeant Sedric Wade told me. After twelve weeks of basic training, Sedric went for three weeks of airborne training. "At first, jumping out of airplanes was scary, but after while it was a piece of cake," he recalled with a laugh.

Sedric was assigned to duty with the 101st Airborne Division. "Yes, it was physically challenging to be sure," Sedric remarked, "but it put you into great *mental* shape as well. You need to stay very alert and pay close attention to details. You have objectives to accomplish in a short time frame and need to find a way to do that with the rest of your team." Sedric mentioned that he was also away from home and on his own for the first time, which helped him learn to rely on himself more.

There was also a classroom component to Sedric's training. On the military side, he learned about the history and heritage of the U.S. Army and core Army values like military courtesy, loyalty and integrity. On the curriculum side, Sedric took advantage of the Army's support to study some basic college courses. More recently, he took a course in personnel management. "You can take a course as long as your commanding officer certifies that it will not interfere with your training. The Army will even pay 75% of the tuition cost," Sedric explained. "Some colleges even have an extension on some of the bases." Continuing education is not a small thing to the Army. Sedric still meets every month with an advisor to discuss his career goals and related tasks.

On the road to becoming a staff sergeant, Sedric certainly has had a chance to travel. With the 101st Airborne, he was in Kentucky, Arkansas and New York. He also served for eight months in Desert Shield and Desert Storm. "Our training had prepared us well for a war-time mission. The biggest change was the climate," Sedric told me. When Sedric re-enlisted, he requested a transfer to the 82nd Airborne. In addition to a $4,000 bonus, he trained in California, Alaska, Germany and Panama. "The 82nd trains you for combat in all kinds of climates and conditions," Sedric said.

As a staff sergeant, Sedric is responsible for the leadership and welfare of a nine person squad. "You need to know your people as well as your weapons," Sedric noted. "You are also responsible for millions of dollars of high tech equipment. For example, I carry a hand held Global Positioning System (GPS) set which gives me information on the fighting terrain around me through a satellite hook-up." The need to make quick and sound decisions has helped Sedric enhance his leadership skills.

In terms of housing, staff sergeants like Sedric have a private room in a "barracks," which is more like a dormitory or apartment. Soldiers below that rank share a room. "There are some nice amenities," Sedric observed. "Each room has a private bathroom and there is a service area with a refrigerator and microwave. We're tough, but we have a comfortable living environment."

Sedric's current duty position is in recruiting. "This is the biggest mission in the Army today," Sedric told me. "To protect the country, we need a strong Army. That means attracting and retaining the best people we can get." Sedric speaks to people from age 17 to age 30 every day about what the Army can mean for them. "I don't sell, I just present the facts," Sedric said. "Our standards are very high, but so are the benefits of an Army career." After Sedric pre-screens a candidate, he or she must still pass the Army's strict moral, mental and medical standards.

Sedric's next step is to study at the Soldier's Support Institute in preparation for his next duty assignment, career counseling. That function focuses on developing and retraining Army personnel.

Sedric could retire from the Army after 20 years of service. "I want to become a teacher or coach in civilian life. Or maybe I'll become a high school ROTC instructor. Today's Army is preparing me for tomorrow as well," Sedric concluded.

WHAT TO DO NOW

To help you prepare for a career in the government, the people interviewed for this chapter recommended organizations you can contact, as well as publications and Web sites that may prove useful in your search:

Organizations:

ESRI (Environmental Systems Research 909/793-2853
Institute, Ind.) .... www.esri.com
URISA (Urban and Regional Information 202/298-1685
Systems Association) .... www.URISA.org
WLIA - Wisconsin Land Information Association 800/344-0421
Environmental Systems Research 909/793-2853
Institute, Inc. .... www.esri.com
Peace Corps .... 800/424-8580; www.peacecorps.gov
Federal Bureau of Investigation .... www.fbi.gov
U.S. Army .... www.goarmy.com

Publications:

Government Executive Magazine .... www.govexec.com

Web Sites:

www.USAjobs.opm.gov
www.epolitics.com
www.statesnews.org
www.magiclink.com/web/jberry

15

Your Own Business

Your Boss is in the Mirror

Many people want to be their own boss. What is that like and how do you get there?

Ed Jajosky had a burning desire to make things since he was a child. While working for others, Ed developed a superb reputation in his field; now clients come to him. Carmen Johnson learned ASL at home and found that she could combine a personal commitment with a career.

Sometimes you start out small. Rex Gore is the president of a large landscape service company, but he started out pushing a lawn mower.

Jon Jorduhl operates a complex, technologically sophisticated business (his farm) without leaving the home he loves. On the other hand, Captain Ernest Richardson manages a complex operation that has taken him from Alaska to the tropics.

Satisfactions can vary. For Rochelle Kaplan, it is providing a problem solving service as an alternative to an adversarial process. The creativity of running her own business and the variety of working with many artists and clients stands out for Crystal Wright.

Making a living while being self-employed is not easy. It is still necessary to satisfy the ultimate boss, economic reality.

Ed Jajosky
Design Model Maker

Coming home from work, you stop off at a drug store to buy a household medical kit, then go next door for a six pack of beer. You come home and sit in your living room chair. Outside a child pedals by on a tricycle while holding an action toy figure. It is quite possible that the point of purchase display which promoted the medical kit, the revolving head which prompted you to buy a certain brand of beer, the tricycle and the toy were all manufactured from models and patterns engineered by Ed Jajosky.

"Since I was five years old, I had a burning desire to make things," Ed told me. "My first creation was a little wooden doll. In seventh grade I made kitchen cabinets and drawers for my mother. Later I built a back porch. To make some money for the family (my mother was a widow with four kids) I did repairs for neighbors." Ed decided to become an industrial arts teacher so "I could earn a living and still build things." In 1964, he earned a degree in that field at what is now Kean University and started teaching Junior High School Shop. "I wanted the kids to be creative, so I didn't let them build from a pre-existing pattern," Ed recalled. "Some of the kids even won awards when I exhibited their work at an Industrial Arts Conference in Atlantic City." During his six years of teaching in junior high schools, Ed earned a Master of Fine Arts degree at Rochester Institute of Technology in furniture making. Ed was also winning awards and receiving publicity for his furniture designs at major exhibits and museums. When Murray State University in Kentucky called RIT seeking a person to teach furniture design, Ed's name was recommended. "I took that job at Murray State and loved it," he recalled. "It really didn't seem like work at all." Outside of teaching, Ed worked for a cultured marble sink company. "I designed molds and the company could then pour in the marble," he explained. "I then applied what I learned and designed a line of marble furniture. I went back to

New Jersey and started my own cultured marble business," Ed recounted, "but the oil embargo of 1973 made polyester resin prohibitively expensive. I had to close my business." Fortunately, good deeds are sometimes rewarded. One of Ed's former junior high school students was working at a toy company which had a molding problem. The student remembered Ed, who was hired to make molds and prototypes from fiberglass. "I worked full time in New York City, plus did contract work for other toy companies," Ed said with a chuckle. "It may seem like a conflict of interest, but I kept everything separate."

After five years as a toy company employee, Ed went freelance and worked for many toy companies over the next thirteen years. "There's a lot of running around and making adjustments as a free-lancer," Ed noted. "I would discuss projects, work with company designers, develop my models, show them to clients, make adjustments based on feed back. It's fun, but it's not a leisurely pace." Based on Ed's prototype, the company could tool-up and go into production. Working in his studio or backyard, Ed made models for about 350 toys, including baby carriages, ride-ons, dolls and robots. "I used every material and every medium," Ed explained. "That's why I always had work." Whatever skills Ed didn't already possess from his education or experience, he learned from other model makers. "We help each other a lot," Ed observed. "What one needs helps with, the other teaches."

When Ed's toy contracts slowed down, he began making point of purchase displays. "Clients usually find me based on reputation," Ed told me. "If things get slow, I remind clients that I'm here. They always have projects for me."

Ed currently works on site with his biggest client. "I needed to get out of my own studio to socialize more. Also, at home I never stopped working since the project was always within reach. Now I put my tools down at 5 PM and finish the project tomorrow." His own studio isn't forming cobwebs, however. An avid skier, Ed has made a huge sculpture for a ski resort and a model mountain coffee table where you can visually relive your ski runs.

Making things by hand and using his creativity is Ed's daily thrill. He also gains a sense of accomplishment when he sees kids playing with toys he designed. "Or their parents selling them at a garage sale," he added. Ed starts a new project every two weeks and might see the results in a store window within six months. "This is a quick turnover profession," he noted.

The basic requirements in Ed's profession are a craftsman's skills in sculpting, molding, drafting and drawing for a range of materials including wood, clay, plaster, rubber and plastics. "Strictly speaking, you don't need a formal college education," Ed observed, "but having that background makes you a professional. You can communicate better and on a wider range of topics. Also you can see how things fit together, and that makes you more valuable. I find it a need to work with my hands and to create something new, beautiful and useful. If feel very fortunate to have been able to develop my talents and achieve such satisfaction."

Carmen Johnson
ASL Interpreter

How about a job which can pay well but you would be willing to do for free? That's how Carmen Johnson of Troy, Michigan described her job as an American Sign Language (ASL) interpreter. Carmen may work on short or long term contracts. For example, she may have a few hours of work in a court or hospital or a long term arrangement at the Michigan Jobs Commission.

Let's take a look at what a short term assignment could be like. Carmen's just sitting down to supper with her husband and four young children. The phone rings. Carmen knows she could be called at any hour, so she answers. A teenager is in the intensive care unit with gun shot wounds. His mother is deaf. Carmen needs to come immediately.

Carmen interprets for the traumatized mother as the doctor is explaining, "The situation is very serious." Shortly after, it gets worse. A nurse tells the mother (Carmen interpreting), "You need to say good-bye to your son." In this situation, Carmen became the voice of the hospital to the grief-stricken mother and, after the son's death, "became the mother" to friends and relatives who had to be notified. Carmen cried as she related her story, "The mother's letter of thanks meant everything to me," she said.

I asked Carmen if she was an advocate for deaf clients and their families in medical settings or elsewhere. "No," she replied, "but sometimes I feel like one." Carmen wants to make sure that they understand the issues involved and can make their wishes known.

Being an ASL interpreter is a job which requires the ability to submerge your own ego. This is a constant requirement which shows itself in many ways. Deaf people themselves often see the interpreter as only a necessary evil. To be effective, the interpreter must not be the center of attention. Rather, s/he has to take a back seat. Carmen's long term contract job at the Michigan Jobs Commission provides an example. She interprets for a deaf counselor. When that individual needs to use the phone, Carmen must make sure that it is her client who shines in phone conversations with peers and clients. Carmen must be perceived as a mere shadow who happens to interpret.

When Carmen appears in court to interpret for deaf witnesses, she herself must be sworn in. This is a protection against an interpreter who might embellish or distort what a witness actually testifies. Not all judges are thrilled about having an interpreter in court. After all, the judge himself probably doesn't understand ASL, so he may feel that he is losing a measure of control. This judicial ambivalence may express itself in determining where Carmen is allowed to sit or stand. For example, it would be best from an ASL point of view for the interpreter to be in the same line of vision as the judge. That way, the witness can read Carmen's signing as well as read the judge's facial expressions. However, some judges simply won't permit that arrangement.

Carmen learned ASL at home from her father, a pioneering pastor who established churches for the deaf in Missouri and Illinois. Although both her parents were hearing, their house was full of people from the deaf community and interns learning ASL. To hone her skills for professional situations, Carmen studied the terminology of engineering and architecture in special courses and seminars.

I was surprised to learn that there are some commonalities when working with the deaf community. For example, Carmen worked in Brazil teaching college students there who were interested in working with deaf people. There are deaf clubs and many sports activities, including a deaf Olympics, the world over. Even so ASL is distinctly an *American* sign language. Those who wish to work with other than English-speaking Americans would need to learn the culture and nuances of that other language.

An interesting down side of interpreting for the deaf is the risk of carpal tunnel syndrome. As a precaution, if Carmen has an interpretation which will require more than two hours, she switches off with another interpreter.

Part of Carmen's involvement with ASL interpreting stemmed from the availability of job opportunities. "When I left college, I had my national certification as an interpreter and a bachelor's degree in Education. When I went looking for a teaching job, I had a hard time, but as soon as interpreter referral agencies knew I was in town, they literally begged me to work for them. There is a severe shortage of interpreters in the United States," Carmen told me.

I asked Carmen what she would ask a person who wanted to learn ASL and become an interpreter. "Why do you want to learn ASL?" Carmen replied. "If you say it's to be a helper, don't do it! Deaf people want to be independent. They resent people who rush to be helpful. Your job is to stay in the shadow and let the deaf person shine. You are an appendage, not a key player, a tolerated instrument and not a patron saint." People should remember that ASL is as difficult to learn as any foreign language. It is not simply a series of hand signs! It is also necessary to adhere to a strict code of ethics, including protecting client confidentiality.

Compensation for Carmen is about $35/hour. In other states she might get paid more. However, remember that Carmen doesn't have a reliable 40 hour week and that she has already attained a high level of certification. A beginner would probably be paid substantially less.

Rex Gore
President
Clean Cut, Inc.

Picture a high achieving, industry experienced MBA pushing a lawn mower to make a living. Now picture that same person as president of a $20+ million company with 400+ employees. There is no disconnection here. The first picture was a necessary step in achieving the second.

Rex Gore is the president of Clean Cut, Inc., a landscape services company based in Austin, Texas. His friend and partner is Dennis Dautel, the founder. Clean Cut is involved in the installation and maintenance of commercial landscapes. Most of their business comes from upper-end commercial clients. Rex is in charge of strategy and operations. "Our typical property is billed at about $25,000 annually, with $4,000-$7,000 more if they want additional service like pruning, annual flowers and mulch. A large property might bill as much as $100,000," Rex told me. We still do some private homes at $30 a pop, though."

Rex studied agricultural economics at Kansas State University and subsequently earned a master's degree in business there. His first job was as a commodities broker and he subsequently did some work in economic research. Rex came to Austin as the trailing spouse when his wife made plans to go to law school. "Because I grew up on a farm, I knew something about fertilizing, planting and irrigation," Rex recalled. "So when my friend Dennis told me about his business plans, I agreed to work with him 'for a little while'," Rex continued with a laugh. "That was thirteen years ago."

The initial business was cutting lawns. "We went door to door, handed out flyers in strip malls, just about anything to get any business at all," Rex explained. "Austin was having a building boom at the time, and we visited sites where buildings were going up and asked for business. We were persistent in asking and consistent in returning phone calls. We earned our first contracts taking care of the exterior of some low-end duplex apartments and small complexes. But it was a start." Rex gave me an example: "One year we had a severe drought in Austin. Some companies didn't bother to check the irrigation systems if it wasn't in their contract. We did! Our theory was the way to earn customer loyalty is to do the job right."

"This wasn't a fabulous job in the beginning," Rex confessed. "There I was pushing a lawn mower in 105 degree weather when my classmates were making megabucks pushing paper in air conditioned offices. My wife and I lived at a very modest life style so we could take the risk of creating an opportunity for something big."

Slowly, the business began to blossom, by "word of appearance," as Rex put it. "We made a point of producing the best product and service, even when we weren't getting paid enough to warrant it. Our strategy was to do the quality of work we would eventually like to be known and paid for. Over time, we started getting bigger clients. Our product is highly visible and the real estate community is fairly tight, so property managers started turning to us."

Rex and his partner also absorbed the pain of dealing with difficult clients. "One property manager wanted us to replace $4,000 worth of flowers because he wanted a deeper shade of pink. With the small margins in the landscape business it would take $100,000 of new business to earn enough profit to cover that loss. But, we couldn't afford the risk that he would question our commitment to customer satisfaction, so we did it."

"Early on, we didn't need a lot of expertise ourselves, although my farm experience was helpful," Rex told me. "We hired technical knowledge like arborists, horticulturists and entomologists. Our sweat was building some equity, and spending it on expertise really impressed potential clients."

As Clean Cut grew from its two owners (Rex and Dennis) to 400+ employees today, a management training program was put into place. "We start trainees where we started—doing basic field tasks. It's good experience, albeit on a small scale, and helps the trainee develop his/her competencies. With 18 months, a trainee may take responsibility for three work crews and half a million dollars in annual business. Mostly we start with recent college graduates. We do talk to more experienced folks, but they need to expect a dip in income, at least in the beginning."

Rex added a note about compensation for management trainees. In 1998 dollars, the starting compensation package is $28,000 to $32,000, plus health insurance, vacation and profit sharing. The anticipated compensation at the end of the second year is $50,000. After 4-7 years compensation is anticipated at $75,000.

Richard Butchko
President
Association Management Solutions

If this were a film, its topic line might be "Guy who wants to work for himself meets associations in need of management services."

Let's start the film in the present. Rich Butchko and his partner, Dianne Farabi, manage the operational aspects of associations ranging from 45 to 1300 members in size. "Our clients are too big to be run by volunteers but too small to pay for full time managers, office space and equipment," Rich explained. "So we do their mailings, newsletters and brochures. We also pay their bills and act as an audited custodian for their funds." By freeing his clients from administrative tasks, they can focus on the goals of the organization. By maintaining extensive databases, Rich can also research important membership issues. "Let's say I discover that new memberships are rising in the Northeast while renewals are declining in the Southwest. The association can then tailor their membership drives accordingly," he explained.

Managing the needs of multiple organizations keeps Rich hopping from one project to another, from mailing out a meeting notice to laying-out a newsletter. "Some days can be rather long, but I don't mind it since I'm working at home and can set my own schedule," Rich offered. His home office is 8'x10' and contains 2 computers, three printers and five telephones. "We work a lot with data, and that doesn't require lots of physical space," Rich noted. "Having a separate phone for each client accentuates the distinct service we give each one."

So is this a tale of the little boy who always wanted to go into association management? Not really. "This is actually a relatively new field. Although everything I ever learned is helping me, I never heard of this profession until I met Dianne." After working in sales for a large photocopying company for five years, Rich earned two graduate degrees, one in social work, the other in psychology. He taught for five years at Christopher Newport University in Virginia and spent six years there as the Director of Student Development. Then Rich had "a personal RIF (reduction in force) experience." He found a position in student development in Ohio. When he met Dianne, who had a small consulting practice and was already managing two associations, Rich left academia and joined her. "I wanted to work for myself and I was very interested in organizational work," Rich recalled. "An organization may be experiencing some difficulty managing rapid growth and change when they come to me. I enjoy helping them become more structured and positioned for future growth."

Rich and his partner are compensated in one of two ways. Some organizations pay him per member. "They know I have an extra incentive to help them grow," Rich quipped. A small organization may pay Rich an annual fee. "Many firms like mine charge by the hour, but that approach would be a record keeping burden we don't want," Rich noted. Association Management Solutions receives an average of five unsolicited requests for proposals each year. He responds to each, but the issue of growth needs to be considered carefully. "If we grow to the point of needing to lease space and hire staff, that would require a different approach to running our business," Rich explained.

Our film on Rich Butchko requires no special effects. Rich is busy and he is happy, so that's a nice story in itself.

Rich Butchko is a member of the American Society of Association Executives, based in Washington D.C., which is a great source for information on this field.

Dianne Farabi is an equal partner to Rich in this enterprise but all our stories focus on just one individual. Maybe we can tell you Dianne's story in our next edition.

Rochelle Kaplan
Mediator/Arbitrator
Dispute Resolution Services

"Did so!"
"Did not!"
"You'll hear from my lawyer."
"See you in court."

One way to handle disputes is for both sides to hire a lawyer and have the case heard before some "government tribunal" — a court, regulatory panel or administrative hearing in an adversarial context. Of course, this is very costly in money and time. Rochelle Kaplan's goal is to provide an alternative. To that end, she provides three basic services.

The first is mediation. "I try to get the people focused on how to solve their problem. That requires moving them from their *position* on the dispute to talking about their respective *interests*," Rochelle explained. "The mediator facilitates bringing the parties to find their own solution."

Whatever Rochelle does, she must be a careful listener. "My approach is listen, absorb, playback," she told me. "I'll say something like 'what you just told me is...' When someone hears their own thoughts expressed by someone else it tells them you're listening. It also tends to prod their thinking a bit." Rochelle can be a reality check for the parties. "I may say something like: "If you push that point, what will it mean to your company? Or, are you so angry that you want this matter tied-up in court?" Rochelle told me. Sometimes Rochelle tries to use humor to break tension or may need to split the parties and listen to them separately.

Both parties must agree to the mediation and often both have agreed to use Rochelle before she even is contacted. She may orient the parties to the mediation process so both understand her approach. If the mediation is productive, either Rochelle or a mutually agreed upon attorney puts their agreement in writing.

Rochelle's second service is to act as an independent fact finder. "The client's main purpose is to clarify the dispute. I am brought in because I have no axes to grind or personal loyalty in the matter," said Rochelle describing this function. "I interview people in a location and manner that does not attract unnecessary attention and I review documents. I am not a detective or a spy." Cases may involve accusations of misconduct, discrimination or sexual harassment." Rochelle needs to cover all the needed bases without speaking to so many people that someone's reputation is tarnished just by the fact finding process. "I ask about specific observed behavior, not for opinions about anyone's character," Rochelle added.

At the end of the process, Rochelle writes her conclusions and perhaps her recommendations. Her report is not a legal document as such, but it could be used in a legal proceeding to prove "due diligence" on the part of an employer. Rochelle's notes will not be used in court because they are destroyed once the report is written.

A third service is arbitration. In this situation, the parties agree that Rochelle's decision is binding on both parties. A typical case may involve a union management dispute. "We all sit around a table and I hear both sides present their case. It is much more informal than a count room, so people tend to be more relaxed. On the other hand, it is more formal than mediation, and each side may bring legal representation," Rochelle explained.

Parties seeking an arbitration usually turn to panels, such as the American Arbitration Association or the Federal Mediation and Conciliation Services, for a list of suggested names. Therefore, it is important for Rochelle to be listed with those organizations, each of which has its own method for identifying arbitrators to suggest. "The public stance of both parties is that they want impartiality. They will often read past rulings or consult with previous parties to determine if the arbitrator has any bias," Rochelle observed.

Rochelle likes helping people find solutions in a non-threatening forum and learning about a variety of businesses as she handles cases. Rochelle makes her own hours, which is a mixed blessing. "You don't want to turn business away, so there is a tendency to book cases very closely," Rochelle noted. "I want to build a successful practice without becoming a workaholic.

Rochelle earned her bachelor's degree at the University of Delaware (1972) and a law degree from Temple University (1975). "I hated my first year," Rochelle remembered. "But when I took courses in employment law I got interested." Studying part-time, she earned a master's degree in labor law in 1981.

Upon graduating from Temple, Rochelle clerked for a trial court judge. "I saw litigation on contract disputes, labor problems, negligence and divorce," she recounted, "and learned that I didn't want to be a litigator." However, Rochelle was impressed by the judges efforts to resolve matters in a pre-trial "settlement conference." After a brief start in a private law firm, Rochelle took a position with a utility company as a labor relations lawyer. In addition to writing personnel policy she also represented the company at labor arbitrations, her first direct exposure to the field. After a few years a steel company hired Rochelle to represent them at arbitrations. The good news was that she met some mediators and arbitrators. The bad news was that Rochelle was laid off when the steel industry became depressed.

For the next three years Rochelle did some law work part time and managed her husband's baseball card business. She also kept involved with arbitrators. In 1985, she became the legal counsel for a national professional association, with a focus on employment. As her dispute resolution service grew, she became part time at the association. "The association job is fun and guarantees a steady paycheck," Rochelle noted. The income is especially important since my practice is still in its infancy."

Rochelle writes for local business journals and makes presentations at workshops and conferences to make her name known.

"I wish I could have a marketing director. Of course, by the time I can afford one, I won't really need one," she joked.

There is no formal licensing process in the dispute resolution field. However, we might suppose that being a lawyer is an asset, Rochelle has a more nuanced opinion. "A lawyer is an advocate who wants to tell his/her client what to do. A mediator can't tell anyone what to do, you can only suggest. A lawyer asks questions and presents arguments; a mediator listens. You need to step back and realize that this is not a dispute but a problem that needs to be resolved," Rochelle said. "If you are a lawyer, that means a good deal of unlearning." Rochelle told me that her graduate degree in labor law may actually have a more direct bearing on her mediation work than her law degree. On the other hand, legal training has helped sharpen Rochelle's analytical and research skills.

"If you were a lawyer, you need to develop good counseling skills. If you came from a counseling background, like many mediators, you need to learn about the business context in which disputes arise," Rochelle suggested.

Whatever your higher education focus or professional experience, Rochelle strongly recommends formal mediation training. Rochelle took at least four courses (over 50 hours) in understanding how disputes are settled, negotiating, mediation process, helping parties prioritize their goals and coming to closure. Since then she has taken higher level courses focusing upon special areas in mediation: employment discrimination and disability discrimination.

"This field is extremely interesting," Rochelle concluded "but it takes a long time and lots of work before you are likely to make a substantial living."

Crystal Wright
The Crystal Agency

"Set the Pace,
Change the Rules
Define the Game and Win"

Is that the slogan of a Super Bowl Coach or an international business tycoon? Not quite. But it is the philosophy of Crystal Wright, who established her own agency to represent free lance artists in hair styling, fashion styling and make-up. "My job is to manage, market and promote them. I manage each artist's calendar so that she or he gets the right 'gigs' to get noticed and move forward. On the business side, the artists shouldn't be both the good guys (artists) and the bad guys (tough business people), so I do the negotiating for them," Crystal told me. "I set them up with fashion magazines, catalogues, record companies and production companies."

Crystal spends a good deal of her time networking with people who can influence or make the decision to retain her clients. Citing an example of placing a make-up artist with Jim Carrey, Crystal traced the connection to being a friend of the actor's publicist. Other connections could be art directors, fashion editors or producers. But most often, Crystal connects with high profile photographers. "The photographer is so central to the final product, that he or she can bring along their own crew, including make-up artists and hair-designers," Crystal explained.

Connections are necessary, but hardly sufficient. Crystal needs to be an astute judge of the match between her artist and her client. "Temperament can be as important as talent," Crystal told me. "Has the artist had exposure to celebrities so s/he will be unobtrusive in general but forceful if necessary? I need to judge who is ready to take the next step in their career. The artist's success is good for him/her, but also a boost to the whole agency." Crystal manages about ten artists at one time and holds exclusive rights to each one's professional activities. "Success can happen quickly for some artists, so you don't want any ambiguity about their agency" Crystal noted.

The field has its own terminology. For example, the term "print" regionally refers to magazine advertisements, editorial (i.e. working on a fashion spread or a cover), music, videos or TV commercials. It has nothing to do with printed words at all. Artists working in "print" need to confront changes everyday. Those doing TV shows or movies tend to work on a specific character whose appearance does not change dramatically from week to week. For that reason, going from "print" to "TV" is easier than trying to move in the other direction.

Crystal is typically up by 6 AM reading the Business, Metro and Lifestyle sections of the LA Times. She is in the office by 7:30 AM trying to find promising photographers with whom to build a connection. Her sources could be magazines or what are called "creative directories." These are books for which photographers pay perhaps $1,500 to have a page of their work displayed. Other sources are breakfast or dinner meetings, happy hours, and industry functions (soirees). "Lunch would be wasting two hours in the middle of the day. I can use that time better in the office," Crystal remarked.

Crystal's workday is often 12-14 hours. "I could cut that down to ten hours if I didn't publish a bi-monthly magazine — *First Hold* — and write a book — *The Hair, Make-up and Styling Career Guide. First Hold* is a trade magazine which artists and industry folk (industry folk include: art directors, fashion editors, publicists, producers) obtain by subscription to keep up with the field.

Talented artists can be expensive. The fee for a full day can run the client $2,500 plus a 20% agency fee. When clients get their bill, Crystal has to turn to her hard-nosed business woman character to make sure the bill is paid in full. "When the bill arrives, I'll sometimes hear all kinds of objections, often stated unpleasantly, but that's part of the business," Crystal said.

The creativity of running her own business and the variety that working with so many artists and clients (particularly marketing each artist individually) produces appeals to Crystal. "Some people are highly temperamental, like you see portrayed on sitcoms," Crystal said. "Working with them is not always fun, but it is always interesting." Crystal also gains satisfaction by growing the career of her artists. "I see a top-flight photo display or advertisement and know that I helped my artist rise to that level in the profession" Crystal explained. "This can be a tightly knit business, almost incestuous. I want to open up worlds to people who think the only avenue for their talent is in a hair salon. This is a passion for me. I want artists like mine to be so numerous throughout the country and highly recognized that the profession will be as well known as doctors or teachers."

Crystal's formal education in fashion began at home with her grandmother, a very fashionable seamstress. She attended a well-known fashion institute, but felt it was the wrong place for her. Crystal transferred to the University of Washington. As a junior, her career counselor pressed her to apply for an internship with Xerox. To mollify the counselor, Crystal took the interview, without a resume but with a bad attitude. In the middle of the interview she said, "I have changed my mind. I want the job." The interviewer gave her a chance to compete for the internship, which she won, and Xerox subsequently offered her a job, to start when she graduated. "I didn't actually graduate, but they hired me anyway. They saw that I had channeled my energy and attitude in a positive way, even if financial problems interfered with completing my degree requirements," Crystal recalled.

At Xerox, Crystal learned that "no is not an option" and the dynamics of marketing a product. She was a top salesperson for five years before leaving to become the agent for a photographer she met at a weekend networking event. "For me, I am selling a commitment to excellence and a philosophy of total concern for your needs, the approach I learned at Xerox. Just as Xerox created a brand for photocopies, I am creating a brand for my agency," Crystal concluded.

Look at www.TheCrystalAgency.Com for anything regarding the agency and its artists.

Captain Ernest E. Richardson
Merchant Marine

The first thing Captain Ernie Richardson said to me was that he has loved his thirty years in the marine industry. The second thing was that opportunities in this field are shrinking and "unless you have salt-water running through your veins" you should think twice before trying to develop a career in it.

Let's start with the good news. Ernie graduated from the US Merchant Marine Academy in Kingspoint, New York, and followed a traditional path by starting at the lowest officer rank, third mate. With that license, Ernie could stand a bridge watch, learning the rules and realities of navigation, safety and how to handle different cargoes. After sailing for a year and passing an exam, Ernie became a second mate. At this stage, Ernie learned how to read navigation charts, lay out a sailing course and use the on board Global Positioning System (GPS), which is a navigation aide connecting the ship to a space satellite. The process continued with another year of experience, taking another exam and becoming a first mate or "cargo mate". Ernie was now responsible for the upkeep of the ship including cargo equipment, life boats and inspections. He also supervised a "deck gang" of "unlicensed seaman" (that means below officer rank; it doesn't mean illegal) who do maintenance work and cargo loading.

When Ernie became a captain, he had ultimate responsibility for his ship. This included everything from general policies and command issues to food supplies and paper work. "I even get up early to check my e-mail, like a guy in an office," Ernie said. "On a lot of voyages there is a thirteen hour differential between the company headquarters and my ship, so you need to be especially alert for messages at any time."

The captain, like his crew, works seven days a week while on a voyage. The daily routine for the captain can actually involve fewer hours during a long ocean crossing, unless there is bad weather. "Then you can have a very long day indeed," Ernie remarked.

One nice thing about his profession is that Ernie truly has seen the world from Alaska to the tropics. The downside is that being at sea "can be a little isolating, especially for the men with families." The crew have a library, videos and on-board sports for their free time. "If you like the crew you're with, it can be a great experience. If not, four months at sea can seem a lot longer," Ernie noted. Being a captain has the advantage "of not having to take any foolishness from your captain—you're the boss," Ernie observed. "On the other hand, you need to maintain a bit of distance from the rest of the crew as part of maintaining your command authority. That means sometimes you are in a club of one." Even so Ernie enjoys seafaring people, from his shipboard crews to the Admirals he worked with ferrying NATO troops to Bosnia. Captain's pay is not bad either. "$90,000 a year for a vessel like mine, plus or minus $10,000," Ernie said. "If I captained a container ship, it might be $150,000."

The ship's officers are hired by the steamship line through their contacts at a Marine academy, previous voyages or headhunters. The unlicensed crew are brought on board through a union hiring hall. The company pays a lump sum to cover wages, union dues, health insurance and retirement. Vacation may seem generous, being from 23 to 30 days of paid vacation for every 30 days at sea. However as Ernie noted, "I work more in six months than most people do in twelve. After four months of continuous long days, you need some vacation time just to recover."

Although the American Merchant Marine has been shrinking, there are thousands of "back-up" jobs in ship yards and engine maintenance. Also, an unlicensed seaman can start climbing the ladder at 3rd Mate after several years of sea experience and passing the appropriate exam.

Jon Jordahl
Farmer

He tries to anticipate the intersection of supply and demand curves a year in advance. He utilizes space age technology to use his assets more effectively, and surfs the internet to find futures information. His partner constantly checks their subscription satellite service for critical information. Each year, he takes a $250,000 perishable investment and literally lays it on the ground unprotected from the elements. Is this a techno-fanatic with unusual investment habits? No! It's Jon Jordahl, a high tech farmer of corn and soybeans in Iowa.

Jon and his wife are partners in their 1,500 acre farm. Their produce is destined for livestock consumption, although they no longer raise livestock of their own. Planting and harvesting are still part of the farmer's life, so let's start there. Jon uses a no-till approach because it requires less equipment, absorbs less time and fosters less erosion. "Before adopting this method, I would have to go over the fields five or six times even before planting," Jon told me.

When it comes time for fertilizer, Jon uses a satellite-fed GPS (Global Positioning System) to pinpoint the amount of fertilizer to apply. "Each farm will have many different soil types," Jon explained. "Before GPS, I used to test the soil in different places, calculate an average and blanket fertilize the fields with that amount. That was more expensive and less productive."

At harvest time, Jon uses a combine, which removes the ear of corn from the plant and then removes the corn from the ear. The combine, also equipped with GPS, constantly calculates and records yield and moisture content through the entire harvest season. Moisture is a critical factor, since corn should be harvested at about 30% or less moisture content. The harvested corn, in order to be sold, needs to be artificially dried to 14-15%. In addition to science and mechanics knowledge, business decisions are involved.

"The new combine replaces two smaller machines. It cost $200,000, so I need to anticipate a significant return in order to buy it. I also need to decide how much produce, if any, I should take straight to market and how much to hold for later sale. If the weather and the grain markets go as I anticipated, it can be a profitable year. If not, well that's a different story," Jon told me.

Between planting and harvesting, the crops need to be tended. Here, too, modern technology can be helpful. "I found a certain microscopic bug in my fields and had to determine what to do about it. By researching on the Internet, I came across a solution someone had used successfully in North Carolina," Jon said.

Of course, not every tool is high tech. Jon has years of experience and can compare notes with fellow farmers and agri-specialists, like vendors for herbicides and insecticides. "Even though we are actually competitors in some sense, farmers share experiences about what works and what doesn't," Jon noted.

There are no full time employees on Jon's farm; it's a family venture. In fact, one of the things Jon likes best about farming is the amount of time he can spend with his family. "Even when I am working, I'm not far away. I was able to be with my five children as they were growing up. My hours may be long during the spring and fall, but they are flexible. If something is going on at the school, I can usually attend," Jon observed.

Unlike most farmers today, Jon did not come from a farming family. He majored in math at college and taught high-school for several years. (Originally, he wanted to be an architect, but that's a different story). Jon married another teacher, who happened to be the daughter of farmers. In 1970 his in-laws interested Jon in a 160 acre farm. With their material support and guidance, Jon purchased the farm and survived his early seasons. "For the two months of my first harvest I was working from 6:30 AM to 2 AM the next morning. I didn't know anybody could work that hard," Jon remembered.

"Meanwhile, my mother just couldn't understand why a college graduate would want to be a farmer," he continued. But Jon did want to be a farmer. In fact, he bought additional land shortly after his initial purchase. "My dream was to live in a country house, on top of a hill with a long lane leading up to it. The house was on that additional land, so we bought it." Jon also helped his in-laws with their 800 acre farm. "What my father-in-law told me to do on his farm I took back and did on mine also. It worked," Jon explained.

Jon is an avid reader of the farm publications which "jam his mailbox" in addition to his Internet and satellite information sources. "You need to grow as a farmer to grow the crops efficiently," he suggested.

Jon advises potential farmers that this career is unique in that you need to "buy your job" i.e. the land and the equipment. If you don't come from a farming family, it is nearly impossible. Your investment of capital and labor is at the mercy of weather conditions and market forces which you can't control. You can do everything right and still have a bad year financially. You take $250,000, every year, put it outside, and hope that Mother Nature treats you well.

Your income is uncertain from year to year. There are other agriculture related professions such as agri-engineering, sales and finance. Those fields require specialized study, but are open to entry without owning land.

WHAT TO DO NOW

To help you prepare for your own business, the people interviewed for this chapter recommended a variety of organizations you can contact, as well as publications and Web sites that may prove useful in your search:

Organizations:

International Asssociation of
Conference Interpreters .... www.aiic.com

Conference for Interpreter Trainers .... http://cit-asl.org

American Society of Association Executives .... www.asaenet.org

American Arbitration Association .... www.adr.org

Keybridge Foundation/Mediation Training and Information Center for ADA .... www.igc.org/medADA/medada/index.htm

American Maritime Officers (AMO) Dania, FL 954/920-3222

Publications:

Inc. .... www.inc.com

Entrepreneur .... www.entrepreneurmag.com

Web Sites:

http:Fambiz.com

www.lowe.org

www.mediate.org

www.imagetools.com

www.photographers.com

Index of Companies

About the Author

Richard Fein is the Director of Placement at the University of Massachusetts (Amherst) School of Management. A career specialist for 18 years, he is widely recognized as a leading authority on developing the core career planning and job search skills — writing effective resumes and cover letters and conducting winning job interviews. He is author of five major career books on these subjects: *100 Great Jobs and How to Get Them, 101 Dynamite Questions to Ask at Your Job Interview; 101 Quick Tips For a Dynamite Resume; 111 Dynamite Ways to Ace Your Job Interview; Cover Letters! Cover Letters! Cover Letters!* and *First Job.*

Richard has been a contributor to the *Wall Street Journal's Managing Your Career* and a columnist for *Employment Review Magazine*. He is a frequent commentator on the job search process for both print and electronic media. He has appeared as a guest on more than 30 radio and television programs and has been quoted in newspapers as diverse as the *Christian Science Monitor* and the *Idaho Statesman*.

Richard holds an MBA from Baruch College in New York, an MA in Political Science from the City University of New York, and a BA in Political Science from the University of Pennsylvania. He can be contacted through Impact Publications or the University of Massachusetts (email: *rfein@som.umass.edu*).

Other Career Resources

Contact Impact Publications for a free annotated listing of career resources or visit the World Wide Web for a complete listing of career resources: www.impactpublications.com. The following career resources are available directly from Impact Publications. Complete the following form or list the titles, include postage (see formula at the end), enclose payment, and send your order to:

IMPACT PUBLICATIONS
9104-N Manassas Drive
Manassas Park, VA 20111-5211
Tel 1-800/361-1055, 703/361-7300, or Fax 703/335-9486
Quick and easy online ordering: *www.impactpublications.com*

Qty.	Titles	Price	Total
INTERNET JOB SEARCH/HIRING			
	Career Exploration On the Internet	15.95	
	Electronic Resumes	19.95	
	Employer's Guide to Recruiting on the Internet	24.95	
	Guide to Internet Job Search.	14.95	
	Heart & Soul Internet Job Search	16.95	
	How to Get Your Dream Job Using the Web	29.99	
	Internet Jobs Kit	149.95	
	Internet Resumes	14.95	
	Job Searching Online for Dummies	24.99	
	Resumes in Cyberspace	14.95	
ALTERNATIVE JOBS & EMPLOYERS			
	100 Best Careers for the 21st Century	15.95	
	100 Great Jobs and How To Get Them	17.95	
	101 Careers	16.95	
	150 Best Companies for Liberal Arts Graduates	15.95	
	50 Coolest Jobs in Sports	15.95	
	Adams Job Almanac 1999	16.95	
	American Almanac of Jobs and Salaries	20.00	
	Back Door Guide to Short-Term Job Adventures	19.95	
	Best Jobs for the 21st Century	19.95	
	Breaking & Entering	17.95	
	Careers in Computers	17.95	
	Careers in Health Care	17.95	
	Careers in High Tech	17.95	
	Career Smarts	12.95	
	College Not Required	12.95	
	Cool Careers for Dummies	16.95	
	Cybercareers	24.95	
	Directory of Executive Recruiters	44.95	
	Flight Attendant Job Finder	16.95	
	Great Jobs Ahead	11.95	
	Health Care Job Explosion!	17.95	
	Hidden Job Market 1999	18.95	
	High-Skill, High-Wage Jobs	19.95	
	JobBank Guide to Computer and High-Tech Companies	16.95	

_____	Jobs 1998	15.00 _____
_____	JobSmarts Guide to Top 50 Jobs	15.00 _____
_____	Liberal Arts Jobs	14.95 _____
_____	Media Companies 2000	18.95 _____
_____	Quantum Companies II	26.95 _____
_____	Sunshine Jobs	16.95 _____
_____	Take It From Me	12.00 _____
_____	Top 100	19.95 _____
_____	Top 2,500 Employers 2000	18.95 _____
_____	Trends 2000	14.99 _____
_____	What Employers Really Want	14.95 _____
_____	Working in TV News	12.95 _____
_____	Workstyles to Fit Your Lifestyle	11.95 _____
_____	You Can't Play the Game If You Don't Know the Rules	14.95 _____

RECRUITERS/EMPLOYERS

_____	Adams Executive Recruiters Almanac	16.95 _____
_____	Directory of Executive Recruiters	44.95 _____
_____	Employer's Guide to Recruiting on the Internet	24.95 _____
_____	Job Seekers Guide to Executive Recruiters	34.95 _____
_____	Job Seekers Guide to Recruiters In. . .Series	36.95 _____

JOB STRATEGIES AND TACTICS

_____	101 Ways to Power Up Your Job Search	12.95 _____
_____	110 Big Mistakes Job Hunters	19.95 _____
_____	24 Hours to Your Next Job, Raise, or Promotion	10.95 _____
_____	Better Book for Getting Hired	11.95 _____
_____	Career Bounce-Back	14.95 _____
_____	Career Chase	17.95 _____
_____	Career Fitness	19.95 _____
_____	Career Intelligence	15.95 _____
_____	Career Starter	10.95 _____
_____	Coming Alive From 9 to 5	18.95 _____
_____	Complete Idiot's Guide to Changing Careers	17.95 _____
_____	Executive Job Search Strategies	16.95 _____
_____	First Job Hunt Survival Guide	11.95 _____
_____	Five Secrets to Finding a Job	12.95 _____
_____	Get a Job You Love!	19.95 _____
_____	Get It Together By 30	14.95 _____
_____	Get the Job You Want Series	37.95 _____
_____	Get Ahead! Stay Ahead!	12.95 _____
_____	Getting from Fired to Hired	14.95 _____
_____	Great Jobs for Liberal Arts Majors	11.95 _____
_____	How to Get a Job in 90 Days or Less	12.95 _____
_____	How to Get Interviews from Classified Job Ads	14.95 _____
_____	How to Succeed Without a Career Path	13.95 _____
_____	How to Get the Job You Really Want	9.95 _____
_____	How to Make Use of a Useless Degree	13.00 _____
_____	Is It Too Late To Run Away and Join the Circus?	14.95 _____
_____	Job Hunting in the 21st Century	17.95 _____
_____	Job Hunting for the Utterly Confused	14.95 _____
_____	Job Hunting Made Easy	12.95 _____
_____	Job Search: The Total System	14.95 _____
_____	Job Search Organizer	12.95 _____
_____	Job Search Time Manager	14.95 _____
_____	JobShift	13.00 _____
_____	JobSmart	12.00 _____
_____	Kiplinger's Survive and Profit From a Mid-Career Change	12.95 _____
_____	Knock 'Em Dead 1999	12.95 _____
_____	Me, Myself, and I, Inc.	17.95 _____
_____	New Rights of Passage	29.95 _____

_____	No One Is Unemployable	29.95	_____
_____	Not Just Another Job	12.00	_____
_____	Part-Time Careers	10.95	_____
_____	Perfect Job Search	12.95	_____
_____	Princeton Review Guide to Your Career	20.00	_____
_____	Perfect Pitch	13.99	_____
_____	Portable Executive	12.00	_____
_____	Professional's Job Finder	18.95	_____
_____	Reinventing Your Career	9.99	_____
_____	Resumes Don't Get Jobs	10.95	_____
_____	Right Fit	14.95	_____
_____	Right Place at the Right Time	11.95	_____
_____	Second Careers	14.95	_____
_____	Secrets from the Search Firm Files	24.95	_____
_____	So What If I'm 50	12.95	_____
_____	Staying in Demand	12.95	_____
_____	Strategic Job Jumping	13.00	_____
_____	SuccessAbilities	14.95	_____
_____	Take Yourself to the Top	13.99	_____
_____	Temping: The Insiders Guide	14.95	_____
_____	Top 10 Career Strategies for the Year 2000 & Beyond	12.00	_____
_____	Top 10 Fears of Job Seekers	12.00	_____
_____	Ultimate Job Search Survival	14.95	_____
_____	VGMs Career Checklist	9.95	_____
_____	Welcome to the Real World	13.00	_____
_____	What Do I Say Next?	20.00	_____
_____	What Employers Really Want	14.95	_____
_____	When Do I Start	11.95	_____
_____	Who Says There Are No Jobs Out There	12.95	_____
_____	Work Happy Live Healthy	14.95	_____
_____	Work This Way	14.95	_____
_____	You and Co., Inc.	22.00	_____
_____	Your Hidden Assets	19.95	_____

TESTING AND ASSESSMENT

_____	Career Counselor's Tool Kit	45.00	_____
_____	Career Discovery Project	12.95	_____
_____	Career Exploration Inventory	29.95	_____
_____	Career Satisfaction and Success	14.95	_____
_____	Career Tests	12.95	_____
_____	Crystal-Barkley Guideto Taking Charge of Your Career	9.95	_____
_____	Dictionary of Holland Occupational Codes	45.00	_____
_____	Discover the Best Jobs For You	14.95	_____
_____	Discover What You're Best At	12.00	_____
_____	Gifts Differing	14.95	_____
_____	Have You Got What It Takes?	12.95	_____
_____	How to Find the Work You Love	10.95	_____
_____	Making Vocational Choices	29.95	_____
_____	New Quick Job Hunting Map	4.95	_____
_____	P.I.E. Method for Career Success	14.95	_____
_____	Putting Your Talent to Work	12.95	_____
_____	Real People, Real Jobs	15.95	_____
_____	Self-Directed Search and Related Holland Career Materials	27.95	_____
_____	Self-Directed Search Form R Combination Package	74.00	_____
_____	Starting Out, Starting Over	14.95	_____
_____	Test Your IQ	6.95	_____
_____	Three Boxes of Life	18.95	_____
_____	Type Talk	11.95	_____
_____	WORKTypes	12.99	_____

ATTITUDE & MOTIVATION

_____	Ways to Motivate Yourself	15.99 _____
_____	Attitude Is Everything	14.99 _____
_____	Change Your Attitude	15.99 _____
_____	Reinventing Yourself	18.99 _____

INSPIRATION & EMPOWERMENT

_____	10 Stupid Things Men Do to Mess Up Their Lives	13.00 _____
_____	10 Stupid Things Women Do	13.00 _____
_____	101 Great Resumes	9.99 _____
_____	101 Simple Ways to Be Good to Yourself	12.95 _____
_____	Awaken the Giant Within	12.00 _____
_____	Beating Job Burnout	12.95 _____
_____	Big Things Happen When You Do the Little Things Right	15.00 _____
_____	Career Busters	10.95 _____
_____	Chicken Soup for the Soul Series	87.95 _____
_____	Do What You Love, the Money Will Follow	11.95 _____
_____	Doing It All Isn't Everything	19.95 _____
_____	Doing Work You Love	14.95 _____
_____	Emotional Intelligence	13.95 _____
_____	First Things First	23.00 _____
_____	Get What You Deserve	23.00 _____
_____	Getting Unstuck	11.99 _____
_____	If It's Going To Be, It's Up To Me	22.00 _____
_____	If Life Is A Game, These Are the Rules	15.00 _____
_____	In Search of Values	8.99 _____
_____	Job/Family Challenge: A 9-5 Guide	12.95 _____
_____	Kick In the Seat of the Pants	11.95 _____
_____	Kiplinger's Taming the Paper Tiger	11.95 _____
_____	Life Skills	17.95 _____
_____	Love Your Work and SuccessWill Follow	12.95 _____
_____	Path, The	14.95 _____
_____	Personal Job Power	12.95 _____
_____	Power of Purpose	20.00 _____
_____	Seven Habits of Highly Effective People	14.00 _____
_____	Softpower	10.95 _____
_____	Stop Postponing the Rest of Your Life	9.95 _____
_____	Suvivor Personality	12.00 _____
_____	To Build the Life You Want, Create the Work You Love	10.95 _____
_____	Unlimited Power	12.00 _____
_____	Wake-Up Calls	18.95 _____
_____	Your Signature Path	24.95 _____

RESUMES & LETTERS

_____	$110,000 Resume	16.95 _____
_____	100 Winning Resumes for $100,000+ Jobs	24.95 _____
_____	101 Best Resumes	10.95 _____
_____	101 More Best Resumes	11.95 _____
_____	101 Quick Tips for a Dynamite Resume	13.95 _____
_____	1500+ Key Words for 100,000+	14.95 _____
_____	175 High-Impact Resumes	10.95 _____
_____	Adams Resume Almanac/Disk	19.95 _____
_____	America's Top Resumes for America's Top Jobs	19.95 _____
_____	Asher's Bible of Exec.utive Resumes	29.95 _____
_____	Best Resumes for $75,000+ Executive Jobs	14.95 _____
_____	Best Resumes for Attorneys	16.95 _____
_____	Better Resumes in Three Easy Steps	12.95 _____
_____	Blue Collar and Beyond	8.95 _____
_____	Blue Collar Resumes	11.99 _____
_____	Building a Great Resume	15.00 _____

_____	Complete Idiot's Guide to Writing the Perfect Resume	16.95	_____
_____	Conquer Resume Objections	10.95	_____
_____	Creating Your High School Resume and Portfolio	13.90	_____
_____	Creating Your Skills Portfolio	10.95	_____
_____	Cyberspace Resume Kit	16.95	_____
_____	Damn Good Resume Guide	7.95	_____
_____	Dynamite Resumes	14.95	_____
_____	Edge Resume and Job Search Strategy	23.95	_____
_____	Electronic Resumes and Onlline Networking	13.99	_____
_____	Encyclopedia of Job-Winning Resumes	16.95	_____
_____	Gallery of Best Resumes	16.95	_____
_____	Gallery of Best Resumes for Two-Year Degree Graduates	16.95	_____
_____	Heart & Soul Resumes	15.95	_____
_____	High Impact Resumes and Letters	19.95	_____
_____	How to Prepare Your Curriculum Vitae	14.95	_____
_____	Just Resumes	11.95	_____
_____	New 90-Minute Resume	15.95	_____
_____	New Perfect Resume	10.95	_____
_____	Overnight Resume	12.95	_____
_____	Portfolio Power	14.95	_____
_____	Power Resumes	14.95	_____
_____	Prof. Resumes/Executives, Managers, & Other Administrators	19.95	_____
_____	Professional "Resumes For..." Career Series	213.95	_____
_____	Quick Resume and Cover Letter Book	12.95	_____
_____	Ready-To-Go Resumes	29.95	_____
_____	Resume Catalog	15.95	_____
_____	Resume Magic	18.95	_____
_____	Resume Power	12.95	_____
_____	Resume Pro	24.95	_____
_____	Resume Shortcuts	14.95	_____
_____	Resume Writing Made Easy	11.95	_____
_____	Resumes for H.S. Grads.	9.95	_____
_____	Resumes for the Over-50 Job Hunter	14.95	_____
_____	Resumes for Re-Entry	10.95	_____
_____	Resume Winners from the Pros	17.95	_____
_____	Resumes for Dummies	12.99	_____
_____	Resumes for the Health Care Professional	14.95	_____
_____	Resumes, Resumes, Resumes	9.99	_____
_____	Resumes That Knock 'Em Dead	10.95	_____
_____	Resumes That Will Get You the Job You Want	12.99	_____
_____	Savvy Resume Writer	10.95	_____
_____	Sure-Hire Resumes	14.95	_____
_____	Winning Resumes	10.95	_____
_____	Wow! Resumes	63.95	_____
_____	Your First Resume	9.99	_____
_____	Your Resume	24.95	_____

COVER LETTERS

_____	101 Best Cover Letters	11.95	_____
_____	175 High-Impact Cover Letters	10.95	_____
_____	200 Letters for Job Hunters	19.95	_____
_____	201 Winning Cover Letters for the $100,000+ Jobs	24.95	_____
_____	201 Dynamite Job Search Letters	19.95	_____
_____	201 Killer Cover Letters	16.95	_____
_____	Complete Idiot's Guide to the Perfect Cover Letters	14.95	_____
_____	Cover Letters, Cover Letters, Cover Letters	9.99	_____
_____	Cover Letters for Dummies	12.99	_____
_____	Cover Letters that Knock 'Em Dead	10.95	_____
_____	Cover Letters That Will Get You the Job You Want	12.99	_____
_____	Dynamite Cover Letters	14.95	_____
_____	Gallery of Best Cover Letters	18.95	_____
_____	Haldane's Best Cover Letters for Professionals	15.95	_____

_____	Perfect Cover Letter	10.95 _____
_____	Winning Cover Letters	10.95 _____

ETIQUETTE AND IMAGE

_____	Business Etiquette and Professionalism	10.95 _____
_____	Dressing Smart in the New Millennium	13.95 _____
_____	Executive Etiquette in the New Workplace	14.95 _____
_____	First Five Minutes	14.95 _____
_____	John Malloy's Dress for Success (For Men)	13.99 _____
_____	Lions Don't Need to Roar	10.99 _____
_____	New Professional Image	12.95 _____
_____	New Women's Dress for Success	12.99 _____
_____	Red Socks Don't Work	14.95 _____
_____	Successful Style	17.95 _____
_____	VGMs Complete Guide to Career Etiquette	12.95 _____
_____	Winning Image	17.95 _____
_____	You've Only Got 3 Seconds	22.95 _____

INTERVIEWING: JOBSEEKERS

_____	101 Dynamite Answers to Interview Questions	12.95 _____
_____	101 Dynamite Questions to Ask at Your Job Interview	14.95 _____
_____	101 Tough Interview Questions. . .	14.95 _____
_____	111 Dynamite Ways to Ace Your Job Interview	13.95 _____
_____	90-Minute Interview Prep (With Software)	15.95 _____
_____	Best Answers/201 Most Frequently Asked Interview Questions	10.95 _____
_____	Complete Q & A Job Interview Book	14.95 _____
_____	Conquer Interview Objectives	10.95 _____
_____	Get Hired	14.95 _____
_____	Haldane's Best Answers to Tough Interview Questions	15.95 _____
_____	Information Interviewing	10.95 _____
_____	Interview for Success	15.95 _____
_____	Interview Strategies ThatWill Get You the Job You Want	12.99 _____
_____	Interview Power	12.95 _____
_____	Job Interviews for Dummies	12.99 _____
_____	Job Interviews That Mean Business	12.00 _____
_____	Killer Interviews	10.95 _____
_____	Savvy Interviewer	10.95 _____
_____	Successful Interviewing for College Seniors	11.95 _____
_____	Sweaty Palms	8.95 _____
_____	Your First Interview	9.95 _____

NETWORKING

_____	52 Ways to Re-Connect, Follow Up, and Stay in Touch	14.95 _____
_____	Dig Your Well Before You're Thirsty	24.95 _____
_____	Dynamite Networking for Dynamite Jobs	15.95 _____
_____	Dynamite Tele-Search	12.95 _____
_____	Effective Networking	10.95 _____
_____	Golden Rule of Schmoozing	12.95 _____
_____	Great Connections	11.95 _____
_____	How to Work a Room	11.99 _____
_____	Network Your Way to Success	19.95 _____
_____	Networking for Everyone	16.95 _____
_____	People Power	14.95 _____
_____	Power Networking	14.95 _____
_____	Power Schmoozing	12.95 _____
_____	Power To Get In	24.95 _____

SALARY NEGOTIATIONS

_____	Dynamite Salary Negotiations	15.95 _____

_____	Get a Raise in 7 Days	14.95	_____
_____	Get More Money on Your Next Job	14.95	_____
_____	Negotiate Your Job Offer	14.95	_____

ENTREPRENEURS AND CONSULTANTS

_____	10 Hottest Consulting Practices	27.95	_____
_____	101 Best Businesses to Start	17.50	_____
_____	101 Best Home Businesses	14.99	_____
_____	101 Best Weekend Businesses	14.99	_____
_____	555 Ways to Earn Extra Money	12.95	_____
_____	Adams Businesses You Can Start Almanac	14.95	_____
_____	Adams Streetwise Small Business Start-Up	16.95	_____
_____	Adams Streetwise Small Business Start-Up CD-ROM	59.95	_____
_____	Be Your Own Business	12.95	_____
_____	Best Home-Based Businesseses for the 90s	12.95	_____
_____	Consultant's Proposal, Fee, and Contract Problem-Solver	19.95	_____
_____	Discovering Your Career in Business (With Disk)	22.00	_____
_____	Finding Your Perfect Work	16.95	_____
_____	Franchise Opportunities Handbook	16.95	_____
_____	Getting Business to Come to You CD-ROM	49.95	_____
_____	How to Raise a Family and Career Under One Roof	15.95	_____
_____	How to Really Start Your Own Business	19.95	_____
_____	How to Start, Run, and Stay in Business	14.95	_____
_____	Howto Succeed as an Independent Consultant	29.95	_____
_____	How to Start and Run a Successful Consulting Business	15.95	_____
_____	Ideal Entrepreneurial Business For You	16.95	_____
_____	Joining the Entrepreneurial Elite	25.95	_____
_____	NBEW's Guide to Self-Employment	12.95	_____
_____	Selling on the Internet	24.95	_____
_____	Start-Up	16.99	_____
_____	Starting on a Shoestring	16.95	_____
_____	Winning Government Contracts	19.95	_____

☞ **SUBTOTAL** $ _____

☞ Virginia residents add 4½% sales tax) _____

☞ Shipping/handling, Continental U.S., $5.00 +   _____ $5.00
plus following percentages when **SUBTOTAL** is:

☐ $30-$100—multiply SUBTOTAL by 8%   _____

☐ $100-$999—multiply SUBTOTAL by 7%   _____

☐ $1,000-$4,999—multiply SUBTOTAL by 6%   _____

☐ Over $5,000—multiply SUBTOTAL by 5%   _____

☞ ☐ If shipped outside Continental US, add another 5%   _____

☞ **TOTAL ENCLOSED** $ _____

SHIP TO: (street address only for UPS or RPS delivery)

Name _____

Address _____

_____

_____

Telephone _____

I enclose ☐ Check ☐ Money Order in the amount of: $ _____

Charge $ _____ to ☐ Visa ☐ MC ☐ AmEx

Card # _____ Exp: _____ /

Signature _____

Discover Hundreds of Additional Resources on the World Wide Web!

Looking for the newest and best books, directories, newsletters, wall charts, training programs, videos, computer software, and kits to help you land a job, negotiate a higher salary, or start your own business? Want to learn the most effective way to find a job in Asia or relocate to San Francisco? Are you curious about how to find a job 24 hours a day using the Internet or about what you'll be doing five years from now? Are you trying to keep up-to-date on the latest career resources, but are not able to find the latest catalogs, brochures, or newsletters on today's "best of the best" resources?

Welcome to the first virtual career bookstore on the Internet. Now you're only a click away with Impact Publications' electronic solution to the resource challenge. Visit this rich site to quickly discover everything you ever wanted to know about finding jobs, changing careers, and starting your own business — including many useful resources that are difficult to find in local bookstores and libraries. The site also includes what's new and hot, tips for job search success, and monthly specials. Check it out today!

www.impactpublications.com